SALADS

The Ultimate Cookbook

SALADS

The Ultimate Cookbook

CIDER MILL PRESS

BOOK
PUBLISHERS

CONTENTS

INTRODUCTION

*J**ust a salad. Just a salad.*

When those words ominously rang in Jerry's head on one episode of *Seinfeld*, it was yet another instance of the show having its finger firmly on the pulse of the public.

To impress his date, Jerry, despite his famously health-conscious nature, eagerly assents to go to dinner at one of those steakhouses where the enthusiasm for meat borders on fanatical. But when the establishment's comically rich entrees are presented to him, he can't help himself, and blurts out the words that led off this introduction as an order.

Immediately, he realizes his error and retreats inward, leaving the audience to chuckle at all of those unsaid things that are informing his anxiety. If given voice, it would sound something like this:

Salads are boring. Salads are something that one can only default to, never desire. Salads are not a proper dinner. Salads are only for the soft. For the vain. For those more interested in slimming down than enjoying themselves.

While so much of *Seinfeld* remains timeless, it is a relief that this one scene has aged poorly.

Simply put, the salad is far from those dark days, with inventive cooks everywhere having transformed its reputation and redefined the roles it is capable of playing in one's diet. Nowadays, you do not have to lower your eyes or turn crimson when you announce you're going to have a salad for dinner. No longer is this a sign that you can't find anything better, or are worried about your waistline. Instead, the salad has become a preparation that is as adept at providing a satisfying meal as any other, full of flavors and textures that will delight even the most fastidious foodie.

This remarkable reversal has done wonders not just for diners, but also for home cooks. For in a world where the demands on our time seem to be ever increasing, the salad, always quick and easy to prepare (it's an ideal option for those who are into making meals ahead of time), stands as a reliable source of salvation, able to get on the table in a hurry and supply the nourishment one needs following a long day. Best of all, since a salad is always centered around nutrient-dense ingredients, they do not pose the threat to one's health that many other efficient options do.

While a catalyst can be difficult to identify in broad, quick-moving movements such as this, here it is pretty easy to identify: the contemporary importance placed on quality ingredients and proper technique. Believing that the reason people tend to dislike certain foods is due more to encountering subpar versions that are poorly prepared rather than an actual aversion, the modern culinary movement has promoted sourcing ingredients of the highest possible quality and employing techniques that allow this quality to make itself apparent. These emphases have done wonders for vegetables' general reputation, lifting them from things that were grudgingly accepted to eagerly pursued in the minds of many. The Brussels sprout may well be the avatar of this shift, moving, almost overnight, from well-worn punchline to being celebrated on menus everywhere, and eagerly gobbled up by the masses.

As the general regard for vegetables improved, as more and more people headed to a local farmers market and discovered foods that had been growing under their noses for years, they began to search for new, inventive preparations to utilize them in—and that old catch-all for all things plant based, the salad, was waiting happily, ready to provide a safe landing spot for all this new enthusiasm. That wave of energy has brought the salad to the once-unthinkable spot where it sits today, where a book such as this, one that celebrates salad and nothing else, is in demand.

What this resurgence has really highlighted is the salad's superpower: versatility. Simply put, it is unmatched in terms of utility, capable of making the strangest mashups of odds and ends work.

It is also capable of providing just about whatever one is looking for a recipe to supply. Perhaps you are looking for a dish to set the right tone at your next party—one of the inventive, palate-awakening salads collected in the first chapter of recipes will fit the bill. Maybe

you've recently made a commitment to improving your health and want to make sure to eat more vegetables at every meal: one of the recipes in the On the Side chapter or the Vegan & Vegetarian Main-Course Salads section would be an excellent fit. Got some leftover rice or stale bread that you're looking to make use of so you can avoid being wasteful? The Salads with Pasta & Grains chapter is here to help. And for those nights where the steak in the butcher's case or the salmon at the fishmonger looks too good to resist, there are two chapters with inventive preparations that will allow you to scratch that carnivorous craving while still making sure your meal possess the proper balance.

Whether you're a longtime salad enthusiast, an avid gardener looking for new ways to utilize the products of their garden, a chef searching for inspiration, or someone who wants to get their quest for better health on track, this book is the ultimate resource, providing a lifetime's worth of salads, ideas, and possibilities.

TO START

While the number of roles the salad is capable of playing has increased dramatically over the course of the last couple of decades, that does not mean that its ability to fill its traditional role—serving as the first course, awakening the palate for the richer fare to come—has suffered in the slightest.

The recipes collected in this chapter are those that shine in this leadoff role, guaranteed to either get an elegant meal off on the right foot or just make a weeknight dinner at home feel like a bit more of an occasion.

ENSALADA DE NOPALES

YIELD: 4 SERVINGS / **ACTIVE TIME:** 30 MINUTES / **TOTAL TIME:** 1 HOUR

A versatile, light, and fresh preparation that can provide a dramatic beginning for any dinner party.

1. Place the nopales in a small bowl and sprinkle the salt over them. Let the nopales rest for 15 minutes.

2. Combine the onion, tomatoes, and cilantro in a separate bowl.

3. Place the nopales and 1 tablespoon of water in a large skillet, cover it, and cook over medium heat until the nopales are tender, about 12 minutes. Remove them from the pan and let them cool. When cool enough to handle, cut the nopales into ¼-inch-thick strips.

4. Stir the nopales into the tomato mixture, add the lemon juice, and season the salad with salt. Garnish with queso fresco or cotija cheese and enjoy.

INGREDIENTS:

3   LARGE NOPALES, SPINES REMOVED

1   TABLESPOON KOSHER SALT, PLUS MORE TO TASTE

½   WHITE ONION, FINELY DICED

2   LARGE TOMATOES, FINELY DICED

½   BUNCH OF FRESH CILANTRO, CHOPPED

JUICE OF 1 LEMON

QUESO FRESCO, CRUMBLED, FOR GARNISH

COTIJA CHEESE, CRUMBLED, FOR GARNISH

FIG & GOAT CHEESE SALAD

YIELD: 2 SERVINGS / **ACTIVE TIME:** 30 MINUTES / **TOTAL TIME:** 30 MINUTES

Pairing the slightly smoky edge the figs pick up on the grill with cheese is a one-way ticket to the Mediterranean.

1. Prepare a gas or charcoal grill for high heat (about 500°F). Place the wine and sugar in a small saucepan and warm the mixture over medium-high heat, stirring until the sugar has dissolved. Simmer until the mixture has reduced to a syrupy consistency. Remove the pan from heat and set it aside.

2. Place the orange slices on the grill and cook until they're caramelized on each side, about 2 minutes. Remove them from heat and set them aside.

3. Place the figs on the grill, cut side down, and cook until they are lightly browned and soft, about 4 minutes.

4. To serve, place the orange slices on a plate, place the figs on top of the orange slices, sprinkle the goat cheese over the dish, and then drizzle the reduction over the top.

INGREDIENTS:

1	CUP PINOT NOIR
¼	CUP SUGAR
8	ORANGE SLICES
12	FRESH FIGS, HALVED
¼	CUP CRUMBLED GOAT CHEESE

SHRIMP & PAPAYA SALAD

YIELD: 4 SERVINGS / **ACTIVE TIME:** 15 MINUTES / **TOTAL TIME:** 20 MINUTES

This tropically inclined salad is the perfect place to kick off a light dinner on a blistering summer day.

1. To prepare the dressing, place all of the ingredients in a small bowl and whisk until combined. Set the dressing aside.

2. To begin preparations for the salad, place the mesclun greens, cucumber, bell pepper, onion, and papaya in a salad bowl and toss to combine. Set the mixture aside.

3. Place the olive oil in a large skillet and warm it over high heat. Add the shrimp to the skillet and cook until they just start to turn pink, about 2 minutes.

4. Remove the skillet from heat, turn the shrimp over, and add the cilantro. Cover the skillet and let the shrimp sit until they are cooked through, about 3 minutes.

5. Add the shrimp and dressing to the salad, toss to combine, and serve.

INGREDIENTS:

FOR THE DRESSING

1½	TABLESPOONS CANOLA OIL
1	TABLESPOON FRESH LIME JUICE
	PINCH OF KOSHER SALT
	BLACK PEPPER, TO TASTE
1	TEASPOON FRESH THYME
	RED PEPPER FLAKES, TO TASTE

FOR THE SALAD

10	OZ. MESCLUN GREENS
½	CUCUMBER, SLICED THIN
½	RED BELL PEPPER, SLICED THIN
½	RED ONION, DICED
1	PAPAYA, PEELED, DESEEDED, AND CUBED
2	TEASPOONS EXTRA-VIRGIN OLIVE OIL
1	LB. LARGE SHRIMP, SHELLS REMOVED, DEVEINED
¼	CUP CHOPPED FRESH CILANTRO, FOR GARNISH

MANGO, RADICCHIO & PEPPER SALAD

YIELD: 4 SERVINGS / **ACTIVE TIME:** 20 MINUTES / **TOTAL TIME:** 20 MINUTES

A beautiful start to an alfresco dinner in the summer, thanks to its refreshing crunch and bittersweet nature.

1. Place the mangoes, radicchio, peppers, cucumber, and scallions in a salad bowl and toss to combine.

2. Add the lime juice and agave nectar, toss to coat, and serve.

INGREDIENTS:

FLESH OF 2 MANGOES, SLICED THIN

5   OZ. RADICCHIO, CHOPPED

1   RED BELL PEPPER, STEMMED, SEEDED, AND SLICED THIN

1   ORANGE BELL PEPPER, STEMMED, SEEDED, AND SLICED THIN

1   CUCUMBER, JULIENNED

6   SCALLIONS, TRIMMED AND CHOPPED

1½   TABLESPOONS FRESH LIME JUICE

1   TABLESPOON AGAVE NECTAR

SALATA MECHOUIA

YIELD: 6 SERVINGS / ACTIVE TIME: 45 MINUTES / TOTAL TIME: 2 HOURS

The smoky char of the grilled vegetables pairs perfectly with a burst of garlicky flavor. If you're planning to serve bread with the entrée, bake an extra loaf and break it out along with this first course.

1. Preheat the oven to 375°F. Use a knife to cut a small slit in the jalapeño.

2. Place the tomatoes, bell peppers, jalapeño, and garlic on an aluminum foil–lined baking sheet. Place it in the oven and roast until the vegetables are well browned and just tender, about 30 minutes for the garlic and 1 hour for the peppers and tomatoes.

3. Remove the vegetables from the oven. Place the garlic cloves on a plate and let them cool. Place the other roasted vegetables in a large bowl and cover it with plastic wrap. Let them rest for about 15 minutes.

4. Peel the garlic cloves and set them aside. Remove the charred skins from the other vegetables, place the vegetables in a colander, and let them drain.

5. Using a fork, mash the roasted garlic.

6. Transfer the drained vegetables to a cutting board. Remove the seeds from the bell peppers and the jalapeño. Finely chop all of the vegetables and place them in a mixing bowl. Add the mashed garlic, salt, pepper, lemon juice, and olive oil and stir well until combined.

7. Enjoy immediately with the Pita Bread.

INGREDIENTS:

1	JALAPEÑO CHILE PEPPER
6	LARGE PLUM TOMATOES
3	GREEN BELL PEPPERS
2	GARLIC CLOVES, UNPEELED
2	TEASPOONS KOSHER SALT
¼	TEASPOON BLACK PEPPER
¼	CUP FRESH LEMON JUICE
3	TABLESPOONS EXTRA-VIRGIN OLIVE OIL
	PITA BREAD (SEE PAGE 660), FOR SERVING

STRAWBERRY & BEET SALAD

YIELD: 4 SERVINGS / **ACTIVE TIME:** 20 MINUTES / **TOTAL TIME:** 2 HOURS

Beets are one of those ingredients that many people—even vegetable lovers—are wary of, a feeling which likely stems from encountering them in some improperly prepared form. But, when cooked correctly, beets are sweet, earthy, and delicious.

1. Preheat the oven to 375°F. Rinse the beets under cold water and scrub them to remove any excess dirt. Pat them dry and place them in a baking dish.

2. Drizzle the olive oil over the beets and season generously with salt and pepper. Place them in the oven and roast until tender, about 1 hour.

3. Remove the beets from the oven and let them cool.

4. When the beets are cool enough to handle, peel and dice them. Place them in a bowl with the pesto and toss to coat. Add the strawberries, cheese, arugula, and annatto oil, toss until evenly distributed, and serve.

INGREDIENTS:

3	LARGE GOLDEN BEETS
½	CUP EXTRA-VIRGIN OLIVE OIL
	SALT AND PEPPER, TO TASTE
	CILANTRO PESTO (SEE PAGE 512)
12	STRAWBERRIES, HULLED AND HALVED
2	CUPS SHREDDED QUESO FRESCO
4	OZ. BABY ARUGULA
2	TABLESPOONS ANNATTO OIL

Strawberry & Beet Salad, see page 23

ROMAINE & CHERRY TOMATO SALAD
WITH FRIED FETA

YIELD: 2 SERVINGS / **ACTIVE TIME:** 25 MINUTES / **TOTAL TIME:** 25 MINUTES

A bit of time in a hot bath amplifies the creamy character of feta cheese and makes this salad a guaranteed crowd-pleaser.

1. Place the flour, salt, baking powder, and water in a small bowl and whisk until the mixture is smooth.

2. Add canola oil to a small saucepan until it is about 1 inch deep and warm it over medium-high heat.

3. Carefully dip the block of feta in the batter until it is completely coated.

4. Submerge half of the feta in the canola oil for 5 seconds, then release it so that it floats. Fry for 1½ minutes on each side, while keeping a close eye on the feta; if the batter doesn't seal, the feta will ooze out, and the dish won't work as designed. Once the feta has browned, remove it from the oil and set it on a wire rack to drain.

5. Place the olive oil in a medium skillet and warm it over high heat. Add the tomatoes and cook until they start to blister, 2 to 3 minutes. Add the lettuce leaves and brown them for about 1 minute. Remove the pan from heat.

6. To serve, place the lettuce in a shallow bowl, scatter the tomatoes on top, and nestle the fried block of feta on top. Drizzle the Balsamic Glaze over the cheese and enjoy.

INGREDIENTS:

1   CUP ALL-PURPOSE FLOUR

1   TEASPOON KOSHER SALT

1   TEASPOON BAKING POWDER

1   CUP WATER

CANOLA OIL, AS NEEDED

1   BLOCK OF FETA CHEESE (½ INCH THICK)

1   TEASPOON EXTRA-VIRGIN OLIVE OIL

1   CUP CHERRY TOMATOES

LEAVES FROM ½ HEAD OF ROMAINE LETTUCE

1   TABLESPOON BALSAMIC GLAZE (SEE PAGE 515)

ROASTED TOMATO CAPRESE SALAD

YIELD: 2 SERVINGS / **ACTIVE TIME:** 25 MINUTES / **TOTAL TIME:** 45 MINUTES

Roasting the tomatoes concentrates their sweetness and adds a note of char that is lovely amid the freshness of a salad.

1. Preheat the oven to 450°F. Place the basil, spinach, garlic, 7 table-spoons of the olive oil, and the Parmesan cheese in a food processor and blitz until smooth. Set the pesto aside.

2. Place the vinegar in a small saucepan and bring it to a simmer over medium-high heat. Reduce the heat to medium and cook the vinegar until it has been reduced by half, 6 to 8 minutes. Remove the pan from heat and let the reduction cool completely.

3. Cut the tomatoes into ⅛-inch-thick slices and place them on a baking sheet in a single layer. Drizzle the remaining olive oil over the top.

4. Distribute the mozzarella around the tomatoes, place the pan in the oven, and bake until the cheese and tomatoes start to brown, about 10 minutes. Remove the pan from the oven and let the tomatoes and mozzarella cool.

5. To serve, arrange the tomatoes and mozzarella on a plate, spoon the pesto over them, and drizzle the balsamic reduction over the top.

INGREDIENTS:

½	CUP FRESH BASIL
½	CUP FRESH SPINACH
2	GARLIC CLOVES
½	CUP EXTRA-VIRGIN OLIVE OIL
½	CUP GRATED PARMESAN CHEESE
½	CUP BALSAMIC VINEGAR
2	TOMATOES
6	OZ. FRESH MOZZARELLA CHEESE, TORN

*Romaine & Cherry Tomato Salad
with Fried Feta, see page 26*

KALE SALAD WITH MINT & HAZELNUTS

YIELD: 4 SERVINGS / **ACTIVE TIME:** 15 MINUTES / **TOTAL TIME:** 35 MINUTES

A citrus-forward dressing would also be a good choice in this salad.

1. Preheat the oven to 350°F. Place the hazelnuts on a baking sheet, place them in the oven, and toast until the hazelnuts are browned, 8 to 10 minutes, stirring occasionally. Remove the hazelnuts from the oven and let them cool.

2. Place the kale, salad greens, toasted hazelnuts, and mint in a salad bowl and toss to combine. Add the dressing, toss to coat, and serve.

INGREDIENTS:

1   CUP HAZELNUTS

1   LB. KALE, STEMMED AND CHOPPED

3   OZ. SALAD GREENS

¼   CUP FINELY CHOPPED FRESH MINT

    GINGER & TAHINI DRESSING (SEE PAGE 635)

OCTOPUS SALAD

YIELD: 8 SERVINGS / **ACTIVE TIME:** 30 MINUTES / **TOTAL TIME:** 2 HOURS AND 30 MINUTES

The key to cooking octopus correctly is to get the tentacles very tender before searing them. This takes time and patience, so try and reserve this salad for an evening when you don't mind lingering in the kitchen.

1. Fill a pot large enough to fully submerge the octopus with water and bring it to a simmer. Add the octopus and cover the pot. Simmer until the octopus is very tender, 45 minutes to 1 hour. Remove the tentacles from the octopus and let them cool.

2. While the octopus is cooking, place the radishes and half of the salt in a bowl and toss to coat. Cover the radishes with some of the vinegar and let them sit.

3. Place the pear in a separate bowl, sprinkle the remaining salt over it, and toss to coat. Cover the pear with the remaining vinegar and let it sit.

4. Warm a large cast-iron skillet over high heat. Brush the pan with the olive oil, pat the octopus tentacles dry, place them in the pan, and sear until slightly charred all over, 3 to 4 minutes.

5. To serve, spread some of the salsa on a plate and place a full tentacle alongside it. Put some of the greens in a small pile beside the tentacle, sprinkle the radishes and pear on top, and enjoy.

INGREDIENTS:

1	WHOLE OCTOPUS
3	RADISHES, SLICED THIN
2	TEASPOONS KOSHER SALT
1	CUP WHITE VINEGAR
1	PEAR, CORED AND SLICED
1	TABLESPOON EXTRA-VIRGIN OLIVE OIL
½	CUP SALSA VERDE, MEDITERRANEAN STYLE (SEE PAGE 517)
2	CUPS MESCLUN GREENS

GRILLED ROMAINE & CRISPY SWEET POTATO SALAD

YIELD: 2 SERVINGS / **ACTIVE TIME:** 30 MINUTES / **TOTAL TIME:** 30 MINUTES

Shredding and frying sweet potato skins is a purely brilliant way to cut down on waste in your kitchen.

1. Prepare a gas or charcoal grill for high heat (about 500°F). Add canola oil to a small saucepan until it is about 2 inches deep and warm it to 350°F. Add the sweet potato skins and fry until they are golden brown and crispy, about 1 minute. Remove the fried sweet potato skins from the oil and place them on a paper towel–lined plate. Season the potato skins with 1 teaspoon of the salt and 1 teaspoon of the pepper.

2. Cut the apple into ½-inch slices, leaving the skin on. Place the apple in a small bowl, add the white vinegar and 1 teaspoon of the salt, and toss to coat. Set the mixture aside.

3. Cut off the bottom from the heart of romaine, separate the leaves, and place them in a bowl. Add the olive oil, remaining salt, and remaining pepper and toss to coat.

4. Place the lettuce on the grill and cook until slightly charred on both sides, but take it off before it starts to wilt, about 1 minute.

5. Arrange the lettuce on a plate and sprinkle the fried sweet potato skins and apple over the top. Drizzle the balsamic vinegar over the dish, sprinkle the feta on top, and enjoy.

INGREDIENTS:

	CANOLA OIL, AS NEEDED
1	CUP SHREDDED BAKED SWEET POTATO SKINS
1	TABLESPOON KOSHER SALT
2	TEASPOONS BLACK PEPPER
½	GREEN APPLE
½	CUP WHITE VINEGAR
1	HEART OF ROMAINE LETTUCE
2	TEASPOONS EXTRA-VIRGIN OLIVE OIL
1	TABLESPOON BALSAMIC VINEGAR
2	TABLESPOONS CRUMBLED FETA CHEESE

*Grilled Romaine & Crispy Sweet
Potato Salad, see page 33*

SHRIMP, CUCUMBER & WATERCRESS SALAD

YIELD: 4 SERVINGS / **ACTIVE TIME:** 15 MINUTES / **TOTAL TIME:** 20 MINUTES

The peppery flavor of watercress supplies a needed punch in this otherwise gentle salad.

1. Bring a few inches of water to a boil in a large saucepan. Thread the shrimp onto the pieces of lemongrass. Place them in a steaming basket, set the basket over the water, and steam the shrimp until they are cooked through, about 5 minutes. Remove the shrimp from the steaming basket and set them aside.

2. Place the cucumber and watercress in a salad bowl and toss to combine.

3. Place half of the pickled ginger, the honey, lime juice, avocado oil, and sour cream in a bowl and whisk until the dressing has emulsified. Season the dressing with salt and pepper.

4. To serve, divide the salad among the plates and place two shrimp skewers on each portion. Top with the remaining pickled ginger and the chile, drizzle the dressing over the salads, and enjoy.

INGREDIENTS:

8   JUMBO SHRIMP, SHELLS REMOVED, DEVEINED

2   LEMONGRASS STALKS, TRIMMED, BRUISED, AND QUARTERED LENGTHWISE

1   LARGE CUCUMBER, PEELED AND SLICED THIN

1   BUNCH OF WATERCRESS, CHOPPED

⅓   CUP PICKLED GINGER

1   TABLESPOON HONEY

     JUICE OF 1 LIME

¼   CUP AVOCADO OIL

1   CUP SOUR CREAM

     SALT AND PEPPER, TO TASTE

1   CHILE PEPPER, STEMMED, SEEDED, AND CHOPPED

ENDIVE SALAD WITH GRAPEFRUIT, SHRIMP & AVOCADO

YIELD: 4 SERVINGS / ACTIVE TIME: 25 MINUTES / TOTAL TIME: 25 MINUTES

While you are segmenting the grapefruit, don't hesitate to add any resulting juices to the vinaigrette. Should you take this route, remember to adjust the amount of white balsamic vinegar you add to it.

1. Place the grapefruit, endives, avocado, red onion, and shrimp in a salad bowl, season with salt and pepper, and gently toss to combine. Set the salad aside.

2. Drizzle the vinaigrette over the salad, garnish with the watercress, and enjoy.

INGREDIENTS:

2	GRAPEFRUIT, SEGMENTED
4	BELGIAN ENDIVES, HALVED LENGTHWISE, CORES REMOVED, AND LEAVES SEPARATED
	FLESH OF 1 AVOCADO, SLICED
¼	CUP FINELY DICED RED ONION
¾	LB. COOKED SHRIMP
	SALT AND PEPPER, TO TASTE
	WHITE BALSAMIC VINAIGRETTE (SEE PAGE 565)
1	BUNCH OF WATERCRESS, RINSED WELL AND DRIED, FOR GARNISH

BUTTER LETTUCE, MANDARIN & WALNUT SALAD

YIELD: 4 SERVINGS / **ACTIVE TIME:** 10 MINUTES / **TOTAL TIME:** 10 MINUTES

Astraightforward, flavorful salad that cries out for a rich, satisfying second course like braised short ribs or grilled rib eyes.

1. Place the lettuce, oranges, and walnuts in a salad bowl and toss to combine. Add half of the dressing, season with salt and pepper, and toss to coat.

2. Garnish with parsley and serve with the remaining dressing.

INGREDIENTS:

½   LB. BUTTER LETTUCE

4   MANDARIN ORANGES, SUPREMED (SEE PAGE 92) AND SLICED THIN

1   CUP WALNUTS, CHOPPED

    BLUE CHEESE DRESSING (SEE PAGE 632)

    SALT AND PEPPER, TO TASTE

    FRESH PARSLEY, CHOPPED, FOR GARNISH

CRAB ROULADE

YIELD: 10 SERVINGS / **ACTIVE TIME:** 25 MINUTES / **TOTAL TIME:** 40 MINUTES

This is about as elegant a salad as you'll find—in this book, or anywhere.

1. Place the crab, shallots, mayonnaise, crème fraîche, and chives in a mixing bowl, season the mixture with salt and pepper, and stir until well combined.

2. Place a piece of plastic wrap on a damp work surface. Place one-tenth of the crab salad on the plastic wrap and roll it up tightly into a cylinder, twisting the ends. Repeat until you have 10 cylinders of the crab salad. Place them in the refrigerator and chill for 15 minutes.

3. Remove the crab salad from the refrigerator and wrap each portion with the slices from half of an avocado.

4. Garnish the roulade with the Passion Fruit Emulsion, chile, sesame seeds, microgreens, and additional chives and enjoy.

INGREDIENTS:

1	LB. CANNED LUMP CRABMEAT, PICKED OVER
¼	CUP MINCED SHALLOTS
¼	CUP MAYONNAISE
¼	CUP CRÈME FRAÎCHE
¼	CUP CHOPPED FRESH CHIVES, PLUS MORE FOR GARNISH
	SALT AND PEPPER, TO TASTE
5	AVOCADOS, HALVED, PITTED, AND SLICED THIN
	PASSION FRUIT EMULSION (SEE PAGE 516), FOR GARNISH
1	FRESNO CHILE PEPPER, STEMMED, SEEDED, AND SLICED THIN, FOR GARNISH
¼	CUP SESAME SEEDS, TOASTED, FOR GARNISH
½	CUP MICROGREENS, FOR GARNISH

MIXED GREENS SALAD
WITH CRANBERRY & ORANGE VINAIGRETTE

YIELD: 4 TO 6 SERVINGS / **ACTIVE TIME:** 20 MINUTES / **TOTAL TIME:** 20 MINUTES

This salad celebrates one of the best developments in modern cooking: the insistence that salads can be bright and stand up, flavor- and imagination-wise, to the rest of the meal.

1. Place all of the ingredients, except for the vinaigrette, in a salad bowl and toss to combine.

2. Add some of the vinaigrette and toss to coat. Serve the salad with the remaining vinaigrette alongside.

INGREDIENTS:

½	LB. MIXED GREENS
½	CUP SHAVED RADISHES
½	CUP SHAVED CARROTS
½	CUP CANDIED PECANS (SEE PAGE 662)
½	RED ONION, SLICED
1	ASIAN PEAR, CORED AND SLICED
	CRANBERRY & ORANGE VINAIGRETTE (SEE PAGE 585)

LATE SUMMER SALAD WITH WILD MUSHROOMS

YIELD: 2 TO 4 SERVINGS / **ACTIVE TIME:** 25 MINUTES / **TOTAL TIME:** 35 MINUTES

The trick to searing mushrooms is to give them plenty of room in the pan and not disturb them, as this gets them nice and brown and concentrates the flavor.

1. Coat the bottom of a saucepan with 2 tablespoons of olive oil and warm it over medium-high heat. Add the mushrooms, taking care not to crowd the pan. Sprinkle a pinch of salt over the mushrooms and then let them cook, undisturbed, until they release their liquid and begin to brown. Gently turn them and repeat on the other side. Remove the mushrooms from the pan and set them aside.

2. Add the onion and garlic to the pan, adding an additional splash of olive oil if the pan looks dry. Cook, stirring frequently, over medium heat until the onion starts to soften, about 5 minutes. Turn off the heat and deglaze the pan with the vinegar, scraping any browned bits from the bottom of the pan. Remove the pan from heat and let it cool to room temperature.

3. Place the pine nuts in a dry skillet and toast them over medium heat for 2 minutes, shaking the pan frequently. Transfer the toasted pine nuts to a bowl and let them cool.

4. Place the cooled onion-and-garlic mixture in a separate bowl along with the remaining olive oil. Whisk until combined, season with salt, and set the dressing aside.

5. Arrange the greens on the serving plates, top with the seared mushrooms, toasted pine nuts, Parmesan, dill, and dressing, and serve.

INGREDIENTS:

½ CUP EXTRA-VIRGIN OLIVE OIL, PLUS MORE AS NEEDED

½ LB. WILD MUSHROOMS, SLICED

SALT, TO TASTE

¼ CUP DICED RED ONION

1 GARLIC CLOVE, CHOPPED

¼ CUP BALSAMIC VINEGAR

1 TABLESPOON PINE NUTS

MESCLUN GREENS, FOR SERVING

2 TABLESPOONS GRATED PARMESAN CHEESE

FRESH DILL, CHOPPED, TO TASTE

KALE SALAD WITH CASHEWS & POPCORN

YIELD: 4 SERVINGS / ACTIVE TIME: 20 MINUTES / TOTAL TIME: 20 MINUTES

This recipe is intended to feature unbuttered popcorn, but tossing it in a bit of melted butter is by no means prohibited. If you opt for this route, add less of the dressing, or forgo it entirely.

1. Preheat the oven to 350°F. Place the cashews on a baking sheet, place them in the oven, and toast until they are well browned, 12 to 15 minutes, stirring occasionally. Remove the cashews from the oven and let them cool.

2. Place the kale, raisins, and cashews in a salad bowl and toss to combine. Add the dressing, season with salt and pepper, and toss to coat.

3. Top the salad with the popcorn and serve.

INGREDIENTS:

1½ CUPS CASHEWS

½ LB. KALE, STEMMED AND TORN

1 CUP RAISINS

TAHINI DRESSING (SEE PAGE 565)

SALT AND PEPPER, TO TASTE

4 CUPS POPPED POPCORN

CRAB & MANGO SALAD

YIELD: 4 SERVINGS / **ACTIVE TIME:** 10 MINUTES / **TOTAL TIME:** 25 MINUTES

Moving past this one because you think you don't have a ring mold? We bet you do—you can just use the band you would use to seal a mason jar.

1. Place the mango, bell pepper, onion, chives, vinegar, and olive oil in a bowl and gently stir to combine. Season with salt and chill the salad in the refrigerator for 15 minutes.

2. Spread some of the dressing over each of the serving plates. Use a ring mold to make four towers out of the salad and place one on each plate. Top each tower with some of the crabmeat and serve.

INGREDIENTS:

½ CUP DICED MANGO

½ RED BELL PEPPER, STEMMED, SEEDED, AND FINELY CHOPPED

3 TABLESPOONS MINCED RED ONION

1 TEASPOON MINCED FRESH CHIVES

1 TEASPOON RICE VINEGAR

2 TABLESPOONS EXTRA-VIRGIN OLIVE OIL

SALT, TO TASTE

AVOCADO & LIME YOGURT DRESSING (SEE PAGE 535)

½ LB. CANNED LUMP CRABMEAT, PICKED OVER

PEA, HEART OF PALM, ARUGULA & PINE NUT SALAD

YIELD: 2 SERVINGS / ACTIVE TIME: 15 MINUTES / TOTAL TIME: 30 MINUTES

The sweet peas are the perfect contrast to the peppery arugula, and the hearts of palm and pine nuts round out the flavors and textures perfectly. The Red Wine Vinaigrette adds just the right amount of zing, and some Parmesan cheese makes it just hearty enough to awaken the appetite.

1. Place the pine nuts in a small, dry skillet and toast over high heat until they are golden brown, about 1 minute, shaking the pan frequently to prevent them from burning. Remove the pine nuts from the pan and let them cool.

2. Bring water to a boil in a saucepan. Add the frozen peas and let the water return to a boil. Drain the peas and run them under very cold water. Drain again and set the peas aside.

3. Place the arugula, hearts of palm, Parmesan, toasted pine nuts, and peas in a salad bowl and toss to combine.

4. Add half of the vinaigrette, toss to coat, taste, and add more dressing as necessary. Serve immediately.

INGREDIENTS:

1	TABLESPOON PINE NUTS
1	CUP FROZEN PEAS
2	CUPS ARUGULA
2	HEARTS OF PALM, SLICED
2	TABLESPOONS GRATED PARMESAN CHEESE
	RED WINE VINAIGRETTE (SEE PAGE 599)

MELON, CUCUMBER & PROSCIUTTO SALAD

YIELD: 4 TO 6 SERVINGS / **ACTIVE TIME:** 15 MINUTES / **TOTAL TIME:** 40 MINUTES

The versatile melon can comfortably straddle the sweet-savory divide. Here it pairs up with crispy, cured prosciutto and creamy feta to carry this dynamic salad.

1. Preheat the oven to 350°F. Place the prosciutto on a parchment-lined rimmed baking sheet. Cover it with another sheet of parchment paper and place another rimmed baking sheet that is the same size on top. Place the prosciutto in the oven and bake until it is crisp, about 12 minutes. Remove it from the oven and let it cool. When the prosciutto is cool enough to handle, chop it into bite-size pieces.

2. Place the cantaloupe, honeydew melon, and cucumber in a salad bowl, season with salt and pepper, and toss to combine. Add the jalapeño and vinaigrette and toss to coat.

3. Top the salad with the prosciutto and feta, garnish with mint, and serve.

INGREDIENTS:

8	SLICES OF PROSCIUTTO
3	CUPS DICED CANTALOUPE
3	CUPS DICED HONEYDEW MELON
1	CUCUMBER, SLICED
	SALT AND PEPPER, TO TASTE
1	JALAPEÑO CHILE PEPPER, STEMMED, SEEDED, AND SLICED
	MINT VINAIGRETTE (SEE PAGE 525)
⅔	CUP CRUMBLED FETA CHEESE
	FRESH MINT, CHOPPED, FOR GARNISH

TUNA SALAD LETTUCE WRAPS

YIELD: 4 SERVINGS / **ACTIVE TIME:** 5 MINUTES / **TOTAL TIME:** 5 MINUTES

This is a light, protein-packed, and fun way to get a party or dinner party started.

1. Place all of the ingredients, except for the lettuce, in a mixing bowl and stir until well combined.

2. Arrange the leaves of lettuce in the serving bowls. Place some of the tuna mixture in the center of each one, garnish with additional parsley, and serve.

INGREDIENTS:

2	(5 OZ.) CANS OF TUNA, DRAINED
⅓	CUP MAYONNAISE
1	SMALL RED ONION, CHOPPED
2	TABLESPOONS CHOPPED PICKLED JALAPEÑO CHILE PEPPERS
2	TEASPOONS WHOLE-GRAIN MUSTARD
2	TABLESPOONS CHOPPED FRESH PARSLEY, PLUS MORE FOR GARNISH
½	TEASPOON KOSHER SALT
1	TEASPOON BLACK PEPPER
	LEAVES FROM 1 HEAD OF BUTTER LETTUCE, RINSED WELL AND PATTED DRY

SOM TAM SALAD

YIELD: 4 SERVINGS / **ACTIVE TIME:** 20 MINUTES / **TOTAL TIME:** 20 MINUTES

Dried shrimp adds a burst of briny flavor and a delicate crunch to this traditional Thai salad.

1. Place the carrot, papaya, and greens beans in a salad bowl and toss to combine. Add the dressing and toss to coat.

2. Top the salad with the shrimp and peanuts and serve with lime wedges.

INGREDIENTS:

1	CARROT, PEELED AND JULIENNED
1	PAPAYA, JULIENNED
1	CUP CHOPPED GREEN BEANS
	SPICY PEANUT DRESSING (SEE PAGE 638)
½	CUP DRIED SHRIMP
1	CUP ROASTED PEANUTS
	LIME WEDGES, FOR SERVING

GRILLED NECTARINE SALAD
WITH PROSCIUTTO & BOCCONCINI

YIELD: 4 SERVINGS / **ACTIVE TIME:** 20 MINUTES / **TOTAL TIME:** 30 MINUTES

Bocconcini are those little balls of fresh mozzarella, and they are a true trump card when it comes to salad making.

1. Prepare a gas or charcoal grill for medium-high heat (about 450°F).

2. Place the nectarines on the grill, cut sides down, and cook until they are lightly charred, about 6 minutes. Turn the nectarines over and cook until they are tender, about 5 minutes. Remove the nectarines from the grill and let them cool slightly.

3. When the nectarines are cool enough to handle, chop them into bite-size pieces and place them in a salad bowl. Add the prosciutto and salad greens and toss to combine. Add the lemon juice and olive oil, season with salt and pepper, and toss to coat.

4. Divide the salad among the serving plates and top each portion with some of the bocconcini. Garnish with lemon zest and serve.

INGREDIENTS:

8   NECTARINES, HALVED AND PITTED

4   OZ. PROSCIUTTO, SLICED THIN AND TORN

5   OZ. SALAD GREENS

2   TABLESPOONS FRESH LEMON JUICE

2   TABLESPOONS EXTRA-VIRGIN OLIVE OIL

    SALT AND PEPPER, TO TASTE

4   OZ. BOCCONCINI (BALLS OF FRESH MOZZARELLA CHEESE), TORN

    STRIPS OF LEMON ZEST, FOR GARNISH

CURED SHRIMP SALAD
WITH AVOCADO PANNA COTTA

YIELD: 4 SERVINGS / ACTIVE TIME: 15 MINUTES / TOTAL TIME: 1 HOUR

Curing shrimp with lime juice is a way to highlight its fresh flavor, and an avocado custard elevates what, in reality, is a simple dish.

1. Place the cucumber, garlic, cilantro, jalapeño, and lime juice in a blender, season with salt and pepper, and puree until smooth.

2. Strain the puree into a bowl, pressing down to push as much of it through as possible.

3. Add the shrimp to the bowl, cover it with plastic wrap, and chill in the refrigerator until the shrimp turn pink, 40 to 50 minutes.

4. Serve alongside the Avocado Panna Cotta.

INGREDIENTS:

½ ENGLISH CUCUMBER

1 GARLIC CLOVE

½ CUP FRESH CILANTRO, CHOPPED

½ JALAPEÑO CHILE PEPPER, STEMMED, SEEDED, AND SLICED

¾ CUP FRESH LIME JUICE

   SALT AND PEPPER, TO TASTE

½ LB. MEXICAN GULF ROCK SHRIMP, SHELLED AND DEVEINED

   AVOCADO PANNA COTTA (SEE PAGE 662), FOR SERVING

SPINACH, BACON, AVOCADO & ORANGE SALAD

YIELD: 4 SERVINGS / **ACTIVE TIME:** 15 MINUTES / **TOTAL TIME:** 25 MINUTES

If you want to make this salad vegetarian, switch out the bacon for generously browned shiitake mushrooms.

INGREDIENTS:

1. Place the bacon in a large skillet and cook over medium heat until it is cooked to your liking. Transfer the bacon to a paper towel–lined plate to drain and cool. When the bacon is cool enough to handle, chop or crumble it into bite-size pieces.

2. Place the spinach in a large salad bowl. Halve the orange segments and add them to the salad bowl, reserving one segment.

3. Squeeze the juice from the reserved orange segment over the avocado slices to keep them from browning and add the avocado to the salad bowl.

4. Add the vinaigrette and toss to coat. Top the salad with the bacon and sunflower seeds and serve.

- 2–4 SLICES OF BACON, COOKED AND CRUMBLED
- 5 OZ. BABY SPINACH
- 1 NAVEL ORANGE, SUPREMED (SEE PAGE 92)
- FLESH FROM 1 AVOCADO, SLICED
- RED WINE & MAPLE VINAIGRETTE (SEE PAGE 560)
- 1 TABLESPOON SUNFLOWER SEEDS

WILD MUSHROOM SALAD
WITH BACON VINAIGRETTE

YIELD: 4 SERVINGS / **ACTIVE TIME:** 25 MINUTES / **TOTAL TIME:** 35 MINUTES

A bacon-centered vinaigrette is a refreshing way to work bacon's beloved flavor into a first course.

1. Preheat the oven to 350°F. Place the pecans on a baking sheet, place them in the oven, and roast until they are fragrant and browned, 8 to 10 minutes. Remove the pecans from the oven and let them cool.

2. Place the olive oil in a large skillet and warm it over medium heat. Add the mushrooms, season with salt and pepper, and cook, without stirring, until they start to brown, about 10 minutes. Stir the mushrooms and cook until they are well browned all over, about 5 minutes.

3. Transfer the mushrooms to a salad bowl, add the greens, pecans, and goat cheese, and toss to combine. Add half of the vinaigrette and toss to coat.

4. Divide the salad among the serving plates and serve with the remaining vinaigrette.

INGREDIENTS:

1	CUP PECANS
2	TABLESPOONS EXTRA-VIRGIN OLIVE OIL
1	LB. WILD MUSHROOMS, STEMMED AND SLICED
	SALT AND PEPPER, TO TASTE
5	OZ. SALAD GREENS
4	OZ. GOAT CHEESE, CRUMBLED
	BACON VINAIGRETTE (SEE PAGE 610)

Wild Mushroom Salad with Bacon Vinaigrette,
see page 61

CUCUMBER & CARROT SALAD WITH MISO DRESSING

YIELD: 4 SERVINGS / ACTIVE TIME: 20 MINUTES / TOTAL TIME: 20 MINUTES

The key to this salad is getting the strips of cucumbers and carrots similarly thin.

1. Place the cucumbers and carrots in a salad bowl and toss to combine. Add the dressing and toss to coat.

2. Top the salad with the sesame seeds, garnish with parsley and basil, and serve.

INGREDIENTS:

3   CUCUMBERS, PEELED AND CUT INTO LONG, THIN STRIPS

4   CARROTS, PEELED AND CUT INTO LONG, THIN STRIPS

     MISO DRESSING (SEE PAGE 571)

2   TABLESPOONS SESAME SEEDS

     FRESH PARSLEY, CHOPPED FOR GARNISH

     FRESH BASIL, CHOPPED, FOR GARNISH

ENDIVE SALAD WITH CINNAMON CROUTONS

YIELD: 4 SERVINGS / **ACTIVE TIME:** 20 MINUTES / **TOTAL TIME:** 20 MINUTES

This is a good one to turn to during the winter months—perhaps even for a holiday party.

1. Preheat the oven to 375°F. Place the bread in a mixing bowl, drizzle the canola oil over it, and sprinkle the cinnamon over the top. Toss until the bread is evenly coated and transfer it to a baking sheet, making sure it is in an even layer.

2. Place the bread in the oven and toast until it is golden brown and crispy, 10 to 15 minutes, stirring once or twice. Remove the croutons from the oven and let them cool slightly.

3. Place the croutons in a salad bowl, add the endive, orange, carrot, and dates, and toss to combine. Add half of the vinaigrette and toss to coat.

4. Garnish with thyme and microgreens and serve with the remaining vinaigrette.

INGREDIENTS:

2	CUPS DAY-OLD BREAD PIECES (½-INCH CUBES)
1	TABLESPOON CANOLA OIL
1	TEASPOON CINNAMON
4	OZ. ENDIVE, CHOPPED
1	ORANGE, PEELED AND DICED
1	CARROT, PEELED AND SHREDDED
½	CUP CHOPPED DATES
	WHITE WINE VINAIGRETTE (SEE PAGE 540)
	FRESH THYME, FOR GARNISH
	MICROGREENS, FOR GARNISH

FENNEL SALAD WITH CARAMELIZED MANGO

YIELD: 4 SERVINGS / **ACTIVE TIME:** 20 MINUTES / **TOTAL TIME:** 40 MINUTES

Herbal, earthy, and tinged with anise, fennel cries out for a sweet mate. The mango more than supplies that, and also balances out the rich prosciutto.

1. Place the canola oil in a large skillet and warm it over medium heat. Working in batches if necessary to avoid crowding the pan, add the mangoes and cook until they are caramelized all over, turning them as necessary. Transfer the mangoes to a salad bowl.

2. Add the fennel and prosciutto to the salad bowl, season with salt and pepper, and toss to combine. Add the vinaigrette and toss until everything is evenly coated.

3. Garnish with fennel fronds and serve.

INGREDIENTS:

1 TABLESPOON CANOLA OIL

FLESH OF 2 MANGOES, SLICED INTO THIN WEDGES

4 BULBS OF FENNEL, TRIMMED AND SLICED VERY THIN

4 OZ. PROSCIUTTO, SLICED THIN AND TORN

SALT AND PEPPER, TO TASTE

WHITE BALSAMIC VINAIGRETTE (SEE PAGE 565)

FENNEL FRONDS, FOR GARNISH

RADICCHIO, POMEGRANATE & PEAR SALAD

YIELD: 4 SERVINGS / **ACTIVE TIME:** 20 MINUTES / **TOTAL TIME:** 20 MINUTES

Doubling up on your chicories means that you've got no shortage of beautiful bitterness to work with, and the creamy, vanilla-edged pears, salty, grassy Gorgonzola, and sweet-tart pomegranate make the most of the opportunity.

1. Preheat the oven to 350°F. Place the pecans on a baking sheet, place them in the oven, and roast until they are fragrant and browned, 8 to 10 minutes. Remove the pecans from the oven and let them cool.

2. Place the radicchio, chicory, pears, Gorgonzola, and pomegranate arils in a salad bowl and toss to combine.

3. Add the olive oil and lemon juice, season with salt and pepper, and toss to coat.

4. Chop the roasted pecans, sprinkle them over the salad, and serve.

INGREDIENTS:

1	CUP PECANS
3	OZ. RADICCHIO, CHOPPED
3	OZ. CHICORY, CHOPPED
4	PEARS, CORED AND SLICED THIN
4	OZ. GORGONZOLA CHEESE, CRUMBLED
1	CUP POMEGRANATE ARILS
2	TABLESPOONS EXTRA-VIRGIN OLIVE OIL
1	TABLESPOON FRESH LEMON JUICE
	SALT AND PEPPER, TO TASTE

MELON, STRAWBERRY & BASIL SALAD
WITH BLUE CHEESE

YIELD: 4 SERVINGS / ACTIVE TIME: 20 MINUTES / TOTAL TIME: 20 MINUTES

Turn to this salad when you're looking for something a bit more substantial and complex during the summer.

1. Place the honey in a microwave-safe bowl, place it in the microwave, and microwave it on high for 10 seconds. Remove the honey from the microwave, add the lime juice, and whisk to combine.

2. Place the watermelon, melon, strawberries, and blue cheese in a salad bowl and toss to combine. Add the honey dressing and toss to coat.

3. Garnish with basil and serve.

INGREDIENTS:

2 TABLESPOONS HONEY

2 TABLESPOONS FRESH LIME JUICE

6 CUPS WATERMELON BALLS

2 CUPS MELON BALLS

2 CUPS SLICED STRAWBERRIES

2 OZ. BLUE CHEESE, CRUMBLED

FRESH BASIL, FOR GARNISH

SWEET POTATO & WATERCRESS SALAD

YIELD: 4 SERVINGS / ACTIVE TIME: 20 MINUTES / TOTAL TIME: 1 HOUR

Sweet potatoes and pumpkin seeds make one think of autumn, but truthfully, this one will be best toward the end of August, on one of those nights when you can feel the summer giving way to what's next.

1. Preheat the oven to 375°F. Place the sweet potatoes in a baking dish, drizzle the olive oil over them, and season with salt and pepper. Toss to combine, cover the dish with aluminum foil, and place the sweet potatoes in the oven. Roast until they are fork-tender, 30 to 45 minutes.

2. Remove the sweet potatoes from the oven and let them cool.

3. Place the sweet potatoes, watercress, cucumber, shallots, goat cheese, and raisins in a salad bowl and toss to combine. Add the vinaigrette, season with salt and pepper, and toss to coat.

4. Garnish with pumpkin seeds and serve.

INGREDIENTS:

2   SWEET POTATOES, PEELED AND DICED

2   TABLESPOONS EXTRA-VIRGIN OLIVE OIL

    SALT AND PEPPER, TO TASTE

5   OZ. WATERCRESS

1   CUCUMBER, DICED

2   SHALLOTS, SLICED THIN

2   OZ. GOAT CHEESE, CRUMBLED

½   CUP RAISINS

    WHITE WINE VINAIGRETTE (SEE PAGE 540)

    ROASTED PUMPKIN SEEDS, FOR GARNISH

POMEGRANATE & SWEET POTATO SALAD

YIELD: 4 SERVINGS / **ACTIVE TIME:** 20 MINUTES / **TOTAL TIME:** 1 HOUR

A salad that serves as a key reminder of what always works in the kitchen—simple ingredients, elegantly deployed and displayed.

1. Preheat the oven to 375°F. Place the sweet potatoes in a baking dish, drizzle the olive oil over them, and season with salt and pepper. Toss to combine and place the sweet potatoes in the oven. Roast until they are fork-tender and well browned, 40 to 45 minutes.

2. Remove the sweet potatoes from the oven and let them cool.

3. Place the sweet potatoes, salad greens, pomegranate arils, figs, and goat cheese in a salad bowl and toss to combine. Add the vinaigrette, toss to coat, and serve.

INGREDIENTS:

4	SWEET POTATOES, HALVED AND SLICED
2	TABLESPOONS EXTRA-VIRGIN OLIVE OIL
	SALT AND PEPPER, TO TASTE
5	OZ. SALAD GREENS
½	CUP POMEGRANATE ARILS
12–16	FIGS, QUARTERED
3	OZ. GOAT CHEESE, CRUMBLED
	CHAMPAGNE VINAIGRETTE (SEE PAGE 592)

TOMATO SALAD WITH BURRATA

YIELD: 4 SERVINGS / **ACTIVE TIME:** 20 MINUTES / **TOTAL TIME:** 20 MINUTES

As far as salad goes, this one requires a bit of a splurge, between the pine nuts and burrata. But the end result is oh so worth it.

1. Place the fennel seeds in a dry skillet and toast over medium heat until they are fragrant, 1 to 2 minutes, shaking the pan frequently to make sure they do not burn. Transfer the toasted fennel seeds to a salad bowl.

2. Add the tomatoes, arugula, chile, and pine nuts to the salad bowl and toss to combine. Add the olive oil, season with salt and pepper, and toss to coat.

3. Divide the salad among the serving plates, top each portion with some of the burrata, garnish with basil, and serve.

INGREDIENTS:

1	TABLESPOON FENNEL SEEDS
2	CUPS CHERRY TOMATOES, HALVED
5	OZ. ARUGULA
1	RED CHILE PEPPER, STEMMED, SEEDED, AND DICED
1	CUP PINE NUTS
2	TABLESPOONS EXTRA-VIRGIN OLIVE OIL
	SALT AND PEPPER, TO TASTE
4	OZ. BURRATA CHEESE, TORN
	FRESH BASIL, FOR GARNISH

SHIITAKE & CHICORY SALAD
WITH RED CURRANT DRESSING

YIELD: 4 SERVINGS / **ACTIVE TIME:** 20 MINUTES / **TOTAL TIME:** 30 MINUTES

Consider adding the cashews to the pan along with the shiitakes, as toasting them a bit will highlight their sweetness.

1. Place the olive oil in a large skillet and warm it over medium heat. Add the mushrooms, season with salt and pepper, and cook until the mushrooms are just tender, 6 to 8 minutes, stirring occasionally. Remove the mushrooms from the pan and let them cool.

2. Place the mushrooms, cashews, and chicory in a salad bowl and toss to combine. Add the dressing and toss to coat.

3. Divide the salad among the serving plates and sprinkle some of the pomegranate arils over each portion. Garnish with fresh herbs and serve.

INGREDIENTS:

2	TABLESPOONS EXTRA-VIRGIN OLIVE OIL
6	OZ. SHIITAKE MUSHROOMS, STEMMED
	SALT AND PEPPER, TO TASTE
½	CUP CASHEWS
5	OZ. CHICORY
	RED CURRANT DRESSING (SEE PAGE 528)
¼	CUP POMEGRANATE ARILS
	FRESH HERBS, FINELY CHOPPED, FOR GARNISH

SEAWEED SALAD

YIELD: 4 SERVINGS / **ACTIVE TIME:** 10 MINUTES / **TOTAL TIME:** 45 MINUTES

A wonderful salad for those evenings when the main course will be something from Japanese cuisine.

1. Place the seaweeds in a bowl and cover with cold water. Let the seaweeds soak until they are soft, about 10 minutes.

2. Drain the seaweeds and pat them dry. Place them in a salad bowl, add the vinegar, sesame oil, soy sauce, ginger, and chile, and toss to combine. Let the seaweeds marinate for 25 minutes.

3. Add the cucumber to the salad, season with salt, and toss to combine. Garnish with sesame seeds and cilantro and serve.

INGREDIENTS:

2	OZ. DRIED RED DULSE SEAWEED
2	OZ. DRIED GREEN WAKAME SEAWEED
2	TABLESPOONS RICE VINEGAR
1	TABLESPOON SESAME OIL
1	TABLESPOON SOY SAUCE
2	TEASPOONS GRATED FRESH GINGER
1½	TEASPOONS MINCED RED CHILE PEPPER
1	CUCUMBER, FINELY DICED
	SALT, TO TASTE
	SESAME SEEDS, FOR GARNISH
	FRESH CILANTRO, CHOPPED, FOR GARNISH

SPRING SALAD WITH ASPARAGUS & GRANOLA

YIELD: 4 SERVINGS / **ACTIVE TIME:** 20 MINUTES / **TOTAL TIME:** 50 MINUTES

You want the granola here primarily for the crunch—the less sweet it is, the better the salad will be.

1. Preheat the oven to 375°F. Place the asparagus in a baking dish, drizzle the olive oil over it, and season with salt and pepper. Toss to combine, place the asparagus in the oven, and roast until the asparagus is tender, 20 to 25 minutes.

2. Remove the asparagus from the oven and let it cool.

3. Chop the asparagus into bite-size pieces and place it in a salad bowl. Add the salad greens, strawberries, and granola and toss to combine. Add the vinaigrette and toss to coat.

4. Garnish with edible flowers and serve.

INGREDIENTS:

6   OZ. ASPARAGUS, TRIMMED

2   TABLESPOONS EXTRA-VIRGIN OLIVE OIL

     SALT AND PEPPER, TO TASTE

4   OZ. SALAD GREENS

1½   CUPS QUARTERED STRAWBERRIES

1   CUP GRANOLA

     MAPLE & MUSTARD VINAIGRETTE (SEE PAGE 572)

     EDIBLE FLOWERS, FOR GARNISH

ON THE SIDE

*I*t can be difficult to distinguish signal from noise when it comes to food research, but pretty much all of the data out there suggests that everyone would benefit from incorporating a few more vegetables into their diet.

These salads make that hurdle effortless to clear, providing dozens of recipes that will provide the nutrients that you need, the flavor that you crave, and the ease that is desirable in a side dish.

WARM ASPARAGUS SALAD

YIELD: 2 TO 4 SERVINGS / **ACTIVE TIME:** 25 MINUTES / **TOTAL TIME:** 35 MINUTES

Few vegetables bring as much joy to gardeners and farmers as asparagus, as its appearance indicates that the winter is completely past, and spring has arrived.

1. Place 1 tablespoon of olive oil in a large skillet and warm it over medium heat. Add the garlic and tomatoes and cook, stirring continually, until the tomatoes start to collapse, about 5 minutes. Transfer the mixture to a bowl and set it aside.

2. Place the remaining olive oil in the skillet and warm it over medium heat. Add the asparagus in a single layer, cover the pan, and cook until the asparagus is bright green, about 5 minutes. Uncover the pan and cook until the asparagus is well browned on one side, about 5 minutes.

3. Add the asparagus to the garlic and tomatoes and season the mixture with salt and pepper. Add the olives, toss to combine, top the salad with the basil and Parmesan, and serve.

INGREDIENTS:

2 TABLESPOONS EXTRA-VIRGIN OLIVE OIL

2 GARLIC CLOVES, MINCED

10 OZ. CHERRY TOMATOES, HALVED

1 LB. ASPARAGUS, TRIMMED

SALT AND PEPPER, TO TASTE

½ CUP KALAMATA OLIVES, PITS REMOVED, CHOPPED

2 TABLESPOONS CHOPPED FRESH BASIL

¼ CUP GRATED PARMESAN CHEESE

GRAPEFRUIT & FENNEL SALAD

YIELD: 4 SERVINGS / ACTIVE TIME: 20 MINUTES / TOTAL TIME: 20 MINUTES

The grapefruit is the key here, as its tang ties the array of other flavors together.

1. Using a mandoline or a sharp knife, cut the white onion, fennel stalks, and apple into very thin slices. Chop the fennel fronds. Place these items in a bowl.

2. Add the fresh herbs, honey, and white vinegar and toss to combine.

3. Trim the top and bottom from the grapefruit and then cut along the contour of the fruit to remove the pith and peel. Cut one segment, lengthwise, between the pulp and the membrane. Make a similar slice on the other side of the segment and then remove the pulp. Set it aside and repeat with the remaining segments. This technique is known as "supreming" and can be used for all citrus fruits.

4. Add the segments to the salad bowl along with the jalapeño, toss to combine, and enjoy.

INGREDIENTS:

½	WHITE ONION
2	FENNEL STALKS, FRONDS REMOVED AND RESERVED
1	APPLE
1	TEASPOON CHOPPED FRESH DILL
1	TEASPOON CHOPPED FRESH MINT
1	TABLESPOON CHOPPED FRESH PARSLEY
1	TABLESPOON HONEY
3	TABLESPOONS WHITE VINEGAR
1	GRAPEFRUIT
1	JALAPEÑO CHILE PEPPER, STEMMED, SEEDED, AND SLICED THIN

OLIVE SALAD

YIELD: 6 SERVINGS / **ACTIVE TIME:** 15 MINUTES / **TOTAL TIME:** 15 MINUTES

Tart and briny, with a slight sweetness and a surprising burst of freshness thanks to the mint, this simple salad is something of a wonder.

1. Place the olives, garlic, and pomegranate arils in a bowl and stir until well combined.

2. Place the pomegranate juice, mint, and olive oil in a separate bowl and stir until combined.

3. Pour the dressing over the olive mixture and stir until evenly coated. Add the salt and pepper, garnish with walnuts and additional mint, and enjoy.

INGREDIENTS:

2 CUPS GREEN OLIVES, PITS REMOVED

2 GARLIC CLOVES, MINCED

1 CUP POMEGRANATE ARILS

⅓ CUP POMEGRANATE JUICE

⅓ CUP CHOPPED FRESH MINT, PLUS MORE FOR GARNISH

⅓ CUP EXTRA-VIRGIN OLIVE OIL

1 TEASPOON KOSHER SALT

¼ TEASPOON BLACK PEPPER

ROASTED WALNUTS, CRUSHED, FOR GARNISH

Grapefruit & Fennel Salad, see page 92

CHICKPEA SALAD

YIELD: 4 SERVINGS / ACTIVE TIME: 20 MINUTES / TOTAL TIME: 24 HOURS

A good option when you need something light yet flavorful beside a particularly savory dish. It is also lovely with some tuna folded in.

1. Drain the chickpeas, place them in a saucepan, and add the stock. Bring to a boil, reduce the heat, and simmer until the chickpeas are tender, about 45 minutes.

2. Drain the chickpeas and let them cool completely.

3. Place the chickpeas and the remaining ingredients in a mixing bowl, toss until combined, and enjoy.

INGREDIENTS:

2 CUPS DRIED CHICKPEAS, SOAKED OVERNIGHT

4 CUPS CHICKEN STOCK (SEE PAGE 663)

1 ONION, CHOPPED

1 CUP CHOPPED FRESH CILANTRO

¼ CUP EXTRA-VIRGIN OLIVE OIL

¼ CUP FRESH LEMON JUICE

¼ TEASPOON SAFFRON

1 TABLESPOON CUMIN

1 TEASPOON CINNAMON

1 TEASPOON RED PEPPER FLAKES

SALT AND PEPPER, TO TASTE

MARINATED EGGPLANT SALAD

YIELD: 4 SERVINGS / **ACTIVE TIME:** 30 MINUTES / **TOTAL TIME:** 2 HOURS AND 30 MINUTES

This super-acidic, herbaceous salad is a complete change of pace from a traditional eggplant salad.

1. Warm a cast-iron skillet over high heat. Brush the eggplant with the olive oil, place it in the pan, and cook until lightly charred on each side, about 6 minutes.

2. Transfer the eggplant to a salad bowl, add the garlic, fresh herbs, salt, vinegar, and any remaining olive oil, and stir to combine.

3. Add the tomatoes and shallots, toss to combine, and refrigerate for at least 2 hours before serving.

INGREDIENTS:

1   EGGPLANT, SLICED INTO ½-INCH-THICK ROUNDS

½   CUP EXTRA-VIRGIN OLIVE OIL

4   GARLIC CLOVES, MINCED

1   TABLESPOON CHOPPED FRESH DILL

1   TABLESPOON CHOPPED FRESH BASIL

1   TABLESPOON KOSHER SALT

½   CUP WHITE VINEGAR

1   CUP CHERRY TOMATOES, HALVED

2   SHALLOTS, JULIENNED

STRAWBERRY & ASPARAGUS SALAD

YIELD: 4 SERVINGS / **ACTIVE TIME:** 20 MINUTES / **TOTAL TIME:** 50 MINUTES

Sweet and with a hint of bitterness, white asparagus is the best variety for this complexly flavored salad.

1. Bring water to a boil in a medium pot.

2. Preheat the oven to 375°F. Place the asparagus in a baking dish, drizzle the olive oil over it, and season with salt and pepper. Toss to combine, place the asparagus in the oven, and roast until it is tender, 15 to 20 minutes.

3. Add salt to the boiling water, let it return to a full boil, and add the peas. Cook until they are just tender, 2 to 4 minutes. Drain the peas, rinse them under cold water, and let them cool.

4. Remove the asparagus from the oven and let it cool.

5. Place the asparagus, peas, spinach, strawberries, and mozzarella in a salad bowl and toss to combine. Add the lemon juice and balsamic vinegar, season with salt and pepper, and toss to coat.

6. Top the salad with the almonds, garnish with mint, and serve.

INGREDIENTS:

½   LB. WHITE ASPARAGUS, TRIMMED AND CHOPPED

2   TABLESPOONS EXTRA-VIRGIN OLIVE OIL

     SALT AND PEPPER, TO TASTE

3   CUPS GREEN PEAS

4   OZ. SPINACH

3   CUPS THINLY SLICED STRAWBERRIES

3   OZ. MOZZARELLA CHEESE, DICED

1   TABLESPOON FRESH LEMON JUICE

3   TABLESPOONS BALSAMIC VINEGAR

1   CUP ALMONDS, CHOPPED

     FRESH MINT, FOR GARNISH

TURKISH EGGPLANT SALAD

YIELD: 4 SERVINGS / **ACTIVE TIME:** 30 MINUTES / **TOTAL TIME:** 1 HOUR AND 30 MINUTES

A salad that highlights the best characteristics of Turkish cuisine: unapologetically garlic heavy, smoky, and earthy.

1. Preheat the oven to 450°F. Poke a few holes in the eggplants, place them on a baking sheet, and place them in the oven. Roast until completely tender and starting to collapse, 40 minutes to 1 hour. Remove the eggplants from the oven and let them cool completely.

2. Place the olive oil in a large skillet and warm it over high heat. Add the tomatoes and onion and cook until the onion is translucent, about 4 minutes. Add the remaining ingredients, except for the parsley, and cook for approximately 20 minutes, stirring occasionally. Transfer the mixture to a mixing bowl.

3. Halve the eggplants and scoop the flesh into the tomato mixture. Stir to combine, adding the parsley as you go. Let the mixture cool to room temperature before serving.

INGREDIENTS:

2	LARGE EGGPLANTS
2	TABLESPOONS EXTRA-VIRGIN OLIVE OIL
3	TOMATOES, DICED
1	WHITE ONION, JULIENNED
4	GARLIC CLOVES, MINCED
1	TABLESPOON PAPRIKA
1	TEASPOON KOSHER SALT
1	TEASPOON CUMIN
1	TEASPOON CAYENNE PEPPER
½	CUP CHOPPED FRESH PARSLEY

BROCCOLINI SALAD

Blanching is a cooking process in which a food, usually a vegetable or fruit, is scalded in boiling water and salt, removed after a brief, timed interval, and finally plunged into iced water or placed under cold running water to halt the cooking process and retain the ingredient's crisp character.

1. Bring salted water to a boil in a large saucepan and prepare an ice bath. Add the broccolini and cook for 4 minutes.

2. Transfer the broccolini to the ice bath and let it cool. Pat the broccolini dry and chop it into bite-size pieces.

3. Place the broccolini in a large salad bowl, add all of the remaining ingredients, except for the olive oil and garlic, and toss to combine. Set the salad aside.

4. Place the olive oil in a medium skillet and warm it over medium heat. Add the garlic and cook, stirring continuously, until it is golden brown, about 1½ minutes.

5. Pour the mixture over the salad and toss to incorporate. Taste, adjust the seasoning as necessary, and serve.

INGREDIENTS:

2	TABLESPOONS KOSHER SALT, PLUS MORE TO TASTE
2	LBS. BROCCOLINI
1	CUP DRIED CRANBERRIES
1	CUP SLICED ALMONDS, TOASTED
½	CUP CRUMBLED FETA OR GOAT CHEESE
1	CUP BLUEBERRIES
½	CUP CHAMPAGNE VINAIGRETTE (SEE PAGE 592)
2	CUPS SLICED RED GRAPES
1	TABLESPOON BLACK PEPPER, PLUS MORE TO TASTE
¼	CUP CHOPPED FRESH HERBS (PARSLEY, MINT, BASIL, AND OREGANO RECOMMENDED)
¼	CUP EXTRA-VIRGIN OLIVE OIL
5	GARLIC CLOVES, MINCED

Turkish Eggplant Salad, see page 100

TOMATO SALAD WITH ROASTED PEPPERS

YIELD: 4 SERVINGS / **ACTIVE TIME:** 20 MINUTES / **TOTAL TIME:** 50 MINUTES

Buy a few bottles of Portuguese wine, grill up some fish or pork, and flank it with this light, richly flavored salad.

1. Preheat the oven to 375°F. Place the peppers in a baking dish and place them in the oven. Roast until they are charred all over, 20 to 25 minutes, turning them as necessary. Remove the roasted peppers from the oven, place them in a heatproof bowl, and cover it with plastic wrap. Let the peppers steam for 10 minutes.

2. Remove the charred skins and the seed pods from the peppers. Slice the remaining flesh into wide strips and place them in a salad bowl. Add the tomatoes and toss to combine.

3. Add the olive oil and vinegar, season with salt and pepper, and toss to coat.

4. Garnish with fresh herbs and serve.

INGREDIENTS:

3   RED BELL PEPPERS

6   TOMATOES, CUT INTO WEDGES

2   TABLESPOONS EXTRA-VIRGIN OLIVE OIL

1   TABLESPOON SHERRY VINEGAR

SALT AND PEPPER, TO TASTE

FRESH HERBS, CHOPPED, FOR GARNISH

SWEET & SPICY CARROT SALAD

YIELD: 4 SERVINGS / **ACTIVE TIME:** 20 MINUTES / **TOTAL TIME:** 20 MINUTES

An excellent salad to incorporate into a mezze platter.

1. Place the carrots, raisins, and pomegranate arils in a salad bowl and toss to combine. Add the vinaigrette and toss to coat.

2. Garnish with cilantro and serve.

INGREDIENTS:

8 CARROTS, PEELED AND JULIENNED

2 CUPS GOLDEN RAISINS

2 CUPS POMEGRANATE ARILS

HARISSA & DIJON VINAIGRETTE (SEE PAGE 584)

FRESH CILANTRO, CHOPPED, FOR GARNISH

RADICCHIO & PEAR SALAD

YIELD: 4 SERVINGS / **ACTIVE TIME:** 20 MINUTES / **TOTAL TIME:** 20 MINUTES

One doesn't often think winter when it comes to salad, but this preparation is a great fit when the weather turns cold.

1. Place the radicchio, arugula, and pears in a salad bowl and toss to combine. Add the vinaigrette and toss to coat.

2. Top with the Candied Walnuts and serve.

INGREDIENTS:

6   OZ. RADICCHIO

4   OZ. ARUGULA

4   PEARS, SLICED THIN

     MAPLE & MUSTARD
     VINAIGRETTE (SEE PAGE
     572)

1   CUP CANDIED WALNUTS
     (SEE PAGE 663), CHOPPED

SHAVED SNAP PEA SALAD

YIELD: 2 SERVINGS / **ACTIVE TIME:** 20 MINUTES / **TOTAL TIME:** 50 MINUTES

A vibrant mix of sweet and tangy, herby and fresh, tender and crunchy.

1. Using a sharp knife, stack 4 snap peas and cut them into thin slices on a bias. Transfer them to a bowl and repeat with the remaining snap peas.

2. Add the remaining ingredients and toss until well combined.

3. Chill the salad in the refrigerator for 30 minutes before serving.

INGREDIENTS:

1	LB. SNAP PEAS
1	TABLESPOON CHOPPED FRESH DILL
1	TABLESPOON CHOPPED FRESH BASIL
1	TABLESPOON CHOPPED FRESH MINT
1	TABLESPOON CRUSHED TOASTED WALNUTS
2	TEASPOONS HONEY
¼	CUP WHITE VINEGAR
1	TEASPOON KOSHER SALT

HEART-BEET SALAD

YIELD: 2 SERVINGS / **ACTIVE TIME:** 20 MINUTES / **TOTAL TIME:** 20 MINUTES

Beets and goat cheese are a classic combination, but the addition of truffle and hazelnuts elevates this salad to something special.

1. Place the arugula, kale, beets, orange, and vinaigrette in a bowl and toss to combine.

2. Spread the truffle goat cheese spread over the serving plates. Top it with the salad, garnish with tarragon, pomegranate arils, hazelnuts, and hemp hearts, and serve.

INGREDIENTS:

2   OZ. ARUGULA

2   OZ. KALE, TORN

½   LB. ROASTED BEETS, DICED

8   ORANGE SEGMENTS

¼   CUP POMEGRANATE VINAIGRETTE (SEE PAGE 592)

3   TABLESPOONS TRUFFLE GOAT CHEESE SPREAD

FRESH TARRAGON, FOR GARNISH

POMEGRANATE ARILS, FOR GARNISH

TOASTED HAZELNUTS, CRUSHED, FOR GARNISH

HEMP HEARTS, FOR GARNISH

Shaved Snap Pea Salad, see page 110

STRAWBERRY FIELDS SALAD

YIELD: 4 SERVINGS / **ACTIVE TIME:** 15 MINUTES / **TOTAL TIME:** 15 MINUTES

D o yourself a favor and hold off on making this salad until strawberries are at the height of their season.

1. Place all of the ingredients in a mixing bowl, toss to coat, and enjoy.

INGREDIENTS:

4	OZ. ARUGULA
½	OZ. TUSCAN KALE, TORN
½	CUP CHERRY TOMATOES, HALVED
¼	CUP SHAVED FENNEL
1	CUP STRAWBERRIES, HULLED AND SLICED
½	CUP CRUMBLED GOAT CHEESE
10	KALAMATA OLIVES, PITTED AND HALVED
	CHAMPAGNE VINAIGRETTE (SEE PAGE 592)
1	TABLESPOON CHOPPED FRESH HERBS
	POMEGRANATE MOLASSES, TO TASTE

RED CABBAGE, DATE & BEET SALAD

YIELD: 6 SERVINGS / **ACTIVE TIME:** 30 MINUTES / **TOTAL TIME:** 1 HOUR AND 30 MINUTES

This salad provides a beautiful burst of deep red hues and sweet and savory flavors.

1. Preheat the oven to 400°F. Line a baking sheet with parchment paper and cover it with the salt.

2. Set the beets on the bed of salt, place them in the oven, and roast until they are fork-tender, 45 minutes to 1 hour.

3. Remove the beets from the oven and let them cool for 30 minutes. Discard the salt.

4. Peel the beets, cut them into 2-inch-long slices that are ⅛ inch thick, and place them in a bowl. You can also grate the beets.

5. Add all of the remaining ingredients to the bowl and stir until well combined. Taste, adjust the seasoning as necessary, and enjoy.

INGREDIENTS:

2	CUPS KOSHER SALT
6	LARGE RED BEETS
½	HEAD OF RED CABBAGE, CORED AND SLICED THIN
5	DRIED MEDJOOL DATES, PITTED AND SLICED THIN LENGTHWISE
½	CUP TAHINI DRESSING (SEE PAGE 565)
⅓	CUP CHOPPED FRESH CILANTRO
⅓	CUP CHOPPED FRESH MINT
⅓	CUP CHOPPED SCALLIONS
¼	CUP EXTRA-VIRGIN OLIVE OIL
¼	CUP FRESH LEMON JUICE

FAVA BEAN SALAD WITH CELERY & PARMESAN

YIELD: 4 SERVINGS / **ACTIVE TIME:** 20 MINUTES / **TOTAL TIME:** 30 MINUTES

When fresh fava beans become available, you want to find as many preparations that utilize them as you can.

1. Bring water to a boil in a medium pot. Add salt, let the water return to a full boil, and add the beans. Cook until they are just tender, 4 to 5 minutes. Drain the beans, rinse them under cold water, and let them cool.

2. Place the beans, celery, and Parmesan in a salad bowl and toss to combine. Add the olive oil and lemon juice, season with salt and pepper, and toss to coat.

3. Garnish with celery leaves and parsley and serve.

INGREDIENTS:

SALT AND PEPPER, TO TASTE

4 CUPS SHELLED FAVA BEANS

2 CELERY STALKS, SLICED THIN

3 OZ. PARMESAN CHEESE, SHAVED

2 TABLESPOONS EXTRA-VIRGIN OLIVE OIL

2 TABLESPOONS FRESH LEMON JUICE

CELERY LEAVES, CHOPPED, FOR GARNISH

FRESH PARSLEY, CHOPPED, FOR GARNISH

HORIATIKI SALAD

YIELD: 4 SERVINGS / **ACTIVE TIME:** 10 MINUTES / **TOTAL TIME:** 10 MINUTES

You know that it's great on the side. But don't hesitate to take it further and use it as a filling for stuffed peppers or tomatoes.

1. Place the cucumber, cherry tomatoes, feta, onion, olives, and dried oregano in a mixing bowl and stir gently until combined.

2. Drizzle the olive oil over the salad, season with salt and pepper, gently toss to combine, and serve.

INGREDIENTS:

1   CUCUMBER, SLICED

1   CUP CHERRY TOMATOES, HALVED

1   CUP CRUMBLED FETA CHEESE

1   RED ONION, SLICED

½   CUP PITTED KALAMATA OLIVES

1   TEASPOON DRIED OREGANO

½   CUP EXTRA-VIRGIN OLIVE OIL

    SALT AND PEPPER, TO TASTE

PICKLED CUCUMBER SALAD

YIELD: 8 SERVINGS / **ACTIVE TIME:** 10 MINUTES / **TOTAL TIME:** 25 MINUTES

Everything a salad should be—easy, refreshing, and delicious.

1. Place the sugar and vinegar in a small saucepan and bring to a simmer, stirring to dissolve the sugar.

2. Place the cucumbers and onion in a shallow bowl and pour the brine over it. Let the vegetables pickle until they are completely cool.

3. Season the salad with salt and pepper, sprinkle the parsley over the top, and serve.

INGREDIENTS:

1	TEASPOON SUGAR
¼	CUP RICE VINEGAR
2	LARGE CUCUMBERS, PEELED AND SLICED INTO THIN ROUNDS
½	RED ONION, SLICED THIN
	SALT AND PEPPER, TO TASTE
1	TABLESPOON CHOPPED FRESH PARSLEY

Horiatiki Salad, see page 118

ROASTED ROOT SALAD
WITH LEMON & CAPER DRESSING

YIELD: 4 SERVINGS / **ACTIVE TIME:** 15 MINUTES / **TOTAL TIME:** 50 MINUTES

Get in the habit of whipping up a big batch of this regularly—it'll make planning meals for the rest of the week a cinch.

1. Preheat the oven to 425°F. Place the parsnips, celeriac, Brussels sprouts, potatoes, shallots, garlic, thyme, rosemary, honey, and ¼ cup of the olive oil in a mixing bowl and toss to coat. Season the mixture with salt and pepper and spread the mixture on a baking sheet in a single layer.

2. Place the vegetables in the oven and roast until they are golden brown and tender, 30 to 35 minutes. Remove the vegetables from the oven and let them cool.

3. Place the parsley, capers, lemon zest, lemon juice, and remaining olive oil in a mixing bowl and whisk to combine.

4. Place the roasted vegetables in a salad bowl and drizzle the dressing over them. Toss to coat and serve.

INGREDIENTS:

½	LB. PARSNIPS, PEELED AND CUT INTO 1-INCH CUBES
1	CELERIAC, PEELED AND CUT INTO 1-INCH CUBES
½	LB. BRUSSELS SPROUTS, TRIMMED AND HALVED
1	LB. NEW POTATOES
6	SHALLOTS, QUARTERED
4	GARLIC CLOVES, MINCED
2	TEASPOONS FRESH THYME
1	TEASPOON CHOPPED FRESH ROSEMARY
1	TABLESPOON HONEY
6	TABLESPOONS EXTRA-VIRGIN OLIVE OIL
	SALT AND PEPPER, TO TASTE
2	TABLESPOONS CHOPPED FRESH PARSLEY
1	TABLESPOON CAPERS, DRAINED AND CHOPPED
	ZEST AND JUICE OF 1 LEMON

SMASHED CUCUMBER SALAD

YIELD: 2 SERVINGS / **ACTIVE TIME:** 15 MINUTES / **TOTAL TIME:** 15 MINUTES

S mashing the cucumbers makes it possible for the soy sauce and other seasonings to permeate them, making this dish far more flavorful.

1. Place the cucumbers in a resealable plastic bag. Press out as much air as possible. Using a rolling pin or a cast-iron skillet, smash the cucumbers.

2. Add the soy sauce, sesame oil, vinegar, and red pepper flakes to the bag, season with salt, and massage the ingredients to combine. Taste and adjust the seasoning as necessary.

3. Transfer the seasoned cucumbers to a serving plate, garnish with the sesame seeds and Rayu, and serve immediately.

INGREDIENTS:

4   PERSIAN OR JAPANESE CUCUMBERS, CHOPPED INTO 3-INCH-LONG PIECES

1½   TABLESPOONS SOY SAUCE

1   TEASPOON SESAME OIL

1   TEASPOON UNSEASONED RICE VINEGAR

½   TEASPOON RED PEPPER FLAKES

    SALT, TO TASTE

1   TABLESPOON TOASTED SESAME SEEDS, FOR GARNISH

    RAYU (SEE PAGE 520), FOR GARNISH

Smashed Cucumber Salad, see page 123

AUTUMN KALE SALAD

YIELD: 6 SERVINGS / ACTIVE TIME: 25 MINUTES / TOTAL TIME: 1 HOUR

The sweet golden raisins contrast the dark, vegetal kale, and the pungent roasted garlic provides a savory kick.

1. Preheat the oven to 400°F. Trim the top 1 inch of the head of the garlic, exposing the cloves. Drizzle 1 teaspoon of olive oil over the garlic and rub it into the cloves. Wrap the garlic in aluminum foil, place it on a baking sheet, and place it in the oven. Roast the garlic until the cloves are completely soft, 30 to 40 minutes. Remove the garlic from the oven and set it aside.

2. While the garlic is roasting, prepare the squash. Place it in a bowl with the remaining olive oil, the salt, and the pepper. Toss to coat, place the squash on a large baking sheet, and place it in the oven. Roast the squash until browned and cooked through, about 20 minutes, turning it over halfway through. Remove the squash from the oven and let it cool.

3. Slice the kale into thin strips, place it in a large bowl, and add the vinaigrette a bit at a time, using your hands to massage the kale leaves until they have softened and look shiny; there may be vinaigrette left over. Add the roasted garlic, raisins, nuts, and squash and toss to combine.

4. Garnish with Parmesan and serve.

INGREDIENTS:

½	HEAD OF GARLIC
2	TABLESPOONS PLUS 1 TEASPOON EXTRA-VIRGIN OLIVE OIL
1	SMALL DELICATA SQUASH, SEEDED AND SLICED THIN
1	TEASPOON KOSHER SALT
	PINCH OF BLACK PEPPER
1	LARGE HEAD OF LACINATO KALE, THICK RIBS REMOVED
	HONEY VINAIGRETTE (SEE PAGE 524)
½	CUP GOLDEN RAISINS
½	CUP CHOPPED HAZELNUTS OR ALMONDS, TOASTED
	PARMESAN CHEESE, SHAVED, FOR GARNISH

CUCUMBER, MINT & SUMAC SALAD

YIELD: 4 SERVINGS / **ACTIVE TIME:** 15 MINUTES / **TOTAL TIME:** 15 MINUTES

Cucumber and mint are sure to lighten any warm-weather meal, and sumac adds an extra layer of sourness and brightness.

1. Place the cucumbers, 1 tablespoon of sumac, the olive oil, lemon juice, and salt in a large bowl and toss to combine.

2. Transfer the salad to a serving bowl, taste, and adjust the seasoning as necessary. Sprinkle the remaining sumac on top, garnish with the mint, and enjoy.

INGREDIENTS:

12 PERSIAN CUCUMBERS, QUARTERED LENGTHWISE ON A BIAS

1½ TABLESPOONS SUMAC

¼ CUP EXTRA-VIRGIN OLIVE OIL

¼ CUP FRESH LEMON JUICE

1 TEASPOON KOSHER SALT, PLUS MORE TO TASTE

¼ CUP FRESH MINT LEAVES, FOR GARNISH

LATE SPRING SALAD WITH CANTALOUPE & CUCUMBERS

YIELD: 4 SERVINGS / ACTIVE TIME: 20 MINUTES / TOTAL TIME: 20 MINUTES

When summer is so close that you can barely stand it, celebrate with some grilled proteins and this refreshing salad.

1. Place the cantaloupe, cucumber, prosciutto, and feta in a salad bowl and toss to combine. Add half of the vinaigrette, season with salt, and toss to coat.

2. Garnish with pea shoots and edible flowers and serve.

INGREDIENTS:

1   CANTALOUPE, PEELED, SEEDED, AND SLICED THIN

1½   CUCUMBER, SLICED INTO LONG, THIN RIBBONS

4   OZ. PROSCIUTTO, TORN

4   OZ. FETA CHEESE, CRUMBLED

      WHITE BALSAMIC VINAIGRETTE (SEE PAGE 565)

      SALT, TO TASTE

      PEA SHOOTS, FOR GARNISH

      EDIBLE FLOWERS, FOR GARNISH

WARM COUSCOUS SALAD

YIELD: 4 SERVINGS / **ACTIVE TIME:** 15 MINUTES / **TOTAL TIME:** 15 MINUTES

A versatile dish that can work well beside both braised chicken legs and roasted seafood.

1. Place the water and 1 tablespoon of the olive oil in a saucepan, season the mixture with salt, and bring to a boil. Add the couscous and cook for 8 minutes.

2. Place the lemon juice, garlic, mustard, and honey in a mixing bowl and whisk until combined. While whisking continually, slowly drizzle in the remaining olive oil until it has emulsified.

3. Drain the couscous and place it in a serving bowl. Add the dressing to taste, season the salad with salt and pepper, and toss to combine. Garnish with mint and parsley and enjoy.

INGREDIENTS:

1¾   CUPS WATER

7   TABLESPOONS EXTRA-VIRGIN OLIVE OIL

SALT AND PEPPER, TO TASTE

1½   CUPS ISRAELI COUSCOUS

1½   TABLESPOONS FRESH LEMON JUICE

1   GARLIC CLOVE, MINCED

2   TEASPOONS MUSTARD

1   TEASPOON HONEY

FRESH MINT, CHOPPED, FOR GARNISH

FRESH PARSLEY, CHOPPED, FOR GARNISH

HONEY-ROASTED VEGETABLE SALAD

YIELD: 4 SERVINGS / **ACTIVE TIME:** 30 MINUTES / **TOTAL TIME:** 1 HOUR

Top with yogurt sauce and mint, and prepare to amaze with this sweet, sour, and savory salad.

1. Preheat the oven to 400°F. Line a large roasting pan with parchment paper.

2. Using a sharp knife, carefully peel the pumpkin and chop it into ¾-inch cubes. Discard the seeds. Trim and cut the cauliflower into florets, halving any large ones. Trim and gently scrub the carrots.

3. Place the vegetables in the roasting pan and drizzle the olive oil and honey over them. Season with the cumin, salt, and pepper and toss to coat.

4. Place the vegetables in the oven and roast until tender and golden brown, 25 to 30 minutes.

5. Remove the pan from the oven, add the spinach and mint, and stir to combine.

6. Place the yogurt and lemon juice in a small bowl, season with salt and pepper, and stir to combine.

7. Transfer the vegetables to a serving dish or salad bowl, drizzle the yogurt over the top, garnish with additional mint, and enjoy.

INGREDIENTS:

1¾	LB. PUMPKIN
1	SMALL HEAD OF CAULIFLOWER
1	BUNCH OF HEIRLOOM BABY CARROTS
2	TABLESPOONS EXTRA-VIRGIN OLIVE OIL
1	TABLESPOON HONEY
1	TEASPOON CUMIN
	SALT AND PEPPER, TO TASTE
4	CUPS BABY SPINACH
1	CUP FRESH MINT LEAVES, PLUS MORE FOR GARNISH
½	CUP PLAIN GREEK YOGURT
1	TABLESPOON FRESH LEMON JUICE

ROASTED PEPPER SALAD

YIELD: 6 SERVINGS / **ACTIVE TIME:** 10 MINUTES / **TOTAL TIME:** 30 MINUTES

A classic Moroccan dish that will fit right in at a summer barbecue.

1. Roast the peppers on a grill or over the flame of a gas burner until they are charred all over and tender. Place the peppers in a baking dish, cover it with plastic wrap, and let them steam for 10 minutes.

2. Remove the charred skins and the seed pods from the peppers and discard them. Slice the roasted peppers into strips and set them aside.

3. Place 1 tablespoon of the avocado oil in a saucepan and warm it over medium heat. Add the onion and cook, stirring occasionally, until it has softened, about 5 minutes. Remove the pan from heat and let the onion cool.

4. Place the peppers, onion, remaining avocado oil, vinegar, salt, pepper, cumin, and cilantro in a bowl, stir until combined, and enjoy.

INGREDIENTS:

3	RED BELL PEPPERS
2	YELLOW BELL PEPPERS
1	GREEN BELL PEPPER
½	CUP PLUS 1 TABLESPOON AVOCADO OIL
½	ONION, SLICED THIN
1	TEASPOON WHITE VINEGAR
¼	TEASPOON KOSHER SALT
⅛	TEASPOON BLACK PEPPER
½	TEASPOON CUMIN
¼	BUNCH OF FRESH CILANTRO, CHOPPED

GREEN BEAN & FAVA BEAN SALAD

YIELD: 4 SERVINGS / **ACTIVE TIME:** 20 MINUTES / **TOTAL TIME:** 30 MINUTES

Consider using rosemary and summer savory for the fresh herb garnish, as they will supply a robust, woodsy element that will shine among these ingredients.

1. Bring water to a boil in a large saucepan. Add salt and the green beans and cook until they are just tender, 3 to 4 minutes. Remove the green beans with a strainer, rinse them under cold water, and let them drain in a colander.

2. Add the fava beans to the boiling water and cook for 2 minutes. Drain the fava beans, rinse them under cold water, and let them cool.

3. Pat the beans dry and add them to a salad bowl. Add the garlic and toss to combine.

4. Add the vinaigrette, season with salt and pepper, and toss to coat.

5. Garnish with fresh herbs and serve.

INGREDIENTS:

SALT AND PEPPER, TO TASTE

6 OZ. GREEN BEANS

3 CUPS SHELLED FAVA BEANS

4 GARLIC CLOVES, MINCED

WHITE BALSAMIC VINAIGRETTE (SEE PAGE 565)

FRESH HERBS, CHOPPED, FOR GARNISH

ROASTED SQUASH & FETA SALAD

YIELD: 4 SERVINGS / **ACTIVE TIME**: 15 MINUTES / **TOTAL TIME**: 40 MINUTES

Feta and bread get roasted alongside winter squash, then tossed with pleasantly bitter greens for a salad that's equal parts warm and cold, soft and crunchy, and sweet and savory.

1. Preheat the oven to 400°F. Halve the squash lengthwise, remove the seeds and discard them, and cut the squash into ¼-inch-thick slices.

2. Place the squash on a baking sheet, season it with the salt and pepper, drizzle the avocado oil over it, and toss to coat. Place the squash in the oven and roast until it is beginning to brown on one side, about 15 minutes.

3. Remove the baking sheet from the oven, turn the squash over, and then sprinkle the bread and feta over the squash. Return the pan to the oven and roast until the bread is lightly toasted and the feta is soft and warmed through, about 10 minutes. Remove the baking sheet from the oven and let the mixture cool slightly.

4. In a small bowl, combine the paprika and cayenne and set the mixture aside.

5. Place the radicchio and warm squash mixture in a salad bowl and toss to combine. Add the vinaigrette and toss to coat.

6. Sprinkle the paprika-and-cayenne mixture over the dish and serve.

INGREDIENTS:

1½   LBS. ACORN SQUASH

1   TEASPOON KOSHER SALT

¼   TEASPOON BLACK PEPPER

2   TABLESPOONS AVOCADO OIL

4   CUPS CUBED FRENCH BREAD

½   LB. FETA CHEESE, CRUMBLED

½   TEASPOON SWEET HUNGARIAN PAPRIKA

½   TEASPOON CAYENNE PEPPER

1   HEAD OF RADICCHIO, LEAVES SEPARATED AND TORN INTO LARGE PIECES

HONEY VINAIGRETTE (SEE PAGE 524)

SHAVED RADISH SALAD WITH WALNUTS & MINT

YIELD: 6 SERVINGS / **ACTIVE TIME:** 20 MINUTES / **TOTAL TIME:** 1 HOUR AND 20 MINUTES

The mandoline was made for recipes like this, as the extra-thin slices it produces will make this straightforward salad look like the work of a pro.

1. Preheat the oven to 375°F. Rinse the beets under cold water and trim away the tops and bottoms. Cut the beets in half, place them in a bowl, and add the olive oil. Season with salt and pepper and toss to coat.

2. Lay out a large piece of aluminum foil, top it with a piece of parchment paper, and wrap the beets in the packet. Place the packet in the oven and roast the beets until they are fork-tender, about 1 hour. Remove the beets from the oven.

3. Reduce the oven's temperature to 350°F. Using rubber gloves or paper towels, rub the beets so that the skins slide right off. Set the beets aside and let them cool.

4. Place the walnuts on a baking sheet, place them in the oven, and toast until golden brown and fragrant, about 10 minutes, tossing them halfway through.

5. Remove the walnuts from the oven and let them cool. Crush the walnuts into small pieces.

6. Place the lemon juice, mustard, lemon zest, honey, and poppy seeds in a blender and pulse until combined. Taste, adjust the seasoning as necessary, and set the dressing aside.

7. Layer the radishes and beets on a large plate and top with the walnuts, Parmesan cheese, mint, and lime zest. Drizzle the dressing over the top and enjoy.

INGREDIENTS:

1	CHIOGGIA BEET
1	GOLDEN BEET
¾	CUP EXTRA-VIRGIN OLIVE OIL, PLUS MORE AS NEEDED
	SALT AND PEPPER, TO TASTE
¼	CUP WALNUTS
¼	CUP FRESH LEMON JUICE
1	TABLESPOON DIJON MUSTARD
1½	TEASPOONS LEMON ZEST
1	TABLESPOON HONEY
1	TABLESPOON POPPY SEEDS
1	WATERMELON RADISH, SLICED THIN
3	RADISHES, SLICED THIN
½	CUP SHAVED PARMESAN CHEESE
1	BUNCH OF FRESH MINT
1½	TEASPOONS LIME ZEST

WARM ZUCCHINI & CORN SALAD

YIELD: 4 SERVINGS / **ACTIVE TIME:** 15 MINUTES / **TOTAL TIME:** 35 MINUTES

A helpful dish for those weeks during the summer when zucchini becomes ubiquitous.

1. Place the olive oil in a skillet and warm it over low heat. Add the chiles and toast lightly until fragrant, taking care not to burn them. Remove the chiles from the pan and set them aside. When cool enough to handle, chop the chiles.

2. Add the onion and garlic to the pan and cook until the onion is translucent, about 3 minutes, stirring frequently.

3. Add the corn and cook for 2 minutes, stirring occasionally. Add the tomatoes and cook until they begin to release their juices.

4. Add the zucchini, season the mixture with salt, and cook until the vegetables are tender, about 10 minutes.

5. Add the cilantro to the pan and cook for 1 minute. Remove the cilantro from the pan, add the chiles, and stir until evenly distributed.

6. To serve, place the mixture in a salad bowl and top it with the queso fresco.

INGREDIENTS:

2 TABLESPOONS EXTRA-VIRGIN OLIVE OIL

3 DRIED CHILES DE ÁRBOL, STEMLESS AND SEEDLESS

½ WHITE ONION, DICED

3 GARLIC CLOVES, SLICED THIN

KERNELS FROM 2 EARS OF CORN

2 LARGE TOMATOES, SEEDLESS AND DICED

4 ZUCCHINI, DICED

SALT, TO TASTE

3 SPRIGS OF FRESH CILANTRO

1 CUP CRUMBLED QUESO FRESCO

CIALLEDDA

YIELD: 4 SERVINGS / **ACTIVE TIME:** 20 MINUTES / **TOTAL TIME:** 1 HOUR AND 20 MINUTES

Also called acquasale, cialledda is a cold bread salad that is popular in Apulia, a region in Southern Italy that forms the "heel" of the famed "boot."

1. Place the onion and vinegar in a bowl, season the mixture with salt, and let it sit for 1 hour.

2. Place the bread in a bowl, gently squeeze the tomatoes over it, and then add the tomatoes. Add the remaining ingredients, season the mixture with salt, and toss to combine.

3. Cover the bowl with plastic wrap and let the salad rest for 1 hour.

4. Drain the onion and rinse it. Add it to the salad, gently toss to incorporate, and enjoy.

INGREDIENTS:

1	SMALL RED ONION, SLICED THIN
2	TABLESPOONS WHITE BALSAMIC VINEGAR
	SALT, TO TASTE
1	LB. STALE BREAD, CHOPPED
4	TOMATOES, CUT INTO WEDGES
1	CUCUMBER, FINELY DICED
1	CELERY STALK, SLICED THIN
	HANDFUL OF FRESH BASIL, CHOPPED
2	TABLESPOONS CAPERS, DRAINED
¼	CUP EXTRA-VIRGIN OLIVE OIL
	DRIED OREGANO, TO TASTE

Warm Zucchini & Corn Salad,
see page 138

INSALATA DI RINFORZO

YIELD: 6 SERVINGS / **ACTIVE TIME:** 15 MINUTES / **TOTAL TIME:** 30 MINUTES

This rich Neapolitan salad is typically served on Christmas Eve and New Year's Eve, and was meant to make sure people could still eat their fill on those days, when the consumption of animal meat was prohibited.

1. Bring salted water to a boil in a large saucepan. Add the cauliflower and cook until it is al dente, about 10 minutes. Drain the cauliflower and let it cool completely.

2. Arrange the cooled cauliflower in a serving dish and top with the anchovies, capers, olives, pickles, and papaccelle.

3. Place the olive oil, vinegar, and a pinch of salt in a bowl and whisk until the mixture has emulsified. Pour the dressing over the salad and enjoy.

INGREDIENTS:

SALT, TO TASTE

1 HEAD OF CAULIFLOWER, CUT INTO FLORETS

8 ANCHOVIES IN OLIVE OIL, DRAINED

½ CUP CAPERS, DRAINED AND SQUEEZED

¾ CUP GREEN OLIVES, PITTED

½ CUP MIXED PICKLES, DRAINED

3½ OZ. PAPACCELLE (STUFFED PEPPERS IN OIL), HALVED

5 TABLESPOONS EXTRA-VIRGIN OLIVE OIL

3 TABLESPOONS RED WINE VINEGAR

CAESAR SALAD

YIELD: 6 SERVINGS / **ACTIVE TIME:** 5 MINUTES / **TOTAL TIME:** 5 MINUTES

As you no doubt have seen, this classic has spawned numerous iterations. But this version, featuring the renowned trio of romaine, croutons, and Caesar dressing, remains without peer.

1. Place the Croutons and lettuce in a salad bowl, add a generous amount of dressing, and toss to coat.

2. Season with salt and pepper, garnish with Parmesan, and serve with any remaining dressing.

INGREDIENTS:

CROUTONS (SEE PAGE 666)

1 LB. ROMAINE LETTUCE

CLASSIC CAESAR DRESSING (SEE PAGE 593)

SALT AND PEPPER, TO TASTE

PARMESAN CHEESE, GRATED, FOR GARNISH

Caesar Salad, see page 143

INSALATA DI ARANCE E FINOCCHIO

YIELD: 4 SERVINGS / **ACTIVE TIME:** 15 MINUTES / **TOTAL TIME:** 30 MINUTES

This extremely simple salad, which is beloved in Sicily, combines oranges and fennel to provide a colorful dish with explosive flavor.

1. Peel the oranges and, using a sharp knife, remove the white pith. Slice the oranges thin and set them aside.

2. Arrange the onion and fennel on a serving platter and top with the oranges and olives.

3. Drizzle the olive oil over the salad and season with salt and pepper.

4. Let the salad marinate for about 15 minutes before serving.

INGREDIENTS:

6 ORANGES

1 SMALL ONION, SLICED THIN

1 SMALL BULB OF FENNEL, TRIMMED AND SLICED THIN

½ CUP BLACK OLIVES, PITTED

¼ CUP EXTRA-VIRGIN OLIVE OIL

SALT AND PEPPER, TO TASTE

INSALATA DI PATATE E FAGIOLINI

YIELD: 4 SERVINGS / **ACTIVE TIME:** 15 MINUTES / **TOTAL TIME:** 50 MINUTES

A cold green bean-and-potato salad that is a very typical summer side dish throughout the whole of Southern Italy.

1. Bring salted water to a boil in a large saucepan. Add the potatoes and boil until they are tender, about 30 minutes. Remove the potatoes from the boiling water and let them cool.

2. Add the green beans and boil until they are tender, about 5 minutes. Drain the green beans and let them cool.

3. When the potatoes and green beans are cool enough to handle, peel the potatoes, chop them, and place them in a bowl. Chop the green beans and add them to the bowl.

4. Add the tomatoes, basil, oregano, and olive oil to the bowl, toss to combine, and either serve the salad immediately or store it in the refrigerator and serve chilled.

INGREDIENTS:

SALT, TO TASTE

4 LARGE POTATOES, SCRUBBED

1½ LBS. GREEN BEANS

1½ CUPS CHERRY TOMATOES, HALVED

FRESH BASIL, CHOPPED, TO TASTE

FRESH OREGANO, CHOPPED, TO TASTE

¼ CUP EXTRA-VIRGIN OLIVE OIL

CAPRESE SALAD

YIELD: 4 SERVINGS / **ACTIVE TIME:** 15 MINUTES / **TOTAL TIME:** 15 MINUTES

The secret of a successful Caprese lies in the freshness and quality of the ingredients, and the precision of the execution, as it is very easy to turn this lovely dish into a wet mess. Just pay attention, follow the steps, and use a sharp knife.

1. Season the tomatoes with salt and let them rest.

2. Pat the mozzarella dry with paper towels. Arrange the mozzarella, tomatoes, and basil on a platter, alternating between them.

3. Drizzle the olive oil over the salad, season it with oregano and pepper, and enjoy.

INGREDIENTS:

5   TOMATOES, CUT INTO ½-INCH-THICK SLICES

    SALT AND PEPPER, TO TASTE

2   BALLS OF FRESH MOZZARELLA CHEESE, CUT INTO ½-INCH-THICK SLICES

    HANDFUL OF FRESH BASIL LEAVES

2   TABLESPOONS EXTRA-VIRGIN OLIVE OIL

    DRIED OREGANO, TO TASTE

Caprese Salad, see page 149

RADICCHIO E BRUCIATINI

YIELD: 4 SERVINGS / **ACTIVE TIME:** 15 MINUTES / **TOTAL TIME:** 30 MINUTES

This lovely radicchio salad is popular on the Romagna side of the Emilia-Romagna region in Italy.

1. Rinse the radicchio and pat it dry.

2. Place the pancetta in a large skillet and cook it over medium heat until the fat has rendered, stirring occasionally.

3. Add the vinegar and cook, stirring occasionally, until the pancetta has browned.

4. Arrange the radicchio leaves on a serving plate, top with the pancetta, and drizzle olive oil over the salad. Season it with salt and serve.

INGREDIENTS:

14 OZ. RADICCHIO

3½ OZ. PANCETTA OR BACON, DICED

2½ TABLESPOONS BALSAMIC VINEGAR

EXTRA-VIRGIN OLIVE OIL, TO TASTE

SALT, TO TASTE

SPICY BEAN SPROUT SALAD

YIELD: 4 SERVINGS / **ACTIVE TIME:** 10 MINUTES / **TOTAL TIME:** 15 MINUTES

This umami-rich, crunchy salad can be served as a side dish, or used to top rice or ramen.

1. In a bowl, combine the soy sauce, canola oil, togarashi, and salt and whisk until well combined.

2. Bring a pot of water to a boil. Add the bean sprouts, blanch for 1 minute, and drain.

3. Add the bean sprouts and sesame seeds to the dressing and stir to combine. Season with pepper, taste the salad, and adjust the seasoning as necessary. Serve immediately.

INGREDIENTS:

2 TEASPOONS SOY SAUCE

2 TABLESPOONS CANOLA OIL

1 TEASPOON SHICHIMI TOGARASHI (SEE PAGE 666)

½ TEASPOON KOSHER SALT

¾ LB. BEAN SPROUTS

1 TABLESPOON TOASTED SESAME SEEDS

FRESHLY GROUND BLACK PEPPER, TO TASTE

SUMMER SALAD WITH WHITE PEACHES & FETA

YIELD: 4 SERVINGS / **ACTIVE TIME:** 20 MINUTES / **TOTAL TIME:** 20 MINUTES

Always overdo it and rush to buy too much during the brief peach season? This salad allows you to turn that error into an opportunity.

1. Place the salad greens, tomatoes, cucumber, peaches, and feta in a salad bowl and toss to combine.

2. Add the lemon juice, season with salt and pepper, and toss to coat.

3. Drizzle the honey over the salad, garnish with mint and edible flowers, and serve.

INGREDIENTS:

5 OZ. SALAD GREENS

2 CUPS HALVED CHERRY TOMATOES

1 CUCUMBER, SLICED INTO LONG, THIN STRIPS

4 WHITE PEACHES, PITTED AND SLICED

4 OZ. FETA CHEESE, CRUMBLED

1 TABLESPOON FRESH LEMON JUICE

SALT AND PEPPER, TO TASTE

2 TABLESPOONS HONEY

FRESH MINT, FOR GARNISH

EDIBLE FLOWERS, FOR GARNISH

SHAVED SQUASH SALAD WITH HERB VINAIGRETTE

YIELD: 6 SERVINGS / ACTIVE TIME: 15 MINUTES / TOTAL TIME: 1 HOUR

This dish provides a crucial bit of instruction: when working with raw vegetables, do your best to make each bite feel effortless.

1. Preheat the oven's broiler to high. Place the cherry tomatoes, olive oil, garlic, thyme, salt, and pepper in a mixing bowl and toss until the tomatoes are evenly coated. Place the tomatoes on a baking sheet, place it in the oven, and broil until the tomatoes' skins begin to blister, 6 to 8 minutes. Remove the pan from the oven and let the mixture cool completely.

2. Place the zucchini, squash, and bell pepper in a large mixing bowl, season with salt and pepper, and add the vinaigrette. Toss to coat, plate the salad, sprinkle the blistered tomatoes over the top, and serve.

INGREDIENTS:

2   CUPS CHERRY TOMATOES

1   TABLESPOON EXTRA-VIRGIN OLIVE OIL

5   GARLIC CLOVES, CRUSHED

    LEAVES FROM 2 SPRIGS OF FRESH THYME

½   TEASPOON KOSHER SALT, PLUS MORE TO TASTE

¼   TEASPOON BLACK PEPPER, PLUS MORE TO TASTE

3   ZUCCHINI, SLICED THIN WITH A MANDOLINE

2   SUMMER SQUASH, SLICED THIN WITH A MANDOLINE

1   RED BELL PEPPER, STEMMED, SEEDED, AND SLICED THIN WITH A MANDOLINE

    HERB VINAIGRETTE (SEE PAGE 643)

RED & GREEN CABBAGE SALAD
WITH GINGER & TAHINI DRESSING

YIELD: 2 SERVINGS / ACTIVE TIME: 15 MINUTES / TOTAL TIME: 15 MINUTES

This is a great recipe for the weekend after Thanksgiving, but it is also delicious enough to make anytime with sliced turkey from the deli. The zesty dressing pairs wonderfully with the cabbage, and the hint of spicy ginger ties it all together.

1. Place all of the ingredients in a salad bowl, except for the dressing and turkey, and toss to combine.

2. Add the dressing and toss to coat. Add the turkey, toss to evenly distribute, and serve.

INGREDIENTS:

2   CUPS SHREDDED GREEN CABBAGE

2   CUPS SHREDDED RED CABBAGE

3   TABLESPOONS CHOPPED PEANUTS

3   SCALLIONS, TRIMMED AND CHOPPED

½   CUP CHOPPED FRESH CILANTRO OR PARSLEY

GINGER & TAHINI DRESSING (SEE PAGE 635)

¼   LB. COOKED TURKEY, DICED

RADICCHIO & RICOTTA SALATA SALAD

YIELD: 4 SERVINGS / **ACTIVE TIME:** 10 MINUTES / **TOTAL TIME:** 10 MINUTES

The key to this salad is to slice everything very thin, so all of the flavors can fit on a single forkful.

1. Arrange the greens on four plates and top with equal amounts of radicchio, fennel, apple, and ricotta salata.

2. Serve with the Apple Cider Vinaigrette.

INGREDIENTS:

3½   CUPS MESCLUN GREENS

½   HEAD OF RADICCHIO, CORED AND SLICED VERY THIN

½   LARGE FENNEL, TRIMMED AND SLICED VERY THIN

1   APPLE, CORED, SEEDED, AND SLICED THIN

2   OZ. RICOTTA SALATA CHEESE

APPLE CIDER VINAIGRETTE (SEE PAGE 561), FOR SERVING

COLD GREEN BEAN SALAD
WITH BLUE CHEESE & WALNUTS

YIELD: 4 SERVINGS / **ACTIVE TIME:** 15 MINUTES / **TOTAL TIME:** 30 MINUTES

When the green beans are coming in strong in midsummer and you are looking for new ways to utilize them, try this salad. It is a cinch to prepare, requiring only that you blanch the beans and then whip up a vinaigrette.

1. Bring water to a boil in a medium saucepan. Add salt and the green beans and cook until the green beans are al dente, about 5 minutes.

2. Drain the green beans and run them under cold water to stop the cooking process. Pat the green beans dry with paper towels.

3. Place the mustard, shallot, vinegar, and olive oil in a bowl and whisk to combine.

4. Place the green beans and remaining ingredients in a bowl and toss to combine. Add the dressing, toss to coat, and refrigerate for 15 minutes before serving.

INGREDIENTS:

SALT, TO TASTE

1 LB. GREEN BEANS, TRIMMED

1 TEASPOON DIJON MUSTARD

1½ TEASPOONS MINCED SHALLOT

2 TABLESPOONS WHITE WINE VINEGAR

⅓ CUP EXTRA-VIRGIN OLIVE OIL

BLACK PEPPER, TO TASTE

2–4 OZ. BLUE CHEESE, CRUMBLED

2 OZ. WALNUTS, ROUGHLY CHOPPED

TOMATO & GRILLED SWEET ONION SALAD

YIELD: 4 SERVINGS / **ACTIVE TIME:** 20 MINUTES / **TOTAL TIME:** 25 MINUTES

Give a traditional tomato salad a little extra boost by adding grilled onions.

1. Prepare a gas or charcoal grill for medium heat (about 400°F) and skewer the onions so they are easy to turn while grilling. Brush both sides of the onions with olive oil and season with salt and pepper.

2. Place the onions on the grill and cook until the edges become slightly soft and the onions start to char, about 10 minutes, turning the skewers over just once.

3. Remove the onions from the grill and cut them in half. Place them in a bowl and toss to separate the layers.

4. Add the tomatoes, basil, olive oil, and vinegar, toss to combine, and serve.

INGREDIENTS:

- 2 SWEET ONIONS, CUT INTO ½-INCH-THICK SLICES
- 2 TABLESPOONS EXTRA-VIRGIN OLIVE OIL, PLUS MORE AS NEEDED
- SALT AND PEPPER, TO TASTE
- 2 CUPS GRAPE TOMATOES, HALVED
- 12 FRESH BASIL LEAVES, SLICED THIN OR TORN
- 2 TEASPOONS BALSAMIC VINEGAR

BROCCOLI & BELL PEPPER SALAD

YIELD: 4 SERVINGS / **ACTIVE TIME:** 20 MINUTES / **TOTAL TIME:** 20 MINUTES

Make sure you take your time mincing the broccoli—you really want to avoid any overly large pieces that will make the experience of actually eating this salad feel like work.

1. Place the broccoli, peppers, and apples in a salad bowl and toss to combine. Add the dressing and toss to coat.

2. Garnish with sunflower seeds and serve.

INGREDIENTS:

½   LB. BROCCOLI FLORETS, MINCED

2   YELLOW BELL PEPPERS, STEMMED, SEEDED, AND DICED

2   GRANNY SMITH APPLES, CORED AND DICED

HONEY MUSTARD & TARRAGON DRESSING (SEE PAGE 596)

SUNFLOWER SEEDS, FOR GARNISH

CELERY, APPLE & BLUE CHEESE SALAD

YIELD: 2 TO 4 SERVINGS / **ACTIVE TIME:** 10 MINUTES / **TOTAL TIME:** 10 MINUTES

Celery gets its aria in this winter salad. There are elements of sweetness from the apples, tanginess from the cranberries, earthiness from the walnuts, and savory creaminess from the blue cheese. And celery is the perfect base to tie all these notes together.

1. Place all of the ingredients in a salad bowl and toss to combine.

2. Taste, adjust the seasoning as necessary, and serve.

INGREDIENTS:

4   CUPS DICED CELERY

2   APPLES, CORED, SEEDED, AND DICED

1   CUP TOASTED WALNUTS, CHOPPED

4   OZ. BLUE CHEESE, CRUMBLED

1   CUP DRIED CRANBERRIES

¼   CUP EXTRA-VIRGIN OLIVE OIL

3   TABLESPOONS FRESH LEMON JUICE

SALT AND PEPPER, TO TASTE

SHAVED BRUSSELS SPROUT & KALE SALAD

YIELD: 4 TO 6 SERVINGS / **ACTIVE TIME:** 10 MINUTES / **TOTAL TIME:** 25 MINUTES

Brussels sprouts are as delicious raw as they are cooked, and pairing their robust, slightly spicy, and savory flavor with bright citrus is the perfect way to highlight this quality.

1. Place the bacon in a large skillet and cook over medium heat until it is crispy, about 8 minutes, turning it as necessary. Transfer the bacon to a paper towel–lined plate to drain. When it is cool enough to handle, chop the bacon into bite-size pieces.

2. Remove the membranes from the segments of the blood oranges and cut each segment in half. Place them in a mixing bowl, add the Brussels sprouts and kale, season with salt and pepper, and toss to combine.

3. Add half of the vinaigrette and toss to coat.

4. Divide the salad among the serving plates and top each portion with some of the bacon. Garnish with the toasted pecans and Parmesan cheese and serve with the remaining vinaigrette on the side.

INGREDIENTS:

- ½ LB. BACON
- 3 BLOOD ORANGES, PEELED
- 1 LB. BRUSSELS SPROUTS, TRIMMED AND SLICED VERY THIN WITH A MANDOLINE
- 2 CUPS BABY KALE

  SALT AND PEPPER, TO TASTE

  BLOOD ORANGE VINAIGRETTE (SEE PAGE 561)
- ½ CUP TOASTED PECANS, FOR GARNISH

  PARMESAN CHEESE, SHAVED, FOR GARNISH

PEAR & RED CABBAGE SALAD

YIELD: 4 SERVINGS / **ACTIVE TIME:** 20 MINUTES / **TOTAL TIME:** 35 MINUTES

A buckwheat-based granola would be a lovely route to take for the topping here.

1. Place the olive oil in a large skillet and warm it over medium heat. Add the cabbage and cook, stirring occasionally, until it is just tender, 6 to 8 minutes.

2. Transfer the cabbage to a salad bowl, cover it with some of the vinaigrette, and let it marinate for 15 minutes.

3. Add the salad greens and pears to the salad bowl and toss to combine.

4. Top with the granola and serve with the remaining vinaigrette.

INGREDIENTS:

2   TABLESPOONS EXTRA-VIRGIN OLIVE OIL

½   HEAD OF RED CABBAGE, SHREDDED

     BALSAMIC VINAIGRETTE (SEE PAGE 573)

5   OZ. SALAD GREENS

2   PEARS, CORED AND SLICED THIN

½   CUP GRANOLA

QUICK SUMMER SALAD

YIELD: 4 SERVINGS / ACTIVE TIME: 10 MINUTES / TOTAL TIME: 15 MINUTES

One for those nights when ease is the priority for dinner, as less time preparing means more time sitting outside, enjoying the glorious evening.

1. Bring water to a boil in a medium saucepan. Add the corn and cook until it turns bright yellow, 3 to 4 minutes. Drain the corn and let it cool completely.

2. Place the cucumber, corn, bell pepper, cherry tomatoes, and onion in a salad bowl, season with salt and pepper, and toss to combine. Add the vinaigrette and toss to coat.

3. Garnish with parsley and serve.

INGREDIENTS:

KERNELS FROM 3 EARS OF CORN

1 ENGLISH CUCUMBER, SLICED

1 LARGE RED BELL PEPPER, STEMMED, SEEDED, AND CHOPPED

2 CUPS CHERRY TOMATOES, HALVED

1 SMALL RED ONION, SLICED THIN

SALT AND PEPPER, TO TASTE

WHITE WINE VINAIGRETTE (SEE PAGE 540)

FRESH PARSLEY, CHOPPED, FOR GARNISH

KACHUMBER SALAD

YIELD: 4 SERVINGS / **ACTIVE TIME:** 5 MINUTES / **TOTAL TIME:** 5 MINUTES

One may not typically use "spicy" and "refreshing" in tandem, but this salad proves that it is possible for them to partner.

1. Place all of the ingredients, except for the chutney, in a salad bowl and toss to combine.

2. Divide the salad among the serving plates, drizzle some chutney over each portion, and serve.

INGREDIENTS:

2   PERSIAN CUCUMBERS

2   PLUM TOMATOES

1   SMALL ONION, DICED

2   TABLESPOONS CHOPPED FRESH CILANTRO

½   TEASPOON KOSHER SALT

½   TEASPOON KASHMIRI CHILI POWDER

JUICE OF ½ LEMON

SPICY GREEN CHUTNEY (SEE PAGE 525)

CELERIAC SALAD WITH APPLES & CASHEWS

YIELD: 4 SERVINGS / ACTIVE TIME: 20 MINUTES / TOTAL TIME: 20 MINUTES

If you're in the mood for something creamy rather than crunchy, simply soak the cashews in some hot water for 30 minutes, blend that mixture, season it to taste, and apply it as a dressing.

1. Place the celeriac, apples, pomegranate arils, and cashews in a salad bowl and toss to combine. Add the lemon juice, season with salt, and toss to coat.

2. Garnish with parsley and serve.

INGREDIENTS:

½   LB. CELERIAC, PEELED AND SLICED INTO LONG, THIN STRIPS

2   APPLES, SLICED

½   CUP POMEGRANATE ARILS

1   CUP CHOPPED CASHEWS

JUICE OF 1 LEMON

SALT, TO TASTE

FRESH PARSLEY, CHOPPED, FOR GARNISH

PURPLE POTATO SALAD

YIELD: 4 SERVINGS / **ACTIVE TIME:** 20 MINUTES / **TOTAL TIME:** 50 MINUTES

An extremely elegant and eye-catching take on potato salad.

1. Bring water to a boil in a large saucepan. Add salt and the potatoes and cook until the potatoes are fork-tender, 15 to 20 minutes.

2. Drain the potatoes, rinse them under cold water, and let them cool completely.

3. Spread some of the dressing over each of the serving plates. Arrange the potatoes on top and then sprinkle the shallots over them.

4. Season with salt and pepper, garnish with fresh herbs and walnuts, and serve.

INGREDIENTS:

SALT AND PEPPER, TO TASTE

4 PURPLE POTATOES, PEELED AND SLICED

GREEN GODDESS DRESSING (SEE PAGE 539)

2 SHALLOTS, DICED

FRESH HERBS, CHOPPED, FOR GARNISH

WALNUTS, TOASTED AND CHOPPED, FOR GARNISH

BAKED POTATO & RADISH SALAD

YIELD: 4 SERVINGS / ACTIVE TIME: 20 MINUTES / TOTAL TIME: 1 HOUR AND 15 MINUTES

Crisping up the potatoes and radishes in the oven adds another layer of texture to this hearty salad.

1. Preheat the oven to 375°F. Place the potatoes and radishes in a baking dish, drizzle the olive oil over them, and season with salt and pepper. Toss to coat, place the vegetables in the oven, and roast until they are browned and tender, 35 to 45 minutes.

2. Remove the potatoes and radishes from the oven and let them cool slightly.

3. Place the potatoes, radishes, eggs, and cucumbers in a salad bowl and toss to combine. Add the sherry vinegar and dill, toss to coat, and serve.

INGREDIENTS:

20 BABY POTATOES, QUARTERED

½ LB. RADISHES, QUARTERED

¼ CUP EXTRA-VIRGIN OLIVE OIL

SALT AND PEPPER, TO TASTE

4 HARD-BOILED EGGS (SEE PAGE 667), SLICED

1½ CUCUMBERS, SLICED

¼ CUP SHERRY VINEGAR

2 TABLESPOONS FINELY CHOPPED FRESH DILL

CHIOGGIA BEET & CARROT SALAD

YIELD: 4 SERVINGS / **ACTIVE TIME:** 20 MINUTES / **TOTAL TIME:** 20 MINUTES

While some cynical folks would point to the appealing aesthetics of Chioggia beets as the primary reason for the uptick in their popularity, in truth their sweeter, slightly peppery flavor compared to other beets is just as big of a reason for the surge.

1. Place the beets, radishes, cucumber, carrots, and salad greens in a salad bowl and toss to combine. Add half of the vinaigrette and toss to coat.

2. Top with the sesame seeds, garnish with fresh herbs, and serve.

INGREDIENTS:

2   CHIOGGIA BEETS, PEELED AND SLICED VERY THIN WITH A MANDOLINE

½   LB. RADISHES, SLICED VERY THIN WITH A MANDOLINE

1   CUCUMBER, SLICED VERY THIN WITH A MANDOLINE

2   YELLOW CARROTS, PEELED AND SLICED INTO VERY THIN STRIPS WITH A MANDOLINE

5   OZ. SALAD GREENS

CHAMPAGNE VINAIGRETTE (SEE PAGE 592)

¼   CUP BLACK SESAME SEEDS

FRESH HERBS, CHOPPED, FOR GARNISH

CUCUMBER & GINGER SALAD

YIELD: 4 SERVINGS / **ACTIVE TIME:** 5 MINUTES / **TOTAL TIME:** 20 MINUTES

One of those lovely summer salads that do not require you to travel anywhere beyond your pantry and the backyard garden.

1. Place the cucumbers, onion, and ginger in a salad bowl and toss to combine. Season with red pepper flakes, salt, and pepper, add the vinegar, and toss to coat. Let the salad marinate in the refrigerator for 15 minutes.

2. Garnish with cilantro and serve.

INGREDIENTS:

3	CUCUMBERS, JULIENNED
½	RED ONION, DICED
1	TABLESPOON GRATED FRESH GINGER
	RED PEPPER FLAKES, TO TASTE
	SALT AND PEPPER, TO TASTE
1½	TABLESPOONS RICE VINEGAR
	FRESH CILANTRO, CHOPPED, FOR GARNISH

ROASTED CAULIFLOWER, FENNEL & ORANGE SALAD

YIELD: 4 SERVINGS / ACTIVE TIME: 20 MINUTES / TOTAL TIME: 1 HOUR

A tahini-based dressing would also be a solid option for this salad.

1. Preheat the oven to 375°F. Place the cauliflower in a baking dish, drizzle the olive oil over it, and season with salt and pepper. Toss to coat, place the cauliflower in the oven, and roast until it is browned and tender, about 30 minutes.

2. Remove the cauliflower from the oven and let it cool completely.

3. Place the cauliflower, fennel, oranges, and almonds in a salad bowl and toss to combine.

4. Top with the raisins, garnish with mint and fennel fronds, and serve with the vinaigrette.

INGREDIENTS:

1	LB. CAULIFLOWER, CUT INTO FLORETS
2	TABLESPOONS EXTRA-VIRGIN OLIVE OIL
	SALT AND PEPPER, TO TASTE
2	BULBS OF FENNEL, TRIMMED AND SLICED VERY THIN WITH A MANDOLINE
2	ORANGES, SUPREMED (SEE PAGE 92)
½	CUP SLIVERED ALMONDS
½	CUP RAISINS
	FRESH MINT, FOR GARNISH
	FENNEL FRONDS, FOR GARNISH
	HONEY VINAIGRETTE (SEE PAGE 524), FOR SERVING

BLOOD ORANGE & CHICORY SALAD

YIELD: 4 SERVINGS / ACTIVE TIME: 5 MINUTES / TOTAL TIME: 5 MINUTES

It's hard to believe that a salad as simple as this could be so eye-catching and filled with bold flavors.

1. Place the oranges and chicory in a salad bowl and toss to combine. Add the honey, season with salt and pepper, toss to coat, and serve.

INGREDIENTS:

4   BLOOD ORANGES, SUPREMED (SEE PAGE 92)

6   OZ. RED CHICORY

2   TABLESPOONS HONEY

SALT AND PEPPER, TO TASTE

SALADS WITH MEAT

The ease of preparing a salad makes it a tempting option to turn to when one's schedule becomes so crammed that the thought of preparing a traditional entree seems overwhelming. But that temptation is often accompanied by the anxiety that just a salad for dinner won't supply the energy we need from our evening meal—to say nothing of the satisfaction we're typically craving at the end of a long day.

These protein-packed salads eliminate both of these concerns, while still maintaining the ease and alacrity that we're after when the world really bears down on us.

THAI BEEF & CUCUMBER SALAD

YIELD: 2 SERVINGS / **ACTIVE TIME:** 15 MINUTES / **TOTAL TIME:** 1 HOUR AND 30 MINUTES

When the weather is hot, even the grill seems too much to bear. This is a light but filling salad, and it is a perfect use for leftover roast beef or steak, or deli-sliced roast beef. The whole recipe requires no cooking, save for boiling water for the noodles.

1. Bring 6 cups of water to a boil in a medium saucepan and place the noodles in a baking dish. Pour the boiling water over the noodles and let them sit until they are tender, about 20 minutes.

2. Drain and place the noodles in a salad bowl. Add the remaining ingredients, except for the sesame seeds, and toss to combine. Chill the salad in the refrigerator for 1 hour.

3. Garnish with sesame seeds and serve.

INGREDIENTS:

2   OZ. THIN RICE NOODLES

1   CARROT, PEELED AND SHREDDED

1   SMALL CUCUMBER, SEEDED AND DICED

ZEST AND JUICE OF 1 LIME

10   FRESH MINT LEAVES, CHOPPED

1½   TABLESPOONS SOY SAUCE

1   TEASPOON PALM SUGAR OR MAPLE SYRUP

½   TEASPOON KOSHER SALT

1   TABLESPOON FISH SAUCE

4   OZ. ROAST BEEF OR LEFTOVER STEAK, SLICED THIN AND CHOPPED

RICE VINEGAR, TO TASTE

HOT SAUCE, TO TASTE

SESAME SEEDS, FOR GARNISH

CHICKEN SALAD

YIELD: 4 SERVINGS / **ACTIVE TIME:** 10 MINUTES / **TOTAL TIME:** 10 MINUTES

The ultimate destination for your leftovers after a roasted chicken dinner.

1. Place the mayonnaise, celery, shallot, mustard, and lemon juice in a mixing bowl and stir to combine.

2. Add the chicken, walnuts, and dried cranberries and stir to incorporate. Season with salt and pepper and serve with bread, wraps, or salad greens.

INGREDIENTS:

⅓ CUP MAYONNAISE

½ CUP CHOPPED CELERY

1 SHALLOT, CHOPPED

1 TEASPOON DIJON MUSTARD

½ TEASPOON FRESH LEMON JUICE

4 CUPS SHREDDED OR DICED LEFTOVER CHICKEN

¼ CUP WALNUTS OR PECANS

½ CUP DRIED CRANBERRIES OR HALVED SEEDLESS RED GRAPES

SALT AND PEPPER, TO TASTE

BREAD, WRAPS, OR SALAD GREENS, FOR SERVING

Chicken Salad, see page 191

ESQUITES CON LONGANIZA

YIELD: 4 SERVINGS / **ACTIVE TIME:** 25 MINUTES / **TOTAL TIME:** 45 MINUTES

A slight refinement of a street food classic. This dish can be made vegetarian by swapping in chopped poblanos for the sausage, and sautéing them for 8 to 10 minutes.

1. Preheat the oven to 375°F. Divide the corn between two baking sheets, season it with salt, and place it in the oven. Roast until the corn is starting to brown, 20 to 25 minutes.

2. While the corn is in the oven, place the olive oil in a skillet and warm it over medium heat. Add the longaniza and cook until it is browned all over and cooked through, 8 to 10 minutes, stirring as necessary. Transfer the cooked longaniza to a large bowl.

3. Remove the corn from the oven and transfer it to the bowl containing the longaniza. Add the remaining ingredients, except for the lettuce, one at a time, stirring until each one is thoroughly incorporated before adding the next.

4. Taste, adjust the seasoning as necessary, and serve with the lettuce (if desired).

INGREDIENTS:

6	CUPS CANNED CORN, DRAINED
	SALT AND PEPPER, TO TASTE
2	TABLESPOONS EXTRA-VIRGIN OLIVE OIL
1	LB. LONGANIZA, CHOPPED
2	TABLESPOONS UNSALTED BUTTER
1	JALAPEÑO CHILE PEPPER, STEMMED, SEEDED, AND DICED
2	TABLESPOONS MAYONNAISE
2	TEASPOONS GARLIC POWDER
¼	CUP SOUR CREAM
½	TEASPOON CAYENNE PEPPER
½	TEASPOON CHILI POWDER
3	TABLESPOONS FETA CHEESE
3	TABLESPOONS GOAT CHEESE
1	TABLESPOON FRESH LIME JUICE
½	CUP FINELY CHOPPED FRESH CILANTRO
6	CUPS LETTUCE OR ARUGULA, FOR SERVING (OPTIONAL)

TACO SALAD

YIELD: 4 SERVINGS / ACTIVE TIME: 25 MINUTES / TOTAL TIME: 25 MINUTES

Aperfect way to trick the fam into eating their vegetables.

1. Place the chili powder, oregano, garlic powder, onion powder, kosher salt, cumin, red pepper flakes, and paprika in a small bowl and stir to combine. Set the seasoning blend aside.

2. Place the avocado oil in a large skillet and warm it over medium heat. Add the onion and cook, stirring occasionally, until it is translucent, about 3 minutes. Add the beef, 1 tablespoon of the seasoning blend, and a splash of water and cook, breaking the beef up with a wooden spoon, until it is just about cooked through, about 8 minutes. Store the remaining seasoning blend in a small mason jar.

3. Add the beans and cook, stirring occasionally, for 5 minutes.

4. Add the pepper and cook, stirring occasionally, until it has softened, about 5 minutes.

5. Divide the lettuce among the serving bowls, top each portion with some of the beef-and-bean mixture, corn, cucumbers, tomatoes, tortilla chips, cheese, and dressing, and serve.

INGREDIENTS:

- 1 TABLESPOON CHILI POWDER
- ½ TEASPOON GROUND OREGANO
- ½ TEASPOON GARLIC POWDER
- ½ TEASPOON ONION POWDER
- ½ TEASPOON KOSHER SALT
- ½ TEASPOON CUMIN
- ½ TEASPOON RED PEPPER FLAKES
- ½ TEASPOON PAPRIKA
- 1 TABLESPOON AVOCADO OIL
- 1 ONION, FINELY DICED
- 1 LB. GROUND BEEF
- 2 CUPS CANNED BLACK BEANS, DRAINED
- 1 RED BELL PEPPER, STEMMED, SEEDED, AND CHOPPED
- 4 CUPS CHOPPED LETTUCE
- 1 CUP CANNED CORN, DRAINED
- 2 CUPS CHOPPED CUCUMBERS
- ½ CUP DICED CHERRY TOMATOES
- ½ CUP CRUSHED TORTILLA CHIPS
- ½ CUP SHREDDED MEXICAN-STYLE CHEESE
- CREAMY CILANTRO DRESSING (SEE PAGE 553)

MEDITERRANEAN GRILLED CHICKEN SALAD

YIELD: 4 SERVINGS / **ACTIVE TIME:** 30 MINUTES / **TOTAL TIME:** 45 MINUTES

The bright, wholesome flavors of the Mediterranean transform the straightforward grilled chicken salad.

1. Prepare a gas or charcoal grill for medium-high heat (about 450°F). Season the chicken with salt and pepper and let it rest at room temperature.

2. Place the peppers on the grill and cook until they are charred all over, turning them as necessary, about 10 minutes. Place the peppers in a bowl, cover it with plastic wrap, and let the peppers steam for 10 minutes.

3. Remove the stems and seeds from the peppers, slice the remaining flesh, and place the strips of roasted peppers in a salad bowl.

4. Place the chicken on the grill and cook until it is cooked through (the interior is 165°F) and seared on both sides, 10 to 15 minutes, turning it over just once. Remove the chicken from the grill and let it rest for 10 minutes.

5. While the chicken is resting, place the zucchini on the grill and cook until it is lightly charred on both sides, about 4 minutes, turning it over halfway through. Place the zucchini in the salad bowl.

6. Slice the chicken into strips and add it to the salad bowl. Add the red onion, arugula, and half of the vinaigrette and gently toss to combine. Add the feta and toss until evenly distributed. Garnish the salad with toasted slivered almonds and serve with the remaining vinaigrette on the side.

INGREDIENTS:

1½   LBS. BONELESS, SKINLESS CHICKEN BREASTS

SALT AND PEPPER, TO TASTE

2   RED BELL PEPPERS

2   ZUCCHINI, SLICED INTO ROUNDS

½   RED ONION, HALVED AND SLICED

5   OZ. ARUGULA

CHAMPAGNE VINAIGRETTE (SEE PAGE 592)

½   CUP CRUMBLED FETA CHEESE

SLIVERED ALMONDS, TOASTED, FOR GARNISH

CURRIED CHICKEN SALAD

YIELD: 6 SERVINGS / **ACTIVE TIME:** 15 MINUTES / **TOTAL TIME:** 15 MINUTES

Prefer sweet over sour? Swap the Granny Smith apples out for a few cups of halved seedless red grapes.

1. Place the chicken, mayonnaise, lime juice, and all of the seasonings in a mixing bowl and stir to combine. Add the celery, apples, and bell pepper, and ½ cup of the pecans and stir to incorporate.

2. Top the chicken salad with the remaining pecans and either serve it over the arugula or use the toasted slices of marble rye to make sandwiches.

INGREDIENTS:

4	CUPS DICED COOKED CHICKEN
¼	CUP MAYONNAISE
3	TABLESPOONS FRESH LIME JUICE
¼	CUP MADRAS CURRY POWDER
1	TABLESPOON CUMIN
1	TABLESPOON GARLIC POWDER
½	TEASPOON CINNAMON
½	TEASPOON TURMERIC
	SALT AND PEPPER, TO TASTE
3	CELERY STALKS, MINCED
2	GRANNY SMITH APPLES, CORED AND MINCED
½	RED BELL PEPPER, STEMMED, SEEDED, AND MINCED
¾	CUP PECANS, CHOPPED
6	OZ. BABY ARUGULA, FOR SERVING (OPTIONAL)
12	SLICES OF MARBLE RYE BREAD, TOASTED, FOR SERVING (OPTIONAL)

PIG EAR SALAD

YIELD: 4 SERVINGS / **ACTIVE TIME:** 30 MINUTES / **TOTAL TIME:** 1 HOUR AND 30 MINUTES

You'll have to head to a good butcher for pig ears, but this classic Mexican salad is worth a special trip.

1. Place the stock in a medium saucepan and add the chiles, white onion, whole cloves of garlic, and bay leaf. Bring to a simmer, add the pig ears, and gently simmer until they are very tender. You want to be able to pass a knife through the pig ears with ease. Drain the pig ears and let them cool. When cool, slice them into ½-inch-thick pieces.

2. Add canola oil to a Dutch oven until it is about 2 inches deep and warm it to 350°F.

3. Place the rice flour in a bowl, dredge the pig ears in the flour until they are coated, and then gently slip them into the hot oil. Fry until the pig ears are crispy on the outside, about 45 seconds. Transfer them to a paper towel–lined plate to drain and season the pig ears with salt.

4. Place all of the remaining ingredients, except for the epazote powder, in a mixing bowl, add the fried pig ears, and toss to combine. Top with the epazote powder and serve.

INGREDIENTS:

4 CUPS CHICKEN STOCK (SEE PAGE 663)

2 CHIPOTLE MORITA CHILE PEPPERS, STEMMED AND SEEDED

½ WHITE ONION, SLICED

4 GARLIC CLOVES, 2 LEFT WHOLE, 2 DICED

1 BAY LEAF

1½ LBS. PIG EARS, TRIMMED

CANOLA OIL, AS NEEDED

2 CUPS RICE FLOUR

SALT AND PEPPER, TO TASTE

¼ RED ONION, SLICED

2 TABLESPOONS TOASTED RICE POWDER (SEE PAGE 667)

15 CURRY LEAVES

10 CHERRY TOMATOES, HALVED

JUICE OF 3 LIMES

2 TABLESPOONS EXTRA-VIRGIN OLIVE OIL

1 TABLESPOON GINGER JUICE

1 TABLESPOON EPAZOTE POWDER

LARB GAI

YIELD: 4 SERVINGS / **ACTIVE TIME:** 20 MINUTES / **TOTAL TIME:** 35 MINUTES

This zippy chicken salad originated in Laos but is commonly found in Thailand, and it's a good example of ingredients common to the region's cuisine. One tip: lemongrass and lime leaves can be very fibrous, so make sure they are both minced very fine. Use an electric herb chopper, if one is available.

1. Warm a large skillet over medium heat and add the chicken and a little water. Cook, using a wooden spoon to break up the chicken, until it starts to brown, about 5 minutes. Add the shallot and cook until the chicken is cooked through. Transfer the mixture to a salad bowl and let it cool completely.

2. When the mixture has cooled, add the lemongrass, lime leaves, chiles, lime juice, fish sauce, soy sauce, Toasted Rice Powder, cilantro, and mint. Season with salt and pepper and stir to combine.

3. Serve with lettuce leaves, using them to scoop the salad.

INGREDIENTS:

1	LB. GROUND CHICKEN
1	SHALLOT, DICED
1	LEMONGRASS STALK, MINCED
2	MAKRUT LIME LEAVES, MINCED
3	RED CHILE PEPPERS, STEMMED, SEEDED, AND CHOPPED
¼	CUP FRESH LIME JUICE
1	TABLESPOON FISH SAUCE
1	TABLESPOON SOY SAUCE
1	TABLESPOON TOASTED RICE POWDER (SEE PAGE 667)
¼	CUP CHOPPED FRESH CILANTRO
12	FRESH MINT LEAVES, CHOPPED
	SALT AND PEPPER, TO TASTE
	BIBB LETTUCE LEAVES, FOR SERVING

Larb Gai, see page 203

CHICKEN FAJITA SALAD

YIELD: 4 SERVINGS / **ACTIVE TIME:** 30 MINUTES / **TOTAL TIME:** 1 HOUR

A salad so good, it alone makes the investment in an air fryer worthwhile.

1. Place the chicken, half of the avocado oil, cumin, chili powder, salt, and lemon juice in a bowl, cover it, and marinate the chicken in the refrigerator for 30 minutes.

2. Preheat an air fryer to 350°F.

3. Place the olive oil in a saucepan and warm it over medium heat. Add the onion, bell peppers, and garlic and cook, stirring occasionally, until the onion starts to brown, 6 to 7 minutes.

4. Add the salt, black beans, jalapeño, and water, cover the pan, and reduce the heat to medium-low. Cook for 5 minutes, remove the pan from heat, and set the beans aside.

5. Layer the chicken in a single layer in the air fryer and brush it with the remaining avocado oil. Cook until the chicken is browned and cooked through (the interior is 165°F), about 15 minutes, turning it over halfway through. Remove the chicken from the air fryer and set it aside.

6. Place the lettuce, avocado, and tomatoes in a salad bowl. Slice the chicken, add it to the salad bowl, and toss to combine.

7. Divide the salad among the serving plates and top each portion with some of the black beans. Garnish with cilantro and cotija and serve with lime wedges and tortilla chips.

INGREDIENTS:

1	LB. CHICKEN THIGHS, TRIMMED
2	TABLESPOONS AVOCADO OIL
1	TEASPOON CUMIN
1	TEASPOON CHILI POWDER
1	TEASPOON KOSHER SALT
	JUICE OF ½ LEMON
1	TABLESPOON EXTRA-VIRGIN OLIVE OIL
1	LARGE ONION, SLICED
2	BELL PEPPERS, STEMMED, SEEDED, AND SLICED
2	GARLIC CLOVES, MINCED
¼	TEASPOON KOSHER SALT
1	(14 OZ.) CAN OF BLACK BEANS, DRAINED
½	JALAPEÑO CHILE PEPPER, DICED
⅓	CUP WATER
5	OZ. ICEBERG LETTUCE, CHOPPED
	FLESH OF 1 AVOCADO, CHOPPED
⅓	CUP HALVED CHERRY TOMATOES
	FRESH CILANTRO, CHOPPED, FOR GARNISH
	COTIJA CHEESE, CRUMBLED, FOR GARNISH
	LIME WEDGES, FOR SERVING
	TORTILLA CHIPS, FOR SERVING

CHICKEN SALAD WITH LABNEH, ROASTED PLUMS & FARRO

YIELD: 4 SERVINGS / ACTIVE TIME: 20 MINUTES / TOTAL TIME: 2 HOURS

Nutty, forgiving of distracted cooks, and in possession of an especially toothsome texture, farro is a great place to turn if you're looking to move away from white rice.

1. Preheat the oven to 375°F. Place the plums in a baking dish, drizzle half of the olive oil over them, and season with salt and pepper. Toss to combine.

2. Place the baking dish in the oven and roast until the plums are tender and caramelized, 30 to 40 minutes.

3. After placing the plums in the oven, place the stock in a saucepan and bring to a boil over medium-high heat. Add the farro, cover the pan, reduce the heat to medium-low, and cook until the farro is al dente, about 30 minutes.

4. While the plums and farro are cooking, place the remaining olive oil in a large skillet and warm it over medium heat. Season the chicken with salt and pepper, place it in the pan, and cook until it is browned on both sides and cooked through (the interior is 165°F), 10 to 12 minutes, turning it over halfway through. Remove the chicken from the pan and let it cool.

5. Remove the plums from the oven and set them aside. Drain the farro and set it aside.

6. When the plums are cool enough to handle, chop them into large chunks.

7. Shred the chicken and place it in a salad bowl. Add the plums, farro, arugula, and onion and toss to combine.

8. Spread the Labneh over a serving dish. Top it with the salad, sprinkle the pistachios over the dish, garnish with orange zest, and serve.

INGREDIENTS:

2	PLUMS, HALVED AND PITTED
¼	CUP EXTRA-VIRGIN OLIVE OIL
	SALT AND PEPPER, TO TASTE
2	CUPS CHICKEN STOCK (SEE PAGE 663)
1	CUP FARRO
1	LB. CHICKEN BREASTS
5	OZ. ARUGULA
1	RED ONION, SLICED THIN
2	CUPS LABNEH (SEE PAGE 653)
½	CUP ROASTED PISTACHIOS
	STRIPS OF ORANGE ZEST, FOR GARNISH

SUMMERY STEAK SALAD

YIELD: 4 SERVINGS / **ACTIVE TIME:** 20 MINUTES / **TOTAL TIME:** 1 HOUR

Try grilling the corn in its husk rather than boiling it—it will preserve the freshness and amplify the corn flavor.

1. Cook the rice according to the directions on the package. Fluff the rice with a fork, cover it, and set it aside.

2. Place the chile, garlic, olive oil, and lime juice in a small bowl, season with salt and pepper, and whisk to combine. Set the dressing aside.

3. Prepare a gas or charcoal grill for medium-high heat (about 450°F). Bring water to a boil in a large pot and add the corn. Cook until it is just tender, 6 to 8 minutes. Remove the corn from the pot and let it drain in a colander.

4. Place the steak on the grill and cook until it is to your liking, turning it over just once. Remove the steak from the grill and set it aside.

5. Pat the corn dry and place it on the grill. Cook until it is lightly charred all over, about 8 minutes, turning it as necessary. Remove the corn from the grill and let it cool slightly. When the corn is cool enough to handle, cut the kernels off of the cobs and place the kernels in a salad bowl.

6. Slice the steak thin against the grain and add it to the salad bowl along with the rice, beans, tomato, and onion. Toss to combine, add the dressing, and toss to coat.

7. Garnish with cilantro and serve.

INGREDIENTS:

- ⅔ CUP JASMINE RICE
- 1 CHILE PEPPER, STEMMED, SEEDED, AND FINELY DICED
- 1 GARLIC CLOVE, FINELY DICED
- ¼ CUP EXTRA-VIRGIN OLIVE OIL
- JUICE OF 1 LIME
- SALT AND PEPPER, TO TASTE
- 2 EARS OF CORN
- 1 LB. STEAK
- 2 CUPS CANNED BLACK BEANS, DRAINED
- 1 TOMATO, DICED
- ¼ RED ONION, DICED
- FRESH CILANTRO, CHOPPED, FOR GARNISH

WARM CHORIZO & CHICKPEA SALAD

YIELD: 4 SERVINGS / ACTIVE TIME: 20 MINUTES / TOTAL TIME: 40 MINUTES

A salad that transports you to Spain's Mediterranean coastline.

1. Preheat the oven to 425°F. Place the peppers in the oven and roast until they are charred all over, about 15 minutes, turning them as necessary. Remove the peppers from the oven and place them in a bowl. Cover it with plastic wrap and let the peppers steam for 10 minutes.

2. Place half of the olive oil in a skillet and warm it over medium heat. Add the chorizo, season with salt and peppers, and cook until it is cooked through and browned all over, 10 to 12 minutes, stirring it as necessary. Remove the chorizo from the pan and set it aside.

3. Remove the stems and seeds from the peppers, slice the remaining flesh, and place the strips of roasted pepper in a salad bowl. Add the chorizo, spinach, chickpeas, tomatoes, and onion to the salad bowl and toss to combine. Add the other half of the olive oil, season with salt and pepper, and toss to coat.

4. Top with the olives, garnish with parsley, and serve.

INGREDIENTS:

2	RED BELL PEPPERS
¼	CUP EXTRA-VIRGIN OLIVE OIL
1	LB. CHORIZO, SLICED
	SALT AND PEPPER, TO TASTE
5	OZ. SPINACH
2	CUPS CANNED CHICKPEAS, DRAINED
½	CUP SUN-DRIED TOMATOES IN OLIVE OIL, DRAINED
½	RED ONION, SLICED VERY THIN
½	CUP PITTED KALAMATA OLIVES
	FRESH PARSLEY, FOR GARNISH

COBB SALAD

YIELD: 4 SERVINGS / ACTIVE TIME: 20 MINUTES / TOTAL TIME: 30 MINUTES

There's been some heated arguments over who created this salad, but no one can quibble with the claim that it's a stone-cold classic.

1. Place the bacon in a skillet and cook over medium heat until it is crispy, about 8 minutes, turning it as necessary. Transfer the bacon to a paper towel–lined plate and let it drain and cool. When it is cool enough to handle, chop the bacon and set it aside.

2. Discard some of the bacon grease that is in the pan. Season the chicken with salt and pepper, place it in the pan, and cook over medium heat until it is browned and cooked through (the interior is 165°F), 10 to 12 minutes, turning it over halfway through. Remove the chicken from the pan and slice it.

3. Place the chicken, bacon, eggs, lettuce, tomatoes, and avocados in a salad bowl and gently toss to combine. Serve with bread and the preferred dressing.

INGREDIENTS:

½   LB. BACON

1   LB. BONELESS, SKINLESS CHICKEN BREASTS

    SALT AND PEPPER, TO TASTE

4   HARD-BOILED EGGS, SLICED (SEE PAGE 667)

5   OZ. ROMAINE LETTUCE, CHOPPED

2   CUPS CHERRY TOMATOES, HALVED

    FLESH OF 2 AVOCADOS, SLICED

    BREAD, FOR SERVING

    RED WINE VINAIGRETTE OR ITALIAN DRESSING (SEE PAGE 599 OR 627), FOR SERVING

MISO DELICATA & BEEF SALAD

YIELD: 4 SERVINGS / **ACTIVE TIME:** 20 MINUTES / **TOTAL TIME:** 1 HOUR AND 30 MINUTES

Delicata is a great squash to cook with because the skin is so ... well, delicate that you don't have to bother to peel it.

1. Preheat the oven to 375°F. Place the mirin and sake in a small saucepan and bring to a boil. Remove the pan from heat, add the miso, brown sugar, and sesame oil, and stir until the sugar has dissolved.

2. Place the squash in a baking dish, brush it all over with the miso glaze, and place it in the oven. Roast until the squash is golden brown and tender, 35 to 45 minutes.

3. While the squash is in the oven, bring water to a boil in a large pot. Add salt, let the water return to a full boil, and add the noodles. Cook until they are al dente, 8 to 10 minutes. Drain the noodles, rinse them under cold water, and set them aside.

4. Remove the squash from the oven and let it cool.

5. Place the olive oil in a large skillet and warm it over medium heat. Add the steak, season with salt and pepper, and cook until it is to your liking. Remove the steak from the pan and let it rest for 2 minutes.

6. Slice the steak thin against the grain and place it in a salad bowl. Add the squash, noodles, steak, peas, and microgreens to the salad bowl and toss to combine. Add the lime juice and toss to coat.

7. Garnish with pickled ginger and serve.

INGREDIENTS:

- 1 TABLESPOON MIRIN
- 1 TABLESPOON SAKE
- 2 TABLESPOONS YELLOW MISO
- 1 TABLESPOON BROWN SUGAR
- 1 TEASPOON SESAME OIL
- 1 DELICATA SQUASH, SEEDED AND SLICED THIN
- SALT AND PEPPER, TO TASTE
- 6 OZ. NOODLES
- 2 TABLESPOONS EXTRA-VIRGIN OLIVE OIL
- 1 LB. RIB EYE STEAK
- 4 OZ. SNOW PEAS, HALVED
- 2 OZ. MICROGREENS
- JUICE OF 1 LIME
- PICKLED GINGER, SLICED THIN, FOR GARNISH

SPICY BEEF SALAD

YIELD: 4 SERVINGS / **ACTIVE TIME:** 20 MINUTES / **TOTAL TIME:** 30 MINUTES

Placing the steak in the freezer for a brief spell is the key to getting slices with the desired thinness here.

1. Place the steak in the freezer and chill for 15 minutes.

2. Remove the steak from the freezer and slice it as thin as possible against the grain.

3. Place the sesame oil in a large skillet and warm it over medium heat. Add the steak, season with salt and pepper, and cook until it is to your liking, stirring as necessary. Remove the pan from heat and set it aside.

4. Place the lettuce, cucumber, sprouts, and carrot in a salad bowl and toss to combine. Add the lime juice and chile and toss to coat.

5. Divide the salad among the serving plates and top each portion with some of the steak. Garnish with cilantro and serve.

INGREDIENTS:

1	LB. FLANK STEAK
1	TABLESPOON SESAME OIL
	SALT AND PEPPER, TO TASTE
6	OZ. LETTUCE, CHOPPED
1	CUCUMBER, SLICED THIN
2	OZ. BEAN SPROUTS
1	CARROT, PEELED AND SHREDDED
	JUICE OF 2 LIMES
1	RED CHILE PEPPER, STEMMED, SEEDED, AND MINCED
	FRESH CILANTRO, CHOPPED, FOR GARNISH

CHICKEN SALAD, VIETNAMESE STYLE

YIELD: 4 SERVINGS / ACTIVE TIME: 20 MINUTES / TOTAL TIME: 1 HOUR

N uoc Cham, a popular Vietnamese dipping sauce, is deployed here as a dressing, and its complex sweet, sour, and savory flavor transforms an otherwise straightforward salad.

1. Cook the rice according to the directions on the package. Fluff the rice with a fork, cover it, and set it aside.

2. Place the olive oil in a large skillet and warm it over medium heat. Season the chicken with salt and pepper, place it in the pan, and cook until it is browned on both sides and cooked through (the interior is 165°F), 10 to 12 minutes, turning it over halfway through. Remove the chicken from the pan and set it aside.

3. Place the rice, cucumber, carrots, sprouts, and chiles in a salad bowl and toss to combine.

4. Divide the salad among the serving plates. Slice the chicken and top each portion with it. Drizzle the Nuoc Cham over the salads, garnish with lemon basil and crispy noodles, and serve.

INGREDIENTS:

⅔ CUP RICE

2 TABLESPOONS EXTRA-VIRGIN OLIVE OIL

1 LB. BONELESS, SKINLESS CHICKEN BREASTS

SALT AND PEPPER, TO TASTE

1 CUCUMBER, JULIENNED

2 CARROTS, PEELED AND JULIENNED

2 OZ. BEAN SPROUTS

2 RED CHILE PEPPERS, SLICED

NUOC CHAM (SEE PAGE 623)

FRESH LEMON BASIL, FOR GARNISH

CRISPY NOODLES, FOR GARNISH

CRISPY DUCK SALAD
WITH PAPAYA & GRAPEFRUIT

YIELD: 4 SERVINGS / **ACTIVE TIME:** 20 MINUTES / **TOTAL TIME:** 1 HOUR

The key to this salad is remaining patient when crisping up the duck's skin, and moving quickly once it gets turned over and reaches the proper temperature.

1. Cut shallow slits in the skin of the duck breasts, taking care not to cut all the way through. Season with salt and pepper, place the duck breasts in a large skillet, skin side down, and cook over medium heat until the skin is golden brown and crispy. Turn the duck breasts over and cook until they are cooked through (the interior is 120°F to 130°F). Remove the duck breasts from the pan and let them rest for 2 minutes.

2. Chop the duck breasts and place the meat in a salad bowl. Add the papayas, cucumber, grapefruit, and scallions and toss to combine. Add half of the dressing and toss to coat.

3. Garnish with basil and cilantro and serve with the remaining dressing.

INGREDIENTS:

1	LB. SKIN-ON DUCK BREASTS
	SALT AND PEPPER, TO TASTE
2	PAPAYAS, SEEDED AND SLICED THIN
1	CUCUMBER, SLICED THIN
1	GRAPEFRUIT, SUPREMED (SEE PAGE 92)
5	SCALLIONS, CHOPPED
	THAI CHILE DRESSING (SEE PAGE 553)
	FRESH BASIL, CHOPPED, FOR GARNISH
	FRESH CILANTRO, CHOPPED, FOR GARNISH

CHORIZO & ROASTED NEW POTATO SALAD

YIELD: 4 SERVINGS / **ACTIVE TIME:** 20 MINUTES / **TOTAL TIME:** 1 HOUR

S weeter than mature potatoes, new potatoes are a good match for the powerfully savory character of chorizo.

1. Bring water to a boil in a large saucepan. Add salt, let the water return to a full boil, and add the potatoes. Cook until they are tender, 15 to 20 minutes.

2. While the potatoes are cooking, place the olive oil in a large skillet and warm it over medium heat. Add the chorizo and cook, breaking it up with a wooden spoon, until it is browned and cooked through, 8 to 10 minutes. Remove the pan from heat and set the chorizo aside.

3. Drain the potatoes and let them cool.

4. Place the potatoes, pickled onion, brine, cornichons, and herbs in a salad bowl and toss to combine. Add the crème fraîche, season with salt and pepper, and toss to coat.

5. Top the salad with the chorizo and serve.

INGREDIENTS:

SALT AND PEPPER, TO TASTE

1   LB. NEW POTATOES, PEELED

1   TABLESPOON EXTRA-VIRGIN OLIVE OIL

½   LB. CHORIZO, CASING REMOVED

¼   CUP PICKLED RED ONION (SEE PAGE 671)

2   TABLESPOONS PICKLED RED ONION BRINE

½   CUP CHOPPED CORNICHONS

½   CUP FINELY CHOPPED FRESH HERBS

½   CUP CRÈME FRAÎCHE

ARUGULA, BLUEBERRY & PROSCIUTTO SALAD

YIELD: 4 SERVINGS / **ACTIVE TIME:** 20 MINUTES / **TOTAL TIME:** 20 MINUTES

Peppery arugula and salty prosciutto are a match made in heaven.

1. Place the arugula, prosciutto, blueberries, and oranges in a salad bowl and toss to combine. Add the lemon juice and olive oil, season with pepper, and toss to coat.

2. Top the salad with the feta cheese and serve.

INGREDIENTS:

5   OZ. ARUGULA

4   OZ. PROSCIUTTO, SLICED THIN AND TORN

2   CUPS BLUEBERRIES

2   ORANGES, SUPREMED (SEE PAGE 92)

1   TABLESPOON FRESH LEMON JUICE

1   TABLESPOON EXTRA-VIRGIN OLIVE OIL

    BLACK PEPPER, TO TASTE

4   OZ. FETA CHEESE, CRUMBLED

GRILLED CHICKEN & STRAWBERRY SALAD WITH PESTO

YIELD: 4 SERVINGS / **ACTIVE TIME:** 20 MINUTES / **TOTAL TIME:** 30 MINUTES

Centered around the brilliant pairing of basil and strawberries, this salad boldly announces that summertime is here.

1. Prepare a gas or charcoal grill for medium heat (about 400°F). Coat the chicken with the olive oil, season with salt and pepper, and place it on the grill. Cook until the chicken is cooked through (the interior is 165°F), 10 to 12 minutes, turning it over half-way through. Remove the chicken from the grill and let it rest for 5 minutes.

2. Place the salad greens, scallions, radishes, and strawberries in a salad bowl, season with salt and pepper, and toss to combine.

3. Slice the chicken into strips. Divide the salad among the serving plates, top each portion with some of the chicken, drizzle some Pesto over the top, and serve.

INGREDIENTS:

1	LB. BONELESS, SKINLESS CHICKEN BREASTS
2	TABLESPOONS EXTRA-VIRGIN OLIVE OIL
	SALT AND PEPPER, TO TASTE
5	OZ. SALAD GREENS
2	OZ. SCALLIONS, SLICED THIN
¼	LB. RADISHES, SLICED VERY THIN
2	CUPS STRAWBERRIES, HULLED AND QUARTERED
	PESTO (SEE PAGE 603)

HARISSA CHICKEN SALAD

YIELD: 4 SERVINGS / **ACTIVE TIME:** 20 MINUTES / **TOTAL TIME:** 1 HOUR AND 30 MINUTES

The bold spice of harissa works wonders with grilled proteins.

1. Place the olive oil, harissa, garlic powder, salt, and cumin in a mixing bowl and whisk to combine. Add the chicken, turn to coat, and let it marinate in the refrigerator for 1 hour.

2. Warm a grill pan over medium heat. Add the chicken and cook until it is browned on both sides and cooked through (the interior is 165°F), about 10 minutes, turning it over halfway through. Remove the chicken from the pan and let it cool.

3. Slice the chicken into strips and place it in a salad bowl. Add the salad greens, pickled onion, corn, dates, avocados, and cucumber and toss to combine. Add the vinaigrette, toss to coat, and serve.

INGREDIENTS:

1	TABLESPOON EXTRA-VIRGIN OLIVE OIL
2	TABLESPOONS HARISSA SAUCE (SEE PAGE 523)
1	TEASPOON GARLIC POWDER
½	TEASPOON KOSHER SALT
1	TEASPOON CUMIN
3	CHICKEN BREASTS
4	CUPS SALAD GREENS MIX
¼	CUP PICKLED RED ONION (SEE PAGE 671)
2	CUPS CANNED CORN, DRAINED
4	PITTED DATES, CHOPPED
	FLESH OF 2 AVOCADOS, DICED
2	CUPS DICED CUCUMBER
	PRESERVED LEMON VINAIGRETTE (SEE PAGE 545)

QUAIL & COUSCOUS SALAD WITH HOT HONEY

YIELD: 4 SERVINGS / **ACTIVE TIME:** 20 MINUTES / **TOTAL TIME:** 1 HOUR

Head to a quality butcher for the quail, as they will understand immediately when you ask for it to be semiboneless.

1. Cook the couscous according to the directions on the package. Fluff it with a fork, cover it, and set it aside.

2. Prepare a gas or charcoal grill for medium-high heat (about 450°F). Clean the grates and brush them with the olive oil.

3. Season the quail with salt and pepper and place them on the grill, breast side down. Cook until they are crispy and caramelized, 2 to 3 minutes. Turn them over and cook until their interiors are 140°F, 1 to 2 minutes. Remove the quail from the grill and let them rest for 10 minutes.

4. Place the couscous and pomegranate arils in a salad bowl and toss to combine. Chop the quail, add it to the salad bowl, and toss to combine.

5. Divide the salad among the serving plates, top each portion with some Hot Honey, garnish with fresh herbs, and serve.

INGREDIENTS:

½ CUP COUSCOUS

2 TABLESPOONS EXTRA-VIRGIN OLIVE OIL

12 SEMIBONELESS QUAIL

SALT AND PEPPER, TO TASTE

1½ CUPS POMEGRANATE ARILS

HOT HONEY (SEE PAGE 599)

FRESH HERBS, FINELY CHOPPED, FOR GARNISH

HERBED CHICKEN, RED CABBAGE & CUCUMBER SALAD

YIELD: 4 SERVINGS / **ACTIVE TIME:** 20 MINUTES / **TOTAL TIME:** 40 MINUTES

Go with your favorite woody, powerfully flavored herbs, like rosemary, thyme, and sage, in this salad.

1. Preheat the oven to 375°F. Rub the chicken with the olive oil, season with salt and pepper, and place it on a baking sheet. Sprinkle the herbs over the top of the chicken, place it in the oven, and roast until it is browned on top and cooked through (the interior is 165°F), 15 to 20 minutes. Remove the chicken from the oven and let it rest for 5 minutes.

2. Slice or chop the chicken and add it to a salad bowl. Add the salad greens, cabbage, cucumbers, and goat cheese and toss to combine.

3. Top the salad with the pepitas, garnish with sesame seeds, and serve with the vinaigrette.

INGREDIENTS:

1   LB. BONELESS, SKINLESS CHICKEN BREASTS

2   TABLESPOONS EXTRA-VIRGIN OLIVE OIL

    SALT AND PEPPER, TO TASTE

¼   CUP FINELY CHOPPED FRESH HERBS

3   OZ. SALAD GREENS

1½ CUPS SHREDDED RED CABBAGE

1½ CUCUMBERS, SLICED INTO LONG, THIN RIBBONS

3   OZ. GOAT CHEESE, CRUMBLED

½   CUP PEPITAS

    SESAME SEEDS, FOR GARNISH

    BALSAMIC VINAIGRETTE (SEE PAGE 573), FOR SERVING

CHICKEN CAESAR SALAD

YIELD: 4 SERVINGS / **ACTIVE TIME:** 20 MINUTES / **TOTAL TIME:** 35 MINUTES

At last, you can stop wasting money at that place around the corner when a chicken Caesar craving strikes.

1. Place the olive oil in a large skillet and warm it over medium heat. Season the chicken with salt and pepper, place it in the pan, and cook until it is browned on both sides and cooked through (the interior is 165°F), 10 to 12 minutes, turning it over halfway through. Remove the chicken from the pan and let it rest for 5 minutes.

2. Chop or slice the chicken and place it in a salad bowl. Add the Croutons, lettuce, scallions, and a generous amount of dressing and toss to coat.

3. Season with salt and pepper and divide the salad among the serving plates. Top each portion with a Hard-Boiled Egg, garnish with Parmesan, and serve with any remaining dressing.

INGREDIENTS:

- 2 TABLESPOONS EXTRA-VIRGIN OLIVE OIL
- 1 LB. BONELESS, SKINLESS CHICKEN BREASTS

  SALT AND PEPPER, TO TASTE

  CROUTONS (SEE PAGE 666)
- 6 OZ. ROMAINE LETTUCE
- 6 SCALLIONS, CHOPPED

  CLASSIC CAESAR DRESSING (SEE PAGE 593)
- 4 HARD-BOILED EGGS (SEE PAGE 667), HALVED

  PARMESAN CHEESE, SHAVED, FOR GARNISH

SALADS WITH SEAFOOD

Seafood's light, fresh flavor and ease of preparation mean that the fruits of the sea are perfect for including in a salad, and they have the added advantage of supplying many vitamins and minerals that will aid one's quest for improved health.

From a handful of inventive tuna- and crab-based salads that require little more of the home cook than opening a few cans and stirring to flavorful recipes built around flavorful treats like smoked salmon and scallops, the preparations collected in this chapter are as capable of serving as a light weeknight dinner as they are of standing at the center of an elegant dinner party.

LOBSTER ESQUITES

YIELD: 4 SERVINGS / **ACTIVE TIME:** 25 MINUTES / **TOTAL TIME:** 50 MINUTES

The slight sweetness present in lobster gets amplified beautifully by this beloved corn-centric Mexican salad.

1. To begin preparations for the salad, preheat the oven to 375°F. Place the mayonnaise, sour cream, lime juice, hot sauce, queso enchilado, salt, and pepper in a salad bowl, stir to combine, and set the mixture aside.

2. Place the corn kernels in a small mixing bowl along with the melted butter and toss to combine. Place the corn kernels in an even layer on a baking sheet, place them in the oven, and roast until the corn is golden brown, 15 to 20 minutes.

3. Stir the corn into the salad bowl and let the mixture cool. Chill the salad in the refrigerator.

4. To begin preparations for the lobster, place the butter in a skillet and melt it over medium-low heat.

5. Remove the meat from the lobster tails using kitchen scissors. Add the meat to the pan and poach until it turns a reddish orange, 4 to 5 minutes. Remove the lobster meat from the pan with a slotted spoon and let it cool.

6. Slice the lobster into small medallions. To serve, spoon the corn salad onto each plate and arrange a few lobster medallions on top of each portion. Sprinkle the Tajín over the dishes, garnish with cilantro, and serve.

INGREDIENTS:

FOR THE SALAD

¼   CUP MAYONNAISE

¼   CUP SOUR CREAM

1   TEASPOON FRESH LIME JUICE

¼   TEASPOON HOT SAUCE

½   CUP GRATED QUESO ENCHILADO

     SALT AND PEPPER, TO TASTE

     KERNELS FROM 5 EARS OF CORN

2   TABLESPOONS UNSALTED BUTTER, MELTED

FOR THE LOBSTER

½   CUP UNSALTED BUTTER

1   LB. LOBSTER TAILS

2   TABLESPOONS TAJÍN

     FRESH CILANTRO, CHOPPED, FOR GARNISH

SALADE NIÇOISE

YIELD: 4 SERVINGS / **ACTIVE TIME:** 45 MINUTES / **TOTAL TIME:** 1 HOUR

A classic salad that transports you directly to the French Riviera.

1. Prepare an ice bath. Place the potatoes in a large saucepan and cover them with water. Season the water with salt and bring the potatoes to a boil. Cook until they are tender, 15 to 20 minutes, and then remove them with a strainer or slotted spoon. Add the potatoes to the ice bath.

2. Add the green beans to the boiling water and cook for 3 minutes. Remove the green beans from the pan and place them in the ice bath. When the green beans are cool, drain the potatoes and green beans and pat them dry.

3. Place the lettuce in a salad bowl and add enough of the dressing to lightly coat the lettuce. Toss to coat, season with salt and pepper, and place the lettuce on a serving dish.

4. Add the tomatoes, Confit Tuna, potatoes, and green beans to the salad bowl, add some dressing, and toss to coat.

5. Place the mixture on top of the lettuce, top the salad with the Hard-Boiled Eggs, red onion, olives, and capers, and serve.

INGREDIENTS:

1   LB. BABY RED POTATOES, QUARTERED

SALT AND PEPPER, TO TASTE

2   CUPS TRIMMED GREEN BEANS

2   HEADS OF BIBB LETTUCE, SEPARATED INTO LEAVES

DIJON DRESSING (SEE PAGE 588)

2   SMALL TOMATOES, CUT INTO ½-INCH WEDGES

CONFIT TUNA (SEE PAGE 672)

2   HARD-BOILED EGGS (SEE PAGE 667), HALVED

½   RED ONION, SLICED THIN

¼   CUP PITTED KALAMATA OLIVES

1   TABLESPOON CAPERS, DRAINED

CHILLED CALAMARI SALAD

YIELD: 4 SERVINGS / **ACTIVE TIME:** 15 MINUTES / **TOTAL TIME:** 45 MINUTES

This salad can work as part of a meal composed of small plates, a first course, or a light dinner.

1. Bring approximately 8 cups of water to a boil in a large saucepan and prepare an ice bath. Season the boiling water generously with salt, add the tentacles of the squid, and cook for 1 minute. Add the bodies, cook for another minute, and use a slotted spoon to transfer the squid to the ice bath.

2. Drain the squid, pat it dry, and chill it in the refrigerator.

3. Place the red wine vinegar, harissa, and mustard in a salad bowl and whisk to combine. While whisking, slowly drizzle in the olive oil until it has emulsified.

4. Add the chilled squid, oranges, bell pepper, and celery and gently toss until combined.

5. Season the salad with salt and pepper, top with the hazelnuts and mint, and enjoy.

INGREDIENTS:

SALT AND PEPPER, TO TASTE

1½ LBS. SMALL SQUID, CLEANED, TENTACLES AND BODIES SEPARATED

3 TABLESPOONS RED WINE VINEGAR

2 TABLESPOONS HARISSA SAUCE (SEE PAGE 523)

1½ TEASPOONS DIJON MUSTARD

⅓ CUP EXTRA-VIRGIN OLIVE OIL

2 ORANGES, PEELED AND CUT INTO SEGMENTS

1 RED BELL PEPPER, STEM AND SEEDS REMOVED, CUT INTO STRIPS

2 CELERY STALKS, CHOPPED

¼ CUP HAZELNUTS, TOASTED

¼ CUP SHREDDED FRESH MINT

SPINACH, FENNEL & APPLE SALAD WITH SMOKED TROUT

YIELD: 4 SERVINGS / ACTIVE TIME: 15 MINUTES / TOTAL TIME: 30 MINUTES

A well-balanced salad that gets sweetness from the apples, anise from the fennel, and salt and freshness from the trout.

1. Place the vinegar, lemon juice, mustard, and honey in a salad bowl and whisk to combine.

2. While whisking continually, slowly drizzle in the olive oil until it has emulsified. Stir in the shallot and tarragon and season the vinaigrette with salt and pepper.

3. Add the spinach, apples, and fennel to the salad bowl and toss to coat.

4. To serve, plate the salad, top each portion with some of the smoked trout, and enjoy.

INGREDIENTS:

2   TABLESPOONS WHITE WINE VINEGAR

1   TABLESPOON FRESH LEMON JUICE

1   TABLESPOON WHOLE-GRAIN MUSTARD

1   TEASPOON HONEY

½   CUP EXTRA-VIRGIN OLIVE OIL

1   SHALLOT, MINCED

2   TEASPOONS CHOPPED FRESH TARRAGON

      SALT AND PEPPER, TO TASTE

4   CUPS BABY SPINACH

2   GRANNY SMITH APPLES, HALVED, CORED, AND SLICED THIN

1   BULB OF FENNEL, TRIMMED AND SLICED THIN

½   LB. SMOKED TROUT, SKIN REMOVED, FLAKED

COUSCOUS & SHRIMP SALAD

YIELD: 6 SERVINGS / **ACTIVE TIME:** 40 MINUTES / **TOTAL TIME:** 50 MINUTES

Regular couscous will also work here, but the toasted nuttiness of Israeli couscous is strongly preferred.

1. Place the shrimp, mint, and garlic in a Dutch oven and cover with water. Bring to a simmer over medium heat and cook until the shrimp are pink and cooked through, about 5 minutes after the water comes to a simmer.

2. Drain, cut the shrimp in half lengthwise, and set them aside. Discard the mint and garlic cloves.

3. Place the stock in the Dutch oven and bring to a boil. Add the couscous, reduce the heat so that the stock simmers, cover, and cook until the couscous is tender and has absorbed the stock, 7 to 10 minutes. Transfer the couscous to a salad bowl.

4. Fill the pot with water and bring to a boil. Add the asparagus and cook until it has softened, 1 to 1½ minutes. Drain, rinse the asparagus under cold water, and chop it into bite-size pieces. Pat the asparagus dry.

5. Add all of the remaining ingredients, except for the feta, to the salad bowl containing the couscous. Add the asparagus and stir to incorporate. Top with the shrimp, sprinkle the feta over the salad, and serve.

INGREDIENTS:

- ¾ LB. SHRIMP, SHELLED AND DEVEINED
- 6 BUNCHES OF FRESH MINT
- 10 GARLIC CLOVES, PEELED
- 3½ CUPS CHICKEN STOCK (SEE PAGE 663)
- 3 CUPS ISRAELI COUSCOUS
- 1 BUNCH OF ASPARAGUS, TRIMMED
- 3 PLUM TOMATOES, DICED
- 1 TABLESPOON FINELY CHOPPED FRESH OREGANO
- ½ PERSIAN CUCUMBER, DICED
- ZEST AND JUICE OF 1 LEMON
- ½ CUP DICED RED ONION
- ½ CUP SUN-DRIED TOMATOES IN OLIVE OIL, DRAINED AND SLICED THIN
- ¼ CUP PITTED AND CHOPPED KALAMATA OLIVES
- ⅓ CUP EXTRA-VIRGIN OLIVE OIL
- SALT AND PEPPER, TO TASTE
- ½ CUP CRUMBLED FETA CHEESE

LOBSTER & BASIL SALAD

The key to this salad is the lemon juice, which provides a memorable brightness.

1. Place the olive oil, garlic, lemon juice, and basil in a small bowl, season the mixture with salt and pepper, and whisk to combine.

2. Divide the salad greens and lobster evenly among the serving plates. Drizzle the dressing over each portion and serve with lemon wedges.

INGREDIENTS:

2 TABLESPOONS EXTRA-VIRGIN OLIVE OIL

1 GARLIC CLOVE, MINCED

3 TABLESPOONS FRESH LEMON JUICE

2 TABLESPOONS CHOPPED FRESH BASIL

SALT AND PEPPER, TO TASTE

6 OZ. SALAD GREENS

2 CUPS COOKED LOBSTER, SLICED

LEMON WEDGES, FOR SERVING

GRILLED LOBSTER & RASPBERRY SALAD

YIELD: 4 SERVINGS / ACTIVE TIME: 15 MINUTES / TOTAL TIME: 30 MINUTES

Any of the soft, leafy herbs will work as part of the mixture this salad calls for, but tarragon, dill, and chives will be the strongest options.

1. Prepare a gas or charcoal grill for high heat (about 500°F).

2. Bring a few inches of water to a boil in a large saucepan. Add the lobsters and parboil them until the shells turn red, about 2 minutes. Remove the lobsters from the water and let them cool.

3. Remove the claws from the lobsters and then cut the lobsters in half lengthwise, starting at the head. Remove the papery sacs from the heads of the lobsters and remove the veins that run the length of the tails.

4. Place the claws on the grill and cook for 3 minutes. Place the split bodies, cut side down, on the grill and cook for another 3 minutes.

5. Turn all of the lobster over and grill until it is cooked through, 6 to 8 minutes, basting the lobster with the melted butter as it cooks. When it is ready, the lobster meat should be firm and white.

6. Remove the lobster meat from the claws. Divide the greens among the serving plates. Place the meat from one claw and half of a lobster body on each plate. Sprinkle the raspberries over the salads.

7. Place the olive oil, lemon juice, salt, and pepper in a mason jar and whisk until combined. Drizzle the dressing over the salads, garnish them with edible flowers, and enjoy.

INGREDIENTS:

2	MAINE LOBSTERS
4	TABLESPOONS UNSALTED BUTTER, MELTED
6	OZ. SALAD GREENS
1	CUP CHOPPED FRESH HERBS
3	CUPS FRESH RASPBERRIES
½	CUP EXTRA-VIRGIN OLIVE OIL
2	TABLESPOONS FRESH LEMON JUICE
	SALT AND PEPPER, TO TASTE
	EDIBLE FLOWERS, FOR GARNISH

SMOKED SALMON & LAMB'S LETTUCE SALAD

YIELD: 4 SERVINGS / ACTIVE TIME: 20 MINUTES / TOTAL TIME: 20 MINUTES

Lamb's lettuce, with its unique nuttiness, provides an ideal foundation for a salad.

1. Place the salmon, lamb's lettuce, radishes, apples, and capers in a salad bowl and toss to combine. Add the vinaigrette, season with salt and pepper, and toss to coat.

2. Garnish with dill and serve.

INGREDIENTS:

¾ LB. SMOKED SALMON, TORN

3 OZ. LAMB'S LETTUCE

¼ LB. RADISHES, SLICED VERY THIN WITH A MANDOLINE

2 GRANNY SMITH APPLES, CORED AND SLICED

2 TABLESPOONS CAPERS, DRAINED

WHITE BALSAMIC VINAIGRETTE (SEE PAGE 565)

SALT AND PEPPER, TO TASTE

FRESH DILL, FOR GARNISH

SHRIMP, CUCUMBER & WATERCRESS SALAD

YIELD: 4 SERVINGS / **ACTIVE TIME:** 15 MINUTES / **TOTAL TIME:** 20 MINUTES

The peppery flavor of watercress supplies a needed punch in this otherwise gentle salad.

1. Bring a few inches of water to a boil in a large saucepan. Thread the shrimp onto the pieces of lemongrass. Place them in a steaming basket, set the basket over the boiling water, and steam the shrimp until they are cooked through, about 5 minutes. Remove the shrimp from the steaming basket and set them aside.

2. Place the cucumber and watercress in a salad bowl and toss to combine.

3. Place half of the pickled ginger, the honey, lime juice, avocado oil, and sour cream in a bowl and whisk until the dressing has emulsified. Season the dressing with salt and pepper.

4. To serve, divide the salad among the plates and then place two shrimp skewers on each portion. Top with the remaining pickled ginger and the chile and serve with the dressing.

INGREDIENTS:

8	JUMBO SHRIMP, SHELLS REMOVED, DEVEINED
2	LEMONGRASS STALKS, TRIMMED, BRUISED, AND QUARTERED LENGTHWISE
1	LARGE CUCUMBER, PEELED AND SLICED THIN
1	BUNCH OF WATERCRESS, CHOPPED
⅓	CUP PICKLED GINGER
1	TABLESPOON HONEY
	JUICE OF 1 LIME
¼	CUP AVOCADO OIL
1	CUP SOUR CREAM
	SALT AND PEPPER, TO TASTE
1	CHILE PEPPER, STEMMED, SEEDED, AND CHOPPED

SCALLOP, DRIED CRANBERRY & PECAN SALAD

YIELD: 4 SERVINGS / ACTIVE TIME: 15 MINUTES / TOTAL TIME: 25 MINUTES

Champagne vinegar is less aggressive than other vinegars, with a fruity and floral flavor that carries notes of vanilla, making it an outstanding option for vinaigrettes.

1. Pat the scallops dry and season them with salt and pepper. Place the olive oil in a large skillet and warm it over medium-high heat. Working in batches to avoid crowding the pan, add the scallops and cook for about 2 minutes on each side, until they are golden brown and cooked through. Remove the scallops from the pan, transfer them to a plate, and tent them with aluminum foil to keep them warm.

2. Pour the vinaigrette into the skillet and cook, stirring continually, until it has reduced slightly, about 3 minutes.

3. Divide the salad greens among the serving plates. Place four scallops on top of each portion. Sprinkle the cranberries and pecans over the top, drizzle the vinaigrette over the salad, and serve.

INGREDIENTS:

- 16 LARGE SCALLOPS
- SALT AND PEPPER, TO TASTE
- 3½ TABLESPOONS EXTRA-VIRGIN OLIVE OIL
- CHAMPAGNE & HERB VINAIGRETTE (SEE PAGE 647)
- 5 OZ. SALAD GREENS
- ½ CUP DRIED CRANBERRIES
- ⅓ CUP TOASTED PECANS, CHOPPED

CRAB SALAD

A light and lovely salad that honors the best elements of crab's flavor.

1. Place the crab, shallot, crème fraîche, mayonnaise, corn, and lemon juice in a bowl and gently stir to combine.

2. Add the chives and salmon roe and gently fold to incorporate. Season with salt and pepper and enjoy.

INGREDIENTS:

½ LB. CANNED LUMP CRABMEAT, PICKED OVER

1 TABLESPOON CHOPPED SHALLOT

1 TABLESPOON CRÈME FRAÎCHE

1 TABLESPOON MAYONNAISE

¼ CUP CORN KERNELS

¼ TEASPOON FRESH LEMON JUICE

2 TABLESPOONS CHOPPED FRESH CHIVES

2 TABLESPOONS SALMON ROE

SALT AND PEPPER, TO TASTE

SHRIMP, AVOCADO, CORN & TOMATO SALAD

YIELD: 4 SERVINGS / **ACTIVE TIME**: 10 MINUTES / **TOTAL TIME**: 10 MINUTES

This salad will work with any herb-laden, summery vinaigrette. The one suggested here is a good option, but by no means mandatory.

1. Place all of the ingredients, except for the vinaigrette, in a salad bowl and toss to combine.

2. Drizzle the vinaigrette over the salad, toss to coat, and serve.

INGREDIENTS:

1   LB. COOKED SHRIMP, CHILLED

1   LB. GRAPE TOMATOES, HALVED

    FLESH OF 1 AVOCADO, CUBED

1   CUP CANNED CORN, DRAINED

6   OZ. MESCLUN GREENS

    BLACK PEPPER, TO TASTE

    HERB VINAIGRETTE (SEE PAGE 643)

SHRIMP, BASIL & AVOCADO SALAD

YIELD: 4 SERVINGS / **ACTIVE TIME:** 15 MINUTES / **TOTAL TIME:** 15 MINUTES

Don't be afraid to inject a little spice into the proceedings here—the dish is so balanced that it can easily accommodate it.

1. Arrange the lettuce leaves around the edges of the serving bowls.

2. Place the lemon juice, water, honey, olive oil, and basil in a small bowl, season the mixture with salt and pepper, and whisk until well combined.

3. Place the shrimp, avocados, and dressing in a bowl and toss gently to coat.

4. Top each portion with some of the shrimp-and-avocado mixture and serve.

INGREDIENTS:

2	HEARTS OF ROMAINE LETTUCE
2	TABLESPOONS FRESH LEMON JUICE
1	TABLESPOON WATER
1	TEASPOON HONEY
5	TABLESPOONS EXTRA-VIRGIN OLIVE OIL
	HANDFUL OF FRESH BASIL, CHOPPED
	SALT AND PEPPER, TO TASTE
1	LB. COOKED SHRIMP, CHILLED
	FLESH OF 2 AVOCADOS, SLICED

MACKEREL, ROASTED FENNEL & APPLE SALAD

YIELD: 4 SERVINGS / **ACTIVE TIME:** 20 MINUTES / **TOTAL TIME:** 1 HOUR

The richness of mackerel needs sweetness and freshness to cut against it, which the apples supply beautifully.

1. Preheat the oven to 375°F. Place the fennel in a baking dish, drizzle half of the olive oil over it, and season with salt. Place the fennel in the oven and roast until it is golden brown and tender, 35 to 40 minutes.

2. Place the mackerel in a baking dish, drizzle the remaining olive oil over it, and sprinkle the pepper and coriander seeds over it. Season with salt, place the mackerel in the oven, and roast until it is just cooked through, 10 to 12 minutes.

3. Remove the fennel and mackerel from the oven and let them cool slightly.

4. Place the mackerel and fennel in a salad bowl, add the apples, and work the mixture with a fork to combine, breaking up the mackerel as you do. Add the vinaigrette and toss to coat.

5. Garnish with parsley and fennel fronds and serve.

INGREDIENTS:

- 2 BULBS OF FENNEL, TRIMMED AND CHOPPED
- 3 TABLESPOONS EXTRA-VIRGIN OLIVE OIL
- SALT, TO TASTE
- 1½ LBS. MACKEREL FILLETS
- 1 TABLESPOON CRUSHED BLACK PEPPER
- 1 TABLESPOON CORIANDER SEEDS, CRUSHED
- 4 GRANNY SMITH APPLES, CORED AND SLICED THIN
- LEMON VINAIGRETTE (SEE PAGE 619)
- FRESH PARSLEY, CHOPPED, FOR GARNISH
- FENNEL FRONDS, FOR GARNISH

ARUGULA, SHRIMP & GRAPEFRUIT SALAD

YIELD: 4 SERVINGS / **ACTIVE TIME:** 15 MINUTES / **TOTAL TIME:** 25 MINUTES

To ramp up the freshness here, swap out the red pepper flakes for some thin slices of Fresno chile.

1. Place the olive oil and red pepper flakes in a large skillet and warm over medium-high heat. Add the shrimp and cook until they turn pink and are cooked through, 3 to 5 minutes, turning them over halfway through. During the last minute of cooking, stir the garlic into the pan.

2. Transfer the shrimp and garlic to a salad bowl. Add the grapefruit, season the mixture with salt and pepper, and gently toss to combine.

3. Divide the arugula among the serving plates. Top with the shrimp-and-grapefruit mixture, drizzle olive oil over each portion, and serve.

INGREDIENTS:

1 TABLESPOON EXTRA-VIRGIN OLIVE OIL, PLUS MORE AS NEEDED

PINCH OF RED PEPPER FLAKES

2 LBS. JUMBO SHRIMP, SHELLS REMOVED, DEVEINED

3 GARLIC CLOVES, MINCED

1 LARGE GRAPEFRUIT, SUPREMED (SEE PAGE 92)

SALT AND PEPPER, TO TASTE

4 OZ. ARUGULA

3½ TABLESPOONS EXTRA-VIRGIN OLIVE OIL

TRUFFLE & CRAB SALAD

YIELD: 4 SERVINGS / **ACTIVE TIME:** 20 MINUTES / **TOTAL TIME:** 20 MINUTES

Finishing off a summery salad with a bit of truffle oil and champagne vinegar is the perfect way to celebrate the season.

1. Using a sharp knife, cut off the bases of the endives. Separate 16 large leaves, rinse them well, and pat them dry.

2. Place the shallot, salt, vinegar, and orange juice in a small bowl. While whisking continually, slowly add the olive oil until it has emulsified.

3. Place the crabmeat and scallion in a small bowl, drizzle the vinaigrette over it, and gently toss until combined. Season the salad with pepper and paprika.

4. Place 1 tablespoon of the crab salad on each endive leaf and top it with a segment of the oranges. Garnish with truffle oil and serve.

INGREDIENTS

2	HEADS OF ENDIVE
1	SHALLOT, FINELY DICED
⅛	TEASPOON KOSHER SALT
2	TEASPOONS CHAMPAGNE VINEGAR
1	TABLESPOON FRESH ORANGE JUICE
3	TABLESPOONS EXTRA-VIRGIN OLIVE OIL
½	LB. CANNED LUMP CRABMEAT, PICKED OVER
1	SCALLION, TRIMMED AND MINCED
	BLACK PEPPER, TO TASTE
	PAPRIKA, TO TASTE
2	ORANGES, SUPREMED (SEE PAGE 929
	TRUFFLE OIL, FOR GARNISH

CHICORY SALAD WITH SCALLOPS & STILTON

YIELD: 4 SERVINGS / **ACTIVE TIME:** 25 MINUTES / **TOTAL TIME:** 25 MINUTES

Blue cheese may seem like an odd choice to pair with seafood, but it can work beautifully, as this preparation shows. Should you happen to have a few slices of bacon lying around, crisp them up in a pan, crumble, and use them to top this salad.

1. Place the avocado oil in a large skillet and warm it over medium heat. Pat the scallops dry with paper towels and season generously with salt and pepper. Add the scallops to the skillet and cook until they are golden brown on one side, 1 to 2 minutes.

2. Turn the scallops over and add the butter. Cook the scallops until they are golden brown on both sides and cooked through, 1 to 2 minutes, basting them with the butter as they cook.

3. Remove the scallops from the pan and set them aside.

4. Add the lemon juice and walnuts to the pan and toss until the nuts are evenly coated.

5. Arrange the chicory on the serving plates, top with the walnuts, scallops, and Stilton, and serve.

INGREDIENTS:

1½ TABLESPOONS AVOCADO OIL

12 LARGE SCALLOPS

SALT AND PEPPER, TO TASTE

1½ TABLESPOONS UNSALTED BUTTER

JUICE OF ½ LEMON

½ CUP SHELLED WALNUTS

2 HEADS OF CHICORY, LEAVES SEPARATED

1 CUP CRUMBLED STILTON CHEESE

TUNA & POTATO SALAD

YIELD: 4 SERVINGS / ACTIVE TIME: 15 MINUTES / TOTAL TIME: 1 HOUR

If you have time, consider baking the potatoes rather than boiling them, as it provides a lighter, more pleasant texture.

1. Bring water to a boil in a medium saucepan. Add salt and the potatoes and cook until the potatoes are fork-tender, about 15 minutes. Drain the potatoes and let them cool.

2. Place the cucumber, tomatoes, onion, tuna, and potatoes in a salad bowl and toss to combine.

3. Add the olive oil, vinegar, and herbs and toss until the salad is coated. Season the salad with salt and pepper and enjoy.

INGREDIENTS:

	SALT AND PEPPER, TO TASTE
2	POTATOES, CHOPPED
1	CUCUMBER, CHOPPED
1	LB. CHERRY TOMATOES, HALVED
¼	RED ONION, SLICED
1	LB. TUNA IN OLIVE OIL, DRAINED
2	TABLESPOONS EXTRA-VIRGIN OLIVE OIL
2	TEASPOONS CHAMPAGNE VINEGAR
1	TABLESPOON CHOPPED FRESH HERBS

CHILE, SHRIMP & BASIL SALAD

YIELD: 6 SERVINGS / **ACTIVE TIME:** 30 MINUTES / **TOTAL TIME:** 30 MINUTES

The dressing here also makes for a wonderful marinade for whitefish such as halibut or cod.

1. Place all of the ingredients, except for the dressing and cashews, in a mixing bowl and stir to combine.

2. Add the dressing, toss to coat, garnish with the chopped cashews, and serve.

INGREDIENTS:

½	HEAD OF NAPA CABBAGE, CHOPPED
1	CUP FRESH MINT, CHOPPED
2	CUPS FRESH BASIL, CHOPPED
1	CUP FRESH CILANTRO, CHOPPED
1	RED ONION, SLICED THIN
3	SCALLIONS, TRIMMED AND SLICED THIN
1	CARROT, PEELED AND SLICED THIN
1	LB. COOKED SHRIMP, CHOPPED
	CHILE & CURRY DRESSING (SEE PAGE 534)
¼	CUP CASHEWS, CHOPPED, FOR GARNISH

TUNA SALAD WITH RICE & AVOCADO

YIELD: 4 SERVINGS / ACTIVE TIME: 20 MINUTES / TOTAL TIME: 40 MINUTES

Tangier and with a deeper flavor than traditional mayo, Kewpie Mayonnaise is a game changer in the tuna salad space.

1. Cook the rice according to the directions on the package. Fluff the rice with a fork, cover it, and set it aside.

2. Place the tuna in a salad bowl, add mayonnaise, season with salt and pepper, and work the mixture to combine. Add the avocado and snow peas and gently toss to combine.

3. Divide the rice among the serving plates and top each portion with some of the tuna salad. Garnish with scallions and serve.

INGREDIENTS:

⅔ CUP RICE

¾ LB. CANNED TUNA, DRAINED

KEWPIE MAYONNAISE, TO TASTE

SALT AND PEPPER, TO TASTE

FLESH OF 1 AVOCADO, DICED

4 OZ. SNOW PEAS, CHOPPED

SCALLIONS, CHOPPED, FOR GARNISH

TUNA & BROCCOLI SALAD WITH TAHINI DRESSING

YIELD: 4 SERVINGS / **ACTIVE TIME:** 20 MINUTES / **TOTAL TIME:** 40 MINUTES

If you'd like a little bit more crunch in this salad, consider roasting some cashews, chopping them up, and sprinkling them over the top.

1. Bring water to a boil in a large pot. Add salt, let the water return to a full boil, and add the broccoli. Cook until it is just tender, 4 to 6 minutes. Drain the broccoli, rinse it under cold water, and let it cool.

2. Place the tuna and olive oil in a salad bowl, season with salt and pepper, and work the mixture to combine. Add the broccoli, spinach, and tomatoes and toss to combine.

3. Add the dressing, toss to coat, and serve.

INGREDIENTS:

SALT AND PEPPER, TO TASTE

4 OZ. BROCCOLI, CHOPPED

¾ LB. CANNED TUNA, DRAINED

2 TABLESPOONS EXTRA-VIRGIN OLIVE OIL

5 OZ. SPINACH

2 CUPS CHERRY TOMATOES, HALVED

TAHINI DRESSING (SEE PAGE 565)

VIETNAMESE SHRIMP & GRAPEFRUIT SALAD

YIELD: 4 SERVINGS / **ACTIVE TIME:** 20 MINUTES / **TOTAL TIME:** 40 MINUTES

Sweet, sour, spicy, and herbal, this salad has all of the hallmarks of a successful dish in Vietnamese cuisine.

1. Bring water to a boil in a large pot. Add salt, let the water return to a full boil, and add the shrimp. Cook until they just turn pink, 2 to 4 minutes. Drain the shrimp, rinse them under cold water, and let them drain again.

2. Pat the shrimp dry with paper towels, place them in a salad bowl, and add the grapefruits, chile, and Nuoc Cham. Toss to combine and top the salad with the peanuts and Crispy Shallots.

3. Garnish with mint and serve.

INGREDIENTS:

SALT, TO TASTE

1 LB. SHRIMP, SHELLED AND DEVEINED

2 GRAPEFRUITS, SUPREMED (SEE PAGE 42) AND CHOPPED

1 RED CHILE PEPPER, SLICED VERY THIN

2 TABLESPOONS NUOC CHAM (SEE PAGE 623)

½ CUP PEANUTS, CHOPPED

½ CUP CRISPY SHALLOTS (SEE PAGE 673)

FRESH MINT, FOR GARNISH

SALMON SALAD WITH BROCCOLI & NUTS

YIELD: 2 SERVINGS / **ACTIVE TIME:** 25 MINUTES / **TOTAL TIME:** 40 MINUTES

When the temperature starts to get the best of you in the summer, prepare this salad in the morning and enjoy a needed break from dining out.

1. Bring a few inches of water to a boil in a large saucepan. Add the broccoli to the boiling water. Place the salmon in a steaming basket and place the basket over the boiling water. Cook until the broccoli is tender and the salmon is just cooked through, 3 to 5 minutes.

2. Remove the steaming basket from heat and let the salmon cool. Drain the broccoli and let it cool.

3. Place the olive oil in a large skillet and warm it over medium heat. Add the chile, scallions, almonds, and pumpkin seeds and cook, stirring occasionally, until the chile starts to brown, about 5 minutes.

4. Stir in the orange zest and orange juice, season the mixture with salt and pepper, and remove the pan from heat.

5. Flake the salmon and place it in a bowl. Add the broccoli and chile-and-nut mixture, toss to combine, and enjoy.

INGREDIENTS:

5   OZ. BROCCOLI

2   SALMON FILLETS, SKIN
     REMOVED, DEBONED

1   TABLESPOON EXTRA-
     VIRGIN OLIVE OIL

½   RED CHILE PEPPER, FINELY
     DICED

2   SCALLIONS, TRIMMED AND
     CHOPPED

¼   CUP ALMONDS, CHOPPED

1   TABLESPOON PUMPKIN
     SEEDS

     ZEST AND JUICE OF 1
     ORANGE

     SALT AND PEPPER, TO
     TASTE

SOUTHWESTERN TUNA SALAD

YIELD: 4 SERVINGS / ACTIVE TIME: 20 MINUTES / TOTAL TIME: 20 MINUTES

If you'd like even more Southwestern-style spice, consider swapping in your favorite salsa for the vinaigrette.

1. Place the tuna and vinaigrette in a salad bowl and work the mixture to combine.

2. Season with salt and pepper, add the tomatoes, chiles, bell pepper, and lettuce, and toss to combine.

3. Garnish with parsley and serve.

INGREDIENTS:

¾ LB. CANNED TUNA, DRAINED

CUMIN & CILANTRO VINAIGRETTE (SEE PAGE 576)

SALT AND PEPPER, TO TASTE

2 CUPS CHERRY TOMATOES, HALVED

2 CHILE PEPPERS, STEMMED, SEEDED, AND MINCED

1 BELL PEPPER, STEMMED, SEEDED, AND SLICED

5 OZ. ICEBERG LETTUCE, CHOPPED

FRESH PARSLEY, CHOPPED, FOR GARNISH

Southwestern Tuna Salad, see page 273

SESAME SALMON & CHIOGGIA BEET SALAD

YIELD: 4 SERVINGS / ACTIVE TIME: 20 MINUTES / TOTAL TIME: 1 HOUR

Wild-caught salmon is always preferrable to farm raised, but it is essential here.

1. Preheat the oven to 350°F. Line a baking sheet with aluminum foil.

2. Rub the salmon with the canola oil. Place the sesame seeds on a plate, coat the salmon with them, and place the salmon on the baking sheet. Season it with salt and pepper, place the salmon in the oven, and roast until the salmon is cooked through, 15 to 20 minutes.

3. Remove the salmon from the oven and let it cool. When it is cool enough to handle, chop the salmon into bite-size pieces.

4. Place the salmon, beets, cucumbers, carrots, spring onions, and radishes in a salad bowl and toss to combine. Add the vinaigrette and toss to coat.

5. Top the salad with dollops of the crème fraîche, garnish with dill, and serve.

INGREDIENTS:

1   LB. SALMON FILLETS

2   TABLESPOONS CANOLA OIL

½   CUP SESAME SEEDS

SALT AND PEPPER, TO TASTE

2   CHIOGGIA BEETS, PEELED AND SLICED VERY THIN WITH A MANDOLINE

2   CUCUMBERS, PEELED AND DICED

2   CARROTS, PEELED AND GRATED

2   SPRING ONIONS, TRIMMED AND DICED

3   RADISHES, SLICED VERY THIN WITH A MANDOLINE

CHAMPAGNE VINAIGRETTE (SEE PAGE 592)

¼   CUP CRÈME FRAÎCHE

FRESH DILL, CHOPPED, FOR GARNISH

TUNA, TOMATO & GREEN BEAN SALAD

YIELD: 4 SERVINGS / **ACTIVE TIME:** 20 MINUTES / **TOTAL TIME:** 35 MINUTES

Y ou might be surprised by how much the addition of a few vegetables livens up a tuna salad.

1. Bring water to a boil in a large pot. Place the tuna, mayonnaise, and tomatoes in a salad bowl, season with salt and pepper, and work the mixture to combine. Set it aside.

2. Add salt to the boiling water, let it return to a boil, and add the green beans. Cook until they are just tender, about 4 minutes. Drain the green beans, rinse them under cold water, and let them drain again.

3. Pat the green beans dry with paper towels, add them to the tuna salad, and toss to combine.

4. Garnish with parsley and serve.

INGREDIENTS:

- ¾ LB. CANNED TUNA, DRAINED
- ¼ CUP MAYONNAISE
- 2 TOMATOES, DICED
- SALT AND PEPPER, TO TASTE
- 6 OZ. GREEN BEANS, CHOPPED
- FRESH PARSLEY, FINELY CHOPPED, FOR GARNISH

RICE & TUNA SALAD

YIELD: 4 SERVINGS / ACTIVE TIME: 20 MINUTES / TOTAL TIME: 1 HOUR AND 30 MINUTES

With added substance from the rice and a considerable flavor boost from a host of Mediterranean-inclined ingredients, this is a long way from your standard tuna salad.

1. Cook the rice according to the directions on the package. Fluff it with a fork, cover it, and set it aside.

2. Place the olive oil in a large skillet and warm it over medium heat. Add the carrot and cook, stirring occasionally, until it is tender, about 10 minutes.

3. Add the corn and peas, season with salt and pepper, and cook until they are warmed through. Remove the pan from heat and set the vegetables aside.

4. Place the rice, tuna, tomatoes, olives, pickled onions, cornichons, Hard-Boiled Eggs, mozzarella, and carrot mixture in a salad bowl and work the resulting mixture until everything is evenly distributed. Add the dressing and toss to coat.

5. Garnish with basil and serve.

INGREDIENTS:

⅔ CUP SHORT-GRAIN RICE

2 TABLESPOONS EXTRA-VIRGIN OLIVE OIL

1 CARROT, PEELED AND FINELY DICED

¼ CUP CANNED CORN, DRAINED

½ CUP PEAS

SALT AND PEPPER, TO TASTE

CONFIT TUNA (SEE PAGE 672), CHOPPED

2 CUPS CHERRY TOMATOES, HALVED

1 CUP BLACK OLIVES, PITTED AND SLICED

½ CUP PICKLED CIPOLLINI ONIONS

¼ CUP CHOPPED CORNICHONS

4 HARD-BOILED EGGS (SEE PAGE 667), QUARTERED

2 OZ. FRESH MOZZARELLA CHEESE, DRAINED AND DICED

ITALIAN DRESSING (SEE PAGE 627)

FRESH BASIL, CHOPPED, FOR GARNISH

GRILLED OCTOPUS & CHORIZO SALAD

YIELD: 4 SERVINGS / **ACTIVE TIME:** 20 MINUTES / **TOTAL TIME:** 4 HOURS

Octopus, perhaps more than any ingredient, rewards patience.

1. Preheat the oven to 300°F.

2. Place the octopus, bay leaves, and head of garlic in a Dutch oven and add stock until half of the octopus is submerged. Cover the Dutch oven and place it in the oven. Braise the octopus for 2 to 3 hours, until the thickest parts of the tentacles are very tender. Remove the octopus from the braising liquid and let it cool.

3. Prepare a gas or charcoal grill for medium-high heat (about 450°F). Place half of the olive oil in a large skillet and warm it over medium heat. Add the chorizo and cook, turning it as necessary, until it is browned and cooked through, 8 to 10 minutes. Remove the pan from heat, cover it, and set the chorizo aside.

4. Brush the grates of the grill with the remaining olive oil. Place the octopus on the grill and cook until it is caramelized and crispy all over, 5 to 7 minutes, turning it as necessary.

5. Remove the octopus from the grill and transfer it to a salad bowl. Add the spinach, chiles, and chorizo and toss to combine. Add the lime juice, season with salt and pepper, toss to coat, and serve.

INGREDIENTS:

- 1 LB. OCTOPUS, BEAK REMOVED AND HEAD CLEANED
- 2 BAY LEAVES
- 1 HEAD OF GARLIC, HALVED AT ITS EQUATOR
- CHICKEN STOCK (SEE PAGE 663), AS NEEDED
- ¼ CUP EXTRA-VIRGIN OLIVE OIL
- ½ LB. CHORIZO, SLICED
- 5 OZ. SPINACH
- 2 RED CHILE PEPPERS, STEMMED, SEEDED, AND SLICED
- 2 TABLESPOONS FRESH LIME JUICE
- SALT AND PEPPER, TO TASTE

SHRIMP & CUCUMBER SALAD
WITH COCONUT & POPPY SEED DRESSING

YIELD: 4 SERVINGS / **ACTIVE TIME:** 20 MINUTES / **TOTAL TIME:** 30 MINUTES

Cashews or macadamias would also be good choices for the nutty component in this salad.

1. Place the sesame oil in a large skillet and warm it over medium heat. Add the shrimp, season with salt, and cook until the shrimp turn pink and are cooked through, 2 to 3 minutes, turning them over halfway through. Transfer the shrimp to a salad bowl.

2. Add the carrots, cucumbers, onion, pomegranate arils, and almonds to the salad bowl and toss to combine. Add the dressing and toss to coat.

3. Drizzle additional sesame oil over the salad and serve.

INGREDIENTS:

1	TABLESPOON SESAME OIL, PLUS MORE FOR GARNISH
1	LB. SHRIMP, SHELLED AND DEVEINED
	SALT, TO TASTE
¼	LB. RAINBOW BABY CARROTS
2	CUCUMBERS, FINELY DICED
1	RED ONION, JULIENNED
1	CUP POMEGRANATE ARILS
1	CUP CHOPPED ALMONDS
	COCONUT & POPPY SEED DRESSING (SEE PAGE 541)

SALMON, QUINOA & BOK CHOY SALAD

YIELD: 4 SERVINGS / ACTIVE TIME: 20 MINUTES / TOTAL TIME: 1 HOUR

B aby bok choy is an underutilized source of greens in the salad world, and this salad seeks to remedy that oversight.

1. Preheat the oven to 350°F. Line a baking sheet with aluminum foil. Rub the salmon with the sesame oil and place it on the baking sheet. Season with salt, place the salmon in the oven, and roast until it is cooked through, 15 to 20 minutes.

2. While the salmon is in the oven, cook the quinoa according to the directions on the package. Spread the cooked quinoa on a rimmed baking sheet in an even layer and let it cool completely.

3. Remove the salmon from the oven and let it cool. When it is cool enough to handle, chop the salmon into bite-size pieces.

4. Bring water to a boil in a large saucepan. Add salt, let the water return to a full boil, and add the bok choy. Cook until it is tender, drain the bok choy, and rinse it under cold water. Pat the bok choy dry with paper towels and place it in a salad bowl.

5. Add the salmon, quinoa, and onion to the salad bowl and toss to combine. Add the dressing and toss to coat.

6. Top the salad with the pomegranate arils, garnish with dill, and serve.

INGREDIENTS:

1	LB. SALMON
2	TABLESPOONS SESAME OIL
	SALT, TO TASTE
⅔	CUP QUINOA
7	OZ. BABY BOK CHOY, TRIMMED AND CHOPPED
1	RED ONION, SLICED THIN
	GINGER & LEMON DRESSING (SEE PAGE 560)
1	CUP POMEGRANATE ARILS
	FRESH DILL, CHOPPED, FOR GARNISH

HERRING SALAD OVER POTATO ROSTI

YIELD: 4 SERVINGS / **ACTIVE TIME:** 20 MINUTES / **TOTAL TIME:** 50 MINUTES

A pair of Central European standards combine to carry this, the rare salad that can serve as comfort food.

1. Preheat the oven to 350°F. Place the potatoes in a bowl, add the salt and pepper, and stir to combine.

2. Place the olive oil in a large cast-iron skillet and warm it over medium-high heat. Carefully place all of the potatoes in the pan and gently press down on them. Cook until the edges of the rosti are golden brown, 8 to 10 minutes.

3. Using a large spatula, carefully flip the rosti over and then cook for another 5 minutes.

4. Place the pan in the oven and bake until the rosti is crispy and golden brown, about 10 minutes. Remove the rosti from the oven and let it cool.

5. Place the rosti on a cutting board and cut it into four pieces.

6. Place the herring, radishes, cucumber, apples, onion, and scallions in a salad bowl, season with salt and pepper, and toss to combine.

7. Divide the rosti among the serving plates and top each portion with some of the herring salad.

8. Garnish with parsley and serve.

INGREDIENTS:

6	CUPS PEELED AND GRATED POTATOES
1	TEASPOON KOSHER SALT, PLUS MORE TO TASTE
½	TEASPOON BLACK PEPPER, PLUS MORE TO TASTE
3	TABLESPOONS EXTRA-VIRGIN OLIVE OIL
1	LB. PICKLED HERRING, SLICED
¼	LB. RADISHES, SLICED VERY THIN WITH A MANDOLINE
1	CUCUMBER, CHOPPED
2	APPLES, CORED AND DICED
½	RED ONION, SLICED THIN
8	SCALLIONS, TRIMMED AND CHOPPED
	FRESH PARSLEY, CHOPPED, FOR GARNISH

SALAD WITH BLUEBERRIES, FENNEL & SMOKED SALMON

YIELD: 4 SERVINGS / ACTIVE TIME: 20 MINUTES / TOTAL TIME: 20 MINUTES

A good salad for the late fall or early spring, when you need a bit of brightness.

1. Place the salmon, greens, blueberries, tomatoes, and fennel in a salad bowl and toss to combine. Add the honey and lemon juice, season with salt and pepper, and toss to coat.

2. Garnish with parsley and serve.

INGREDIENTS:

½   LB. SMOKED SALMON, TORN

6   OZ. SALAD GREENS

2   CUPS BLUEBERRIES

2   CUPS CHERRY TOMATOES, HALVED

1   BULB OF FENNEL, TRIMMED AND SLICED VERY THIN WITH A MANDOLINE

2   TABLESPOONS HONEY

1½   TABLESPOONS FRESH LEMON JUICE

     SALT AND PEPPER, TO TASTE

     FRESH PARSLEY, CHOPPED, FOR GARNISH

SHRIMP, MANGO & PINEAPPLE SALAD

YIELD: 4 SERVINGS / **ACTIVE TIME:** 20 MINUTES / **TOTAL TIME:** 30 MINUTES

One sees this tropically inclined salad and thinks summer, but in truth it will supply brightness, refreshment, and energy all year long.

1. Bring water to a boil in a large pot.

2. Cook the rice according to the directions on the package. Fluff the rice with a fork, cover it, and set it aside.

3. Add salt to the boiling water, let the water return to a full boil, and add the shrimp. Cook until they turn pink and are cooked through, 2 to 3 minutes. Drain the shrimp and transfer them to a salad bowl.

4. Add the rice, avocados, mango, pineapple, and onion to the salad bowl and toss to combine. Add the lime juice and agave nectar and toss to coat.

5. Garnish with cilantro and serve.

INGREDIENTS:

⅔   CUP RICE

     SALT, TO TASTE

1   LB. SHRIMP, SHELLED AND DEVEINED

     FLESH OF 2 AVOCADOS, DICED

½   CUP DICED MANGO

½   CUP PINEAPPLE

¼   RED ONION, FINELY DICED

2   TABLESPOONS FRESH LIME JUICE

1   TABLESPOON AGAVE NECTAR

     FRESH CILANTRO, CHOPPED, FOR GARNISH

VEGAN & VEGETARIAN MAIN-COURSE SALADS

*P*erhaps no recipes in this book have benefitted from the recent salad revolution than those collected in this chapter, as they prove that even a plant-based salad can provide the substance and flavor we want from a main course.

One easy way to achieve this satisfying quality is to center a salad around pulses like lentils or legumes such as chickpeas, since their protein and fiber-rich nature means that any salad featuring them checks the substantial-enough box. But many other plant-based options, such as cauliflower, Brussels sprouts, and tofu, to name just a few, prove that they are more than capable of standing at the center of a main-course salad, providing vegans, vegetarians, and those who just want a few more veggies in their diet with plenty of options when the time comes to get dinner on the table.

WARM POTATO & FENNEL SALAD

YIELD: 4 SERVINGS / **ACTIVE TIME:** 20 MINUTES / **TOTAL TIME:** 1 HOUR

Dressing the potatoes while they are still warm allows them to absorb more of the sherry vinegar's flavor, a key to tying all of the elements in this salad together.

1. Preheat the oven to 375°F. Place the potatoes in a baking dish, drizzle half of the olive oil over them, and season with salt, pepper, and sage. Toss to coat, place the potatoes in the oven, and roast until a knife inserted into them passes easily to their centers, 35 to 45 minutes, stirring occasionally.

2. Place the bacon in a large skillet and cook over medium heat until it is crispy, 6 to 8 minutes, turning it as necessary. Transfer the bacon to a paper towel–lined plate to drain.

3. Discard some of the bacon fat in the skillet and add the fennel and radicchio. Cook, stirring occasionally, until they are tender and browned, about 10 minutes. Remove the pan from heat and set the fennel and radicchio aside.

4. Remove the potatoes from the oven and place them in a salad bowl.

5. Add the fennel and radicchio to the salad bowl and toss to combine. Add the vinegar and remaining olive oil, season with salt and pepper, and toss to coat.

6. Chop the bacon into bite-size pieces, top the salad with it and the walnuts, garnish with sage, and serve.

INGREDIENTS:

1	LB. BABY POTATOES, HALVED
¼	CUP EXTRA-VIRGIN OLIVE OIL
	SALT AND PEPPER, TO TASTE
	FRESH SAGE, CHOPPED, TO TASTE
½	LB. BACON, CHOPPED
1	BULB OF FENNEL, TRIMMED AND CHOPPED
3	OZ. RADICCHIO, CHOPPED
1½	TABLESPOONS SHERRY VINEGAR
½	CUP CHOPPED WALNUTS

VEGAN LARB GAI

YIELD: 4 SERVINGS / ACTIVE TIME: 20 MINUTES / TOTAL TIME: 30 MINUTES

A vegan take on the refreshing and beloved Thai salad.

1. Place the sesame oil in a large skillet and warm it over medium heat. Add the vegan meat, season with salt and pepper, and cook until it is browned and warmed through, breaking it up with a wooden spoon as it cooks, 6 to 8 minutes.

2. Place the vegan meat, chile, shallot, and cucumber in a salad bowl and toss to combine.

3. Divide the lettuce leaves among the serving plates and top each leaf with some of the salad.

4. Top the salad with some of the peanuts, garnish with cilantro, and serve with the Thai Chile Dressing and lime wedges.

INGREDIENTS:

1	TABLESPOON SESAME OIL
1	LB. VEGAN GROUND MEAT
	SALT AND PEPPER, TO TASTE
1	RED CHILE PEPPER, STEMMED, SEEDED, AND SLICED TFIN
1	SHALLOT, PEELED AND SLICED TFIN
½	CUCUMBER, SLICED AND CHOPPED
12	LETTUCE LEAVES
1	CUP SALTED PEANUTS, CHOPPED
	FRESH CILANTRO, CHOPPED, FOR GARNISH
	THAI CHILE DRESSING (SEE PAGE 553), FOR SERVING
	LIME WEDGES, FOR SERVING

ROASTED CAULIFLOWER SALAD
WITH RAISINS & PINE NUTS

YIELD: 2 SERVINGS / **ACTIVE TIME:** 20 MINUTES / **TOTAL TIME:** 50 MINUTES

A bit of honey, if you like things sweet, or sumac, if you prefer some sourness, would be a welcome addition here.

1. Preheat the oven to 375°F. Place the cauliflower in a baking dish, drizzle the olive oil over it, and season with the turmeric, paprika, salt, and pepper. Toss to coat, place the cauliflower in the oven, and roast until the cauliflower is golden brown and tender, 35 to 40 minutes.

2. Remove the cauliflower from the oven and place it in a salad bowl.

3. Add the onion, chile, pine nuts, and raisins to the salad bowl and toss to combine. Add the lemon juice, season with salt and pepper, and toss to coat.

4. Garnish with parsley and serve.

INGREDIENTS:

1	LARGE HEAD OF CAULIFLOWER, CUT INTO FLORETS
2	TABLESPOONS EXTRA-VIRGIN OLIVE OIL
1	TEASPOON TURMERIC
1	TABLESPOON PAPRIKA
	SALT AND PEPPER, TO TASTE
½	RED ONION, SLICED VERY THIN
1	RED CHILE PEPPER, STEMMED, SEEDED, AND MINCED
½	CUP PINE NUTS
½	CUP RAISINS
2	TABLESPOONS FRESH LEMON JUICE
	FRESH PARSLEY, CHOPPED, FOR GARNISH

BRUSSELS SPROUT & RADICCHIO SALAD

YIELD: 4 SERVINGS / **ACTIVE TIME:** 20 MINUTES / **TOTAL TIME:** 20 MINUTES

The sweetness from the apples and vinaigrette is needed to counter the bold spice of raw Brussels sprouts and the bitter radicchio.

1. Place the radicchio, Brussels sprouts, and apples in a salad bowl and toss to combine.

2. Add the vinaigrette, season with salt and pepper, and toss to coat.

3. Top the salad with the almonds and serve.

INGREDIENTS:

4	OZ. RADICCHIO, CHOPPED
½	LB. BRUSSELS SPROUTS, TRIMMED AND SHAVED
2	APPLES, CORED AND CHOPPED
	HONEY MUSTARD VINAIGRETTE (SEE PAGE 557)
	SALT AND PEPPER, TO TASTE
1	CUP CHOPPED ALMONDS

GREEN BEAN & BELUGA LENTIL SALAD

YIELD: 4 SERVINGS / **ACTIVE TIME:** 20 MINUTES / **TOTAL TIME:** 40 MINUTES

Named for their resemblance to the famed caviar, beluga lentils are a wonderful choice for use in salads, because they maintain their texture when cooked properly, rather than becoming mushy.

1. Bring water to a boil in two large pots.

2. Add the lentils to one of the pots and cook until they are tender, 20 to 25 minutes.

3. Add salt to the other pot, let the water return to a full boil, and add the green beans. Cook until they are just tender, 3 to 4 minutes. Drain the green beans, rinse them under cold water, and let them drain again.

4. Drain the lentils, spread them on a baking sheet in an even layer, and season with salt. Let the lentils cool completely.

5. Place the lentils, green beans, and pickled onion in a salad bowl and toss to combine. Add the dressing, season with salt and pepper, and toss to coat.

6. Divide the salad among the serving plates and top each portion with a Hard-Boiled Egg. Garnish with fresh herbs and edible flowers and serve.

INGREDIENTS:

1½   CUPS BELUGA LENTILS

SALT AND PEPPER, TO TASTE

5   OZ. GREEN BEANS, TRIMMED

PICKLED RED ONION (SEE PAGE 671)

GREEN GODDESS DRESSING (SEE PAGE 539)

4   HARD-BOILED EGGS (SEE PAGE 667), HALVED

FRESH HERBS, CHOPPED, FOR GARNISH

EDIBLE FLOWERS, FOR GARNISH

Schnittlauch — Sauerampfer — Kresse — Kerbel — Borretsch — Petersilie

WINTER SALAD WITH POMEGRANATE, PEARS & HEMP SEEDS

YIELD: 4 SERVINGS / ACTIVE TIME: 20 MINUTES / TOTAL TIME: 20 MINUTES

This salad is a good place to turn around the holidays, when you desperately need something to counter the continual indulgences.

1. Bring water to a boil in a large pot. Add salt, let the water return to a full boil, and add the kale. Cook until it is just tender, 3 to 4 minutes. Drain the kale, rinse it under cold water, and let it drain again.

2. Place the kale, salad greens, microgreens, pears, and clementines in a salad bowl and toss to combine. Add half of the vinaigrette, season with salt and pepper, and toss to coat.

3. Top the salad with the pomegranate arils and hemp seeds and serve with the remaining vinaigrette.

INGREDIENTS:

SALT AND PEPPER, TO TASTE

5 OZ. KALE, STEMMED AND CHOPPED

5 OZ. SALAD GREENS

1 OZ. MICROGREENS

2 PEARS, CORED AND SLICED THIN

4 CLEMENTINES, SUPREMED (SEE PAGE 92)

CRANBERRY & ORANGE VINAIGRETTE (SEE PAGE 585)

1 CUP POMEGRANATE ARILS

3 TABLESPOONS HEMP SEEDS

BROCCOLINI & ASPARAGUS SALAD
WITH MOZZARELLA

YIELD: 4 SERVINGS / ACTIVE TIME: 20 MINUTES / TOTAL TIME: 50 MINUTES

The mild flavor of the breakfast radish is best suited to this salad, but any variety will do.

1. Bring water to a boil in a large pot. Place the pine nuts in a dry skillet and toast them over medium heat for 1 to 2 minutes, shaking the pan frequently. Transfer the pine nuts to a bowl and set them aside.

2. Add salt to the boiling water, let it return to a full boil, and add the asparagus and broccolini. Cook until they are just tender, 5 to 7 minutes. Drain, rinse the vegetables under cold water, and let them drain again.

3. Pat the asparagus and broccolini dry with paper towels and place them in a salad bowl. Add the spinach and radishes and toss to combine. Add the vinaigrette, season with salt and pepper, and toss to coat.

4. Top the salad with the mozzarella and toasted pine nuts, garnish with basil, and serve.

INGREDIENTS:

1	CUP PINE NUTS
	SALT AND PEPPER, TO TASTE
¼	LB. ASPARAGUS, TRIMMED AND CHOPPED
½	LB. BROCCOLINI, TRIMMED
3	OZ. SPINACH
4	OZ. BREAKFAST RADISHES, SLICED
	WHITE BALSAMIC VINAIGRETTE (SEE PAGE 565)
4	OZ. FRESH MOZZARELLA CHEESE, DRAINED AND TORN
	FRESH BASIL, CHOPPED, FOR GARNISH

LENTIL SALAD WITH KING OYSTER MUSHROOMS & FENNEL

YIELD: 4 SERVINGS / ACTIVE TIME: 20 MINUTES / TOTAL TIME: 40 MINUTES

Take your time and be careful cutting the fennel, as it is imperative to get it as thin as possible.

1. Bring water to a boil in a large pot. Add the lentils and cook until they are tender, 20 to 25 minutes.

2. Place the olive oil in a large skillet and warm it over medium heat. Add the mushrooms, season with salt and pepper, and cook, without stirring, until they start to brown, about 10 minutes. Stir the mushrooms and cook until they are browned all over, about 5 minutes. Remove the pan from heat.

3. Drain the lentils, spread them on a baking sheet in an even layer, season with salt, and let them cool completely.

4. Place the lentils, mushrooms, salad greens, microgreens, and fennel in a salad bowl and toss to combine. Top the salad with the cranberries and pepitas.

5. Divide the salad among the serving plates and top each portion with dollops of the yogurt. Garnish with dill and serve.

INGREDIENTS:

1½ CUPS BELUGA LENTILS

2 TABLESPOONS EXTRA-VIRGIN OLIVE OIL

½ LB. KING OYSTER MUSHROOMS, SLICED

SALT AND PEPPER, TO TASTE

3 OZ. SALAD GREENS

1 OZ. MICROGREENS

1 BULB OF FENNEL, TRIMMED AND SLICED VERY THIN WITH A MANDOLINE

½ CUP DRIED CRANBERRIES

½ CUP PEPITAS

2 CUPS COCONUT YOGURT

FRESH DILL, CHOPPED, FOR GARNISH

BEAN & TOMATO SALAD

YIELD: 4 SERVINGS / **ACTIVE TIME:** 20 MINUTES / **TOTAL TIME:** 30 MINUTES

Arugula is a good option if you're looking to use something other than cabbage here.

1. Preheat the oven to 350°F. Place the hazelnuts on a baking sheet, place them in the oven, and roast until they are golden brown, 8 to 10 minutes. Remove the hazelnuts from the oven and set them aside.

2. Bring water to a boil in a large pot. Add salt, let the water return to a full boil, and add the beans. Cook until they are just tender, 4 to 6 minutes. Drain the beans, rinse them under cold water, and let them drain again.

3. Place the beans, tomatoes, and cabbage in a salad bowl and toss to combine. Add half of the dressing and toss to coat.

4. Chop the hazelnuts and top the salad with them. Garnish with fresh herbs and serve with the remaining dressing.

INGREDIENTS:

1   CUP HAZELNUTS

    SALT, TO TASTE

4   OZ. GREEN BEANS, TRIMMED AND CHOPPED

4   OZ. WAX BEANS, TRIMMED AND CHOPPED

3   OZ. FAVA BEANS, CHOPPED

2   CUPS CHERRY TOMATOES, HALVED

3   OZ. RED CABBAGE, SHREDDED

    DIJON DRESSING (SEE PAGE 588)

    FRESH HERBS, CHOPPED, FOR GARNISH

PEA & SMOKY TOFU SALAD

YIELD: 4 SERVINGS / **ACTIVE TIME:** 20 MINUTES / **TOTAL TIME:** 30 MINUTES

If you'd prefer to smoke the tofu yourself, place it in a roasting pan, place some wood chips in a cast-iron skillet, ignite the wood chips, and place the skillet inside the roasting pan. Cover the roasting pan with aluminum foil and let the tofu smoke for 15 to 20 minutes.

1. Bring water to a boil in a medium pot.

2. Place the olive oil in a large skillet and warm it over medium heat. Add the tofu, season with salt and pepper, and cook until it is browned, stirring occasionally, 5 to 8 minutes. Add the liquid smoke and cook until the tofu has absorbed it. Remove the pan from heat and let the tofu cool.

3. Add salt to the boiling water, let it return to a full boil, and add the peas. Cook until they are just tender, 2 to 4 minutes. Drain the peas, rinse them under cold water, and let them drain again.

4. Place the tofu, peas, radishes, scallions, eggs, and cheese in a salad bowl and toss to combine. Add the lemon juice, season with salt, pepper, and red pepper flakes, and toss to coat.

5. Sprinkle the lemon zest over the salad, garnish with mint, and serve.

INGREDIENTS:

2 TABLESPOONS EXTRA-VIRGIN OLIVE OIL

4 OZ. TOFU, DRAINED AND DICED

SALT AND PEPPER, TO TASTE

1 TEASPOON LIQUID SMOKE

3 CUPS GREEN PEAS

3 OZ. BREAKFAST RADISHES, SLICED THIN

6 SCALLIONS, TRIMMED AND CHOPPED

4 HARD-BOILED EGGS (SEE PAGE 667), SLICED

4 OZ. CHEDDAR CHEESE, DICED

2 TABLESPOONS FRESH LEMON JUICE

RED PEPPER FLAKES, TO TASTE

1 TABLESPOON LEMON ZEST

FRESH MINT, FOR GARNISH

PUMPKIN & LENTIL SALAD
WITH TOASTED GOAT CHEESE

YIELD: 4 SERVINGS / **ACTIVE TIME:** 20 MINUTES / **TOTAL TIME:** 1 HOUR AND 20 MINUTES

Slightly caramelized goat cheese is all it takes to turn this straightforward salad into an instant autumnal classic.

1. Preheat the oven to 375°F. Place the pumpkin in a baking dish, drizzle the olive oil over it, and season with salt and pepper. Toss to coat and place it in the oven. Roast until the pumpkin is tender, about 45 minutes, stirring it occasionally.

2. Place the walnuts on a baking sheet, place them in the oven, and toast until they are golden brown, 8 to 10 minutes. Remove the walnuts from the oven and set them aside.

3. Bring water to a boil in a large pot and add the lentils. Cook until they are tender, 20 to 25 minutes. Drain the lentils, spread them on a baking sheet in an even layer, season with salt, and let them cool completely.

4. Remove the pumpkin from the oven and let it cool.

5. Line a baking sheet with aluminum foil and set the oven's broiler to high. Place the goat cheese on the baking sheet and place it under the broiler. Broil until it is softened and lightly browned on top. Remove the goat cheese from the oven and set it aside.

6. Place the pumpkin, lentils, and walnuts in a salad bowl and toss to combine. Add the vinaigrette, season with salt and pepper, and toss to coat.

7. Top with the toasted goat cheese, garnish with parsley, and serve.

INGREDIENTS:

1	SMALL PUMPKIN, PEELED, SEEDED, AND DICED
2	TABLESPOONS EXTRA-VIRGIN OLIVE OIL
	SALT AND PEPPER, TO TASTE
1	CUP WALNUTS
1½	CUPS LENTILS
5	OZ. GOAT CHEESE, CUT INTO ROUNDS
	HERB VINAIGRETTE (SEE PAGE 643)
	FRESH PARSLEY, CHOPPED, FOR GARNISH

SWEET POTATO & KALE SALAD
WITH SEA BUCKTHORN DRESSING

YIELD: 4 SERVINGS / **ACTIVE TIME:** 20 MINUTES / **TOTAL TIME:** 1 HOUR

Sea buckthorns are especially tart, so you'll want to add the dressing in increments here.

1. Preheat the oven to 375°F. Place the sweet potatoes and kale in a baking dish, drizzle the olive oil over the top, and season with salt and pepper. Toss to coat, place the vegetables in the oven, and roast until the sweet potatoes are browned and tender, about 40 minutes.

2. Remove the roasted vegetables from the oven and let them cool.

3. Place the flaxseeds in a dry skillet and toast them over medium heat for 2 to 4 minutes, shaking the pan frequently. Remove the pan from heat and set the flaxseeds aside.

4. Place the sweet potatoes, kale, oranges, and avocados in a salad bowl and toss to combine. Add one-quarter of the dressing, season with salt and pepper, and toss to coat. Taste the salad and add dressing to taste.

5. Top the salad with the almonds and toasted flaxseeds and serve with any remaining dressing.

INGREDIENTS:

2   LARGE SWEET POTATOES, SLICED

6   OZ. KALE, STEMMED AND CHOPPED

2   TABLESPOONS EXTRA-VIRGIN OLIVE OIL

     SALT AND PEPPER, TO TASTE

¼   CUP FLAXSEEDS

2   ORANGES, PEELED AND SLICED THIN

     FLESH OF 2 AVOCADOS, SLICED THIN

     SEA BUCKTHORN DRESSING (SEE PAGE 517)

1   CUP CHOPPED ALMONDS

ROASTED RHUBARB & RADISH SALAD

YIELD: 4 SERVINGS / **ACTIVE TIME:** 20 MINUTES / **TOTAL TIME:** 1 HOUR

M ost salads will call for pine nuts to be toasted, but here you can skip that step, since you really just want them for the pleasant crunch that they'll supply.

1. Preheat the oven to 375°F. Place the rhubarb and radishes in a baking dish, drizzle the olive oil over them, and season with salt and pepper. Toss to combine, place the vegetables in the oven, and roast until they are tender, 35 to 45 minutes.

2. Remove the rhubarb and radishes from the oven and let them cool.

3. Place the rhubarb, radishes, salad greens, and mozzarella in a salad bowl and toss to combine. Add the dressing, season with salt and pepper, and toss to coat.

4. Top the salad with the Parmesan, pine nuts, and chia seeds, garnish with edible flowers, and serve.

INGREDIENTS:

½   LB. RHUBARB, SLICED

½   LB. RADISHES, HALVED

2   TABLESPOONS EXTRA-VIRGIN OLIVE OIL

SALT AND PEPPER, TO TASTE

6   OZ. SALAD GREENS

4   OZ. FRESH MOZZARELLA CHEESE, DRAINED AND TORN

APRICOT & ROSE WATER DRESSING (SEE PAGE 656)

2   OZ. PARMESAN CHEESE, SHAVED

1   CUP PINE NUTS

1   TABLESPOON CHIA SEEDS

EDIBLE FLOWERS, FOR GARNISH

BABY POTATO, ASPARAGUS & PESTO SALAD

YIELD: 4 SERVINGS / **ACTIVE TIME:** 20 MINUTES / **TOTAL TIME:** 1 HOUR

Of course you can purchase pesto from the store, but it's easy enough to prepare your own while the potatoes are roasting, and the control you get over the taste and texture is well worth the extra bit of effort.

1. Preheat the oven to 375°F. Place the potatoes in a baking dish, drizzle the olive oil over them, and season with salt and pepper. Toss to combine, place the potatoes in the oven, and roast until they are tender and crispy, 40 to 45 minutes, stirring occasionally.

2. Bring water to a boil in a large saucepan. Add salt, let the water return to a full boil, and add the asparagus. Cook the asparagus until it is just tender, 4 to 6 minutes. Remove the asparagus with a strainer and let it drain. Add the radishes to the boiling water and cook until they are tender, 8 to 10 minutes. Drain the radishes and let them cool.

3. Remove the potatoes from the oven and let them cool slightly.

4. Chop the asparagus into bite-size pieces.

5. Place the potatoes, asparagus, radishes, arugula, and bocconcini in a salad bowl and toss to combine. Add the Pesto and toss to coat.

6. Garnish with basil and serve.

INGREDIENTS:

- 1 LB. BABY POTATOES, HALVED
- 2 TABLESPOONS EXTRA-VIRGIN OLIVE OIL

  SALT AND PEPPER, TO TASTE
- ½ LB. ASPARAGUS, TRIMMED
- 3 OZ. RADISHES, HALVED
- 2 OZ. ARUGULA
- 4 OZ. BOCCONCINI (BALLS OF FRESH MOZZARELLA CHEESE), DRAINED

  PESTO (SEE PAGE 603)

  FRESH BASIL, CHOPPED, FOR GARNISH

LENTIL, POTATO & GREEN BEAN SALAD

YIELD: 4 SERVINGS / **ACTIVE TIME:** 20 MINUTES / **TOTAL TIME:** 1 HOUR

I f you'd like a milder onion-y flavor here, finely dice half of a shallot and swap it in for the scallions.

1. Bring water to a boil in two large pots.

2. Preheat the oven to 375°F. Place the potatoes and scallions in a baking dish, drizzle the olive oil over them, and season with salt and pepper. Toss to combine, place the baking dish in the oven, and roast until the potatoes are golden brown and tender, 35 to 45 minutes, stirring occasionally.

3. Add the lentils to one of the pots and cook until they are tender, 20 to 25 minutes. Drain the lentils, spread them on a baking sheet in an even layer, season with salt, and let them cool completely.

4. Add salt to the other pot of boiling water, let it return to a full boil, and add the green beans. Cook until they are just tender, 4 to 6 minutes. Drain the green beans, rinse them under cold water, and let them drain again.

5. Remove the potatoes and scallions from the oven and let them cool slightly.

6. Place the potatoes, scallions, lentils, green beans, arugula, tomatoes, and feta in a salad bowl and toss to combine. Add the vinaigrette and toss to coat.

7. Top the salad with the peanuts and serve.

INGREDIENTS:

½   LB. RED CREAMER POTATOES, QUARTERED

8   SCALLIONS, TRIMMED AND CHOPPED

2   TABLESPOONS EXTRA-VIRGIN OLIVE OIL

    SALT AND PEPPER, TO TASTE

1½   CUPS LENTILS

6   OZ. GREEN BEANS, TRIMMED AND HALVED

3   OZ. ARUGULA

2   TOMATOES, CHOPPED

3   OZ. FETA CHEESE, CRUMBLED

    ROASTED RED PEPPER VINAIGRETTE (SEE PAGE 619)

1   CUP ROASTED PEANUTS, CHOPPED

ROASTED PEAR & POTATO SALAD
WITH BLUE CHEESE DRESSING

YIELD: 4 SERVINGS / **ACTIVE TIME:** 20 MINUTES / **TOTAL TIME:** 1 HOUR

Two charcuterie stalwarts, blue cheese and pears, bring their noted affinity for each other to the salad bowl.

1. Bring water to a boil in a large pot.

2. Preheat the oven to 375°F. Place the potatoes and pears in a baking dish, drizzle the olive oil over them, and season with salt and pepper. Toss to combine, place the potatoes and pears in the oven, and roast until they are browned and the potatoes are tender, 35 to 45 minutes, stirring occasionally.

3. Add salt to the boiling water, let it return to a full boil, and add the green beans. Cook until they are just tender, 4 to 6 minutes. Drain the green beans, rinse them under cold water, and let them drain again.

4. Remove the potatoes and pears from the oven and let them cool slightly.

5. Place the potatoes, pears, green beans, radicchio, and eggs in a salad bowl and toss to combine. Add half of the dressing, season with salt and pepper, and toss to coat.

6. Top the salad with the walnuts and serve with the remaining dressing.

INGREDIENTS:

1	LB. RED CREAMER POTATOES, QUARTERED
2	PEARS, SLICED
2	TABLESPOONS EXTRA-VIRGIN OLIVE OIL
	SALT AND PEPPER, TO TASTE
6	OZ. GREEN BEANS, HALVED
4	OZ. RADICCHIO, CHOPPED
3	HARD-BOILED EGGS (SEE PAGE 667), SLICED
	BLUE CHEESE DRESSING (SEE PAGE 632)
1	CUP WALNUTS, CHOPPED

EGG SALAD WITH GREEK YOGURT

YIELD: 4 SERVINGS / ACTIVE TIME: 20 MINUTES / TOTAL TIME: 20 MINUTES

Using Greek yogurt instead of mayo amplifies the protein in this egg salad, without sacrificing any of the tang you're after.

1. Place the eggs and celery in a mixing bowl and work the mixture with a fork, breaking up the eggs. Add the yogurt, season with salt and pepper, and work the mixture until well combined.

2. Garnish with dill and serve on toasted bread.

INGREDIENTS:

10 HARD-BOILED EGGS (SEE PAGE 667), CHOPPED

2 CELERY STALKS, CHOPPED

1 CUP GREEK YOGURT

SALT AND PEPPER, TO TASTE

FRESH DILL, CHOPPED, FOR GARNISH

SLICES OF BREAD, TOASTED, FOR SERVING

PUMPKIN & APPLE SALAD WITH SEARED HALLOUMI

YIELD: 4 SERVINGS / **ACTIVE TIME:** 20 MINUTES / **TOTAL TIME:** 1 HOUR AND 20 MINUTES

Halloumi's miraculous ability to withstand high heat makes it a wonder in the world of salads.

1. Preheat the oven to 375°F. Place the pumpkin and apples in a baking dish, drizzle half of the olive oil over them, and season with salt and pepper. Place the dish in the oven and roast until the pumpkin and apples are browned and the pumpkin is tender, 45 minutes to 1 hour, stirring occasionally.

2. Place the remaining olive oil in a large skillet and warm it over medium-high heat. Add the halloumi and cook until it is well browned on both sides, 5 to 7 minutes, turning it over just once. Remove the halloumi from the pan and set it aside.

3. Remove the pumpkin and apples from the oven and let them cool.

4. Place the pumpkin, apples, salad greens, chickpeas, and avocados in a salad bowl and toss to combine. Add the vinaigrette, season with salt and pepper, and toss to coat.

5. Chop the halloumi, top the salad with it, the pomegranate arils, and walnuts, and serve.

INGREDIENTS:

- 1   SMALL PUMPKIN, PEELED, SEEDED, AND DICED
- 2   APPLES, CORED AND SLICED
- ¼   CUP EXTRA-VIRGIN OLIVE OIL
-    SALT AND PEPPER, TO TASTE
- ½   LB. HALLOUMI CHEESE
- 6   OZ. SALAD GREENS
- 2   CUPS CANNED CHICKPEAS, DRAINED AND RINSED
-    FLESH OF 2 AVOCADOS, SLICED
-    RED WINE VINAIGRETTE (SEE PAGE 599)
- 1   CUP POMEGRANATE ARILS
- 1   CUP WALNUTS, ROASTED

YELLOW LENTIL, BROCCOLINI & ZUCCHINI SALAD

YIELD: 4 SERVINGS / **ACTIVE TIME:** 20 MINUTES / **TOTAL TIME:** 40 MINUTES

The blueberries, goat cheese, and Citrus Vinaigrette supply the brightness this satisfying salad needs.

1. Bring water to a boil in two large pots.

2. Add the lentils to the boiling water in one of the pots and cook until they are tender, 20 to 25 minutes.

3. Add salt to the boiling water in the other pot, let it return to a full boil, and add the broccolini. Cook until it is just tender, 2 to 3 minutes. Drain the broccolini, rinse it under cold water, and let it drain again.

4. Place the olive oil in a large skillet and warm it over medium heat. Add the zucchini, season with salt and pepper, and cook, stirring occasionally, until it has browned and is tender, 8 to 10 minutes. Remove the pan from heat and let the zucchini cool.

5. Drain the lentils, spread them on a baking sheet in an even layer, season with salt, and let them cool completely.

6. Place the lentils, broccolini, zucchini, spinach, scallions, avocados, blueberries, and goat cheese in a salad bowl and toss to combine. Add the vinaigrette, season with salt and pepper, and toss to coat.

7. Garnish with basil and serve with lemon wedges.

INGREDIENTS:

1½ CUPS YELLOW LENTILS

SALT AND PEPPER, TO TASTE

¼ LB. BROCCOLINI, CHOPPED

2 TABLESPOONS EXTRA-VIRGIN OLIVE OIL

2 ZUCCHINI, CHOPPED

4 OZ. SPINACH

4 SCALLIONS, TRIMMED AND CHOPPED

FLESH OF 2 AVOCADOS, SLICED

1½ CUPS BLUEBERRIES

4 OZ. GOAT CHEESE, CRUMBLED

CITRUS VINAIGRETTE (SEE PAGE 610)

FRESH BASIL, CHOPPED, FOR GARNISH

LEMON WEDGES, FOR SERVING

CHARRED CHICORY, LENTIL & PINEAPPLE SALAD

YIELD: 4 SERVINGS / ACTIVE TIME: 20 MINUTES / TOTAL TIME: 50 MINUTES

C harring chicory sweetens it slightly, and the pineapple supplies additional sweetness plus the acidity necessary to provide balance to this salad.

1. Bring water to a boil in a large pot. Add the lentils and cook until they are tender, 20 to 25 minutes. Drain the lentils, spread them on a baking sheet in an even layer, season with salt, and let them cool completely.

2. Warm a large cast-iron skillet over medium heat for 5 minutes. Add the olive oil and place the chicory in the pan, cut side down. Cook until it is lightly charred, turn it over, and cook until it is charred on that side. Remove the chicory from the pan and let it cool. When it is cool enough to handle, chop the chicory.

3. Place the chicory, lentils, lettuce, and pineapple in a salad bowl and toss to combine. Add half of the dressing, season with salt and pepper, and toss to coat.

4. Sprinkle the almonds over the salad and serve with the remaining dressing.

INGREDIENTS:

- 1½ CUPS LENTILS
- SALT AND PEPPER, TO TASTE
- 1 TABLESPOON EXTRA-VIRGIN OLIVE OIL
- 5 OZ. CHICORY, HALVED LENGTHWISE
- 3 OZ. LETTUCE, CHOPPED
- 1½ CUPS DICED PINEAPPLE
- LEMON & THYME DRESSING (SEE PAGE 606)
- 1½ CUPS CHOPPED ALMONDS

KOHLRABI & POTATO SALAD

YIELD: 4 SERVINGS / **ACTIVE TIME:** 20 MINUTES / **TOTAL TIME:** 35 MINUTES

If you are at the farmers market and can't resist the intriguing look of the kohlrabies, but also aren't quite sure what you should do with them once you've gotten them home, just make this salad.

1. Bring water to a boil in a large pot. Add salt, let the water return to a full boil, and add the potatoes and kohlrabi. Cook until they are tender, about 20 minutes, drain the vegetables, and let them cool slightly.

2. Place the potatoes, kohlrabi, scallions, eggs, and feta in a salad bowl and toss to combine. Add the vinaigrette, season with salt and pepper, and toss to coat.

3. Garnish with fresh herbs and serve.

INGREDIENTS:

SALT AND PEPPER, TO TASTE

1 LB. BABY POTATOES, HALVED

½ LB. KOHLRABI, PEELED AND DICED

8 SCALLIONS, TRIMMED AND CHOPPED

2 HARD-BOILED EGGS (SEE PAGE 667), DICED

4 OZ. FETA CHEESE, CUBED

HERB VINAIGRETTE (SEE PAGE 643)

FRESH HERBS, CHOPPED, FOR GARNISH

FAVA BEAN & EDAMAME SALAD WITH BURRATA

YIELD: 4 SERVINGS / **ACTIVE TIME:** 20 MINUTES / **TOTAL TIME:** 30 MINUTES

A brilliant salad, both in terms of look and taste.

1. Bring water to a boil in a large pot. Add the fava beans, edamame, and peas and cook until they are just tender, 4 to 6 minutes. Drain the fava beans, edamame, and peas, rinse them under cold water, and let them drain again.

2. Place the fava beans, edamame, and peas in a salad bowl, add half of the vinaigrette, and toss to combine.

3. Season with salt and pepper, top the salad with the burrata, garnish with fresh herbs, and serve with the remaining vinaigrette.

INGREDIENTS:

4 OZ SHELLED FAVA BEANS

4 OZ SHELLED EDAMAME

1½ CUPS GREEN PEAS

OLIVE & WHOLE LEMON VINAIGRETTE (SEE PAGE 429)

SALT AND PEPPER, TO TASTE

5 OZ BURRATA CHEESE, TORN

FRESH HERBS, CHOPPED, FOR GARNISH

LENTIL, CAULIFLOWER & SUMAC SALAD

YIELD: 4 SERVINGS / **ACTIVE TIME:** 20 MINUTES / **TOTAL TIME:** 1 HOUR

Here's a wonderful opportunity to make use of the many colors of cauliflower that are available.

1. Preheat the oven to 375°F. Place the cauliflower in a baking dish, drizzle the olive oil over it, and season with salt and pepper. Toss to combine, place the cauliflower in the oven, and roast until it is tender, about 35 minutes, stirring occasionally.

2. Bring water to a boil in a large pot and add the lentils. Cook until they are tender, 20 to 25 minutes. Drain the lentils, spread them on a baking sheet in an even layer, season with salt, and let them cool completely.

3. Remove the cauliflower from the oven and let it cool.

4. Place the cauliflower and lentils in a salad bowl and toss to combine. Add half of the vinaigrette, the sumac, and red pepper flakes and toss to coat.

5. Garnish with cilantro and serve with the remaining vinaigrette.

INGREDIENTS:

½ LB. CAULIFLOWER, CUT INTO FLORETS

2 TABLESPOONS EXTRA-VIRGIN OLIVE OIL

SALT AND PEPPER, TO TASTE

1½ CUPS LENTILS

PEAR & BALSAMIC VINAIGRETTE (SEE PAGE 614)

1 TABLESPOON SUMAC

1 TEASPOON RED PEPPER FLAKES

FRESH CILANTRO, CHOPPED, FOR GARNISH

MOROCCAN KIDNEY BEAN SALAD

YIELD: 4 SERVINGS / **ACTIVE TIME:** 10 MINUTES / **TOTAL TIME:** 25 MINUTES

The warm, earthy taste of ras el hanout, a popular Moroccan spice blend, transforms a simple bean salad.

1. Place the kidney beans, chickpeas, carrots, and cilantro in a salad bowl and toss to combine.

2. Add the olive oil, vinegar, and ras el hanout, season with salt, and toss to coat.

3. Cover the bowl with plastic wrap and let the salad marinate for 15 minutes.

4. Toss the salad and divide it among the serving plates. Garnish with mint and serve.

INGREDIENTS:

- 2 CUPS CANNED KIDNEY BEANS, DRAINED AND RINSED
- 2 CUPS CANNED CHICKPEAS, DRAINED AND RINSED
- 2 CARROTS, PEELED AND FINELY DICED
- 1 CUP FRESH CILANTRO, CHOPPED
- 2 TABLESPOONS EXTRA-VIRGIN OLIVE OIL
- 2 TABLESPOONS SHERRY VINEGAR
- 2 TABLESPOONS RAS EL HANOUT
- SALT, TO TASTE
- FRESH MINT, FOR GARNISH

LENTIL, BEET & BLUE CHEESE SALAD

YIELD: 4 SERVINGS / **ACTIVE TIME:** 20 MINUTES / **TOTAL TIME:** 2 HOURS

Jasper Hill Farm's Bayley Hazen Blue, with its subtle nutty flavor, is a good choice in this salad.

1. Preheat the oven to 375°F. Place the beets in a baking dish, add a little water, and cover the dish with aluminum foil. Place the beets in the oven and roast until a knife inserted into them passes easily to their centers, about 1 hour.

2. Place the lentils in a pot, cover with water, and bring to a boil. Cook until the lentils are tender, 20 to 25 minutes.

3. Remove the beets from the oven and let them cool.

4. Drain the lentils, spread them on a baking sheet in an even layer, season with salt, and let them cool completely.

5. Peel the beets and dice them.

6. Place the lentils, beets, and salad greens in a salad bowl and toss to combine. Add the lime juice and toss to coat.

7. Top the salad with the blue cheese and pecans and serve.

INGREDIENTS:

2   CHIOGGIA BEETS

2   CUPS LENTILS

     SALT, TO TASTE

5   OZ. SALAD GREENS

1   TABLESPOON FRESH LIME JUICE

2   OZ. BLUE CHEESE, CRUMBLED

1   CUP ROASTED PECANS, CHOPPED

ROASTED ROOT VEGETABLE & CARAMELIZED ONION SALAD

YIELD: 6 SERVINGS / **ACTIVE TIME:** 45 MINUTES / **TOTAL TIME:** 1 HOUR AND 45 MINUTES

A preparation that will have you considering how to work in caramelized onions whenever you're making a salad.

1. Place 6 tablespoons of the avocado oil in a large skillet and warm it over medium heat. Add the onions and salt and cook, stirring frequently, until the onions are caramelized and a deep golden brown, about 30 minutes.

2. Transfer the onions to a large bowl. Add the prunes, apricots, figs, walnuts, sugar, and cinnamon and stir to combine. Season the mixture with salt and pepper.

3. Preheat the oven to 375°F. Place the sweet potatoes, turnips, and butternut squash in a roasting pan and rub them with the remaining avocado oil. Sprinkle the turmeric over the top, season the vegetables with salt and pepper, and toss to combine. Spread the vegetables in an even layer in the pan and spoon the fruit mixture over and around them.

4. Add 1½ cups of water to the pan and place it in the oven. Roast until the vegetables are well browned and cooked through, about 1 hour, stirring halfway through. Add more water if the pan starts to look dry.

5. Toast the almonds in a dry skillet over medium-low heat, stirring often, until they are lightly browned, about 6 minutes. Remove the pan from heat.

6. Remove the vegetables from the oven, sprinkle the toasted almonds on top, and serve with the vinaigrette.

INGREDIENTS:

½   CUP AVOCADO OIL

2   LBS. YELLOW ONIONS, SLICED THIN

1   TEASPOON KOSHER SALT, PLUS MORE TO TASTE

½   CUP PITTED PRUNES, HALVED

½   CUP DRIED APRICOTS, HALVED

½   CUP DRIED FIGS, STEMS REMOVED, HALVED

½   CUP SHELLED WALNUTS

2   TABLESPOONS SUGAR

1   TEASPOON CINNAMON

    BLACK PEPPER, TO TASTE

1   LB. SWEET POTATOES, PEELED AND CUT INTO 2-INCH-LONG PIECES

1   LB. TURNIPS, PEELED AND CUT INTO 2-INCH-LONG PIECES

2   LBS. BUTTERNUT SQUASH, PEELED, SEEDED, AND CUT INTO 2-INCH-LONG PIECES

½   TEASPOON TURMERIC

½   CUP SLIVERED ALMONDS

    CHAMPAGNE VINAIGRETTE (SEE PAGE 592), FOR SERVING

ARUGULA SALAD WITH PICKLED BEETS

YIELD: 4 SERVINGS / ACTIVE TIME: 20 MINUTES / TOTAL TIME: 5 HOURS

This bright salad is perfect for almost any time of the year, although peppery arugula is usually at its best in the spring and fall. The real treat here is the vinaigrette, which enlivens all of the other ingredients.

1. Place each beet in its own small saucepan, cover with water, and simmer until a knife can easily pierce them, about 45 minutes.

2. Drain the beets and let them cool. When they are cool enough to handle, peel the beets, slice them into thin half-moons, and place each one in its own bowl to ensure that the red beet doesn't stain the golden one.

3. Place the rice vinegar, sugar, and 1 cup water in a small saucepan, bring to a boil, and then remove the pan from heat. Cover the beets with the brine and let them sit at room temperature until they are pickled, 3 to 4 hours.

4. Preheat the oven to 300°F. In a small mixing bowl, whip the egg white until it is frothy. Add the pistachios and Cajun seasoning, toss to coat, and spread the pistachios on a parchment-lined baking sheet. Place the pistachios in the oven and roast until they are golden and fragrant, about 15 minutes. Remove them from the oven and let the pistachios cool.

5. Place the arugula in a salad bowl, add half of the vinaigrette, and toss to coat.

6. Arrange the pickled beets in a serving dish and place the dressed arugula on top. Sprinkle the pistachios over the dish, drizzle the balsamic vinegar over the top, season with salt and pepper, and serve with the remaining vinaigrette.

INGREDIENTS:

1	LARGE RED BEET
1	LARGE GOLDEN BEET
1	CUP RICE VINEGAR
1	CUP SUGAR
1	EGG WHITE
½	CUP SHELLED RAW PISTACHIOS
1½	TEASPOONS CAJUN SEASONING
5	OZ. ARUGULA
	PRESERVED LEMON VINAIGRETTE (SEE PAGE 545)
2	TABLESPOONS QUALITY AGED BALSAMIC VINEGAR
	SALT AND PEPPER, TO TASTE

PEPPERS STUFFED WITH GREEK SALAD

YIELD: 4 SERVINGS / ACTIVE TIME: 15 MINUTES / TOTAL TIME: 15 MINUTES

One usually thinks of stuffed peppers as a comfort dish, but this recipe shows that the approach can be healthy as well.

1. Preheat the oven to 375°F and place the peppers on a parchment-lined baking sheet.

2. Place the cherry tomatoes, garlic, olive oil, feta, and black olives in a mixing bowl and stir to combine. Divide the mixture among the peppers, place them in the oven, and roast until the peppers start to collapse, about 10 minutes.

3. Remove the peppers from the oven, season with salt and pepper, top with the basil leaves, and enjoy.

INGREDIENTS:

4 YELLOW BELL PEPPERS, SEEDED AND HALVED

12 CHERRY TOMATOES, HALVED

2 GARLIC CLOVES, MINCED

2 TABLESPOONS EXTRA-VIRGIN OLIVE OIL

½ CUP CRUMBLED FETA CHEESE

1 CUP BLACK OLIVES, PITTED

SALT AND PEPPER, TO TASTE

LEAVES FROM 1 BUNCH OF FRESH BASIL

JERK ACORN SQUASH & BABY KALE SALAD

YIELD: 4 SERVINGS / **ACTIVE TIME:** 25 MINUTES / **TOTAL TIME:** 2 HOURS

The famed spice blend from Jamaican cuisine works wonders when paired with the sweet, earthy flavor of squash.

1. Preheat the oven to 400°F. Halve the squash lengthwise, remove the seeds, and reserve them. Trim the ends of the squash so that each half can sit evenly, flesh side up, on a baking sheet.

2. Score the squash's flesh in a crosshatch pattern, cutting approximately ⅛ inch into the flesh. Brush some of the marinade on the squash and then fill the cavities with ⅓ cup of the marinade.

3. Place the baking sheet in the oven and roast until the squash is tender, 45 minutes to 1 hour. As the squash is cooking, baste the flesh with some of the marinade in the cavity every 15 minutes.

4. Remove the squash from the oven and let it cool. Reduce the oven's temperature to 350°F.

5. Run the squash seeds under water to remove any pulp. Pat the seeds dry, place them in a mixing bowl, and add the olive oil, salt, pepper, and paprika. Toss to combine and then place the seeds on a baking sheet. Place it in the oven and bake until the seeds are light brown and crispy, about 7 minutes.

6. Place the toasted seeds, kale, cranberries, and feta in a salad bowl and toss to combine. Add half of the vinaigrette and toss to coat.

7. Divide the salad among the serving plates, place one of the roasted halves of squash on top of each portion, and serve with the remaining vinaigrette.

INGREDIENTS:

2 ACORN SQUASH

JERK MARINADE (SEE PAGE 673)

1 TABLESPOON EXTRA-VIRGIN OLIVE OIL

½ TEASPOON KOSHER SALT

¼ TEASPOON BLACK PEPPER

¼ TEASPOON PAPRIKA

6 CUPS BABY KALE

½ CUP DRIED CRANBERRIES

4 OZ. FETA CHEESE, CRUMBLED

MAPLE VINAIGRETTE (SEE PAGE 556)

CHARRED BRASSICA SALAD
WITH BUTTERMILK CAESAR

YIELD: 4 SERVINGS / **ACTIVE TIME:** 20 MINUTES / **TOTAL TIME:** 20 MINUTES

Charring brassicas such as cauliflower, broccoli, and cabbage brings out their sweet side, an element that pairs beautifully with the acidity of the dressing.

1. Bring water to a boil in a large pot. Add salt, let the water return to a full boil, and add the cauliflower. Cook for 1 minute, remove it with a strainer, and transfer it to a paper towel–lined plate. Wait for the water to return to a boil, add the broccoli, and cook for 30 seconds. Use a strainer to remove the broccoli and let the water drip off before transferring it to the paper towel–lined plate.

2. Place the olive oil and Brussels sprouts, cut side down, in a large cast-iron skillet. Add the broccoli and cauliflower, season with salt and pepper, and cook over high heat without moving the vegetables. Cook until they are charred, turn them over, and cook until they are charred on that side. Remove the vegetables from the pan and transfer them to a salad bowl.

3. Add the dressing and toss to coat. Garnish with pickled onion, Parmesan, and red pepper flakes and serve.

INGREDIENTS:

SALT AND PEPPER, TO TASTE

1   SMALL HEAD OF CAULIFLOWER, CUT INTO BITE-SIZE PIECES

1   HEAD OF BROCCOLI, CUT INTO FLORETS

¼   CUP EXTRA-VIRGIN OLIVE OIL

4   OZ. BRUSSELS SPROUTS, TRIMMED AND HALVED

BUTTERMILK CAESAR DRESSING (SEE PAGE 598)

PICKLED RED ONION (SEE PAGE 671), FOR GARNISH

PARMESAN CHEESE, GRATED, FOR GARNISH

RED PEPPER FLAKES, FOR GARNISH

CHIPOTLE-DUSTED CAULIFLOWER & CHICKPEA SALAD

YIELD: 4 TO 6 SERVINGS / ACTIVE TIME: 25 MINUTES / TOTAL TIME: 45 MINUTES

The cauliflower renaissance has been powered by its ability to shape-shift, and take on whatever flavor one wishes to freight it with.

1. Preheat the oven to 400°F. Place all of the ingredients, except for the dressing, in a mixing bowl and toss to coat. Place the mixture in a 13 x 9–inch baking dish, place it in the oven, and roast until the cauliflower is slightly charred, about 40 minutes.

2. Remove the dish from the oven and let the mixture cool slightly.

3. Place the mixture in a salad bowl, add the dressing, toss to coat, and serve.

INGREDIENTS:

- 1   (14 OZ.) CAN OF CHICKPEAS, DRAINED AND RINSED
- 3   CUPS CHOPPED CAULIFLOWER FLORETS
- 3   GARLIC CLOVES, SLICED THIN
- 1   SHALLOT, SLICED THIN
- ⅓   CUP EXTRA-VIRGIN OLIVE OIL
- ½   TEASPOON DARK CHILI POWDER
- ½   TEASPOON CHIPOTLE CHILE POWDER
- ½   TEASPOON BLACK PEPPER
- ½   TEASPOON ONION POWDER
- ½   TEASPOON GARLIC POWDER
- ¼   TEASPOON PAPRIKA
- 1   TABLESPOON KOSHER SALT

    RED WINE & CHILE DRESSING (SEE PAGE 556)

SMASHED POTATO & SUMMER BEAN SALAD

YIELD: 4 TO 6 SERVINGS / ACTIVE TIME: 10 MINUTES / TOTAL TIME: 45 MINUTES

Cast iron is a wonder at supplying contrasting textures, as these smashed potatoes, which carry the creamy interior of boiled potatoes and the crispy exterior of French fries, exhibit.

1. Rinse the potatoes under cold water and place them in a large pot. Cover them with water and add about 2 tablespoons of salt, the garlic, thyme, and peppercorns. Bring to a boil and then reduce the heat so that the water simmers. Cook until the potatoes are fork-tender, 15 to 20 minutes.

2. Drain the potatoes and place them on paper towels to dry.

3. Bring water to a boil in a medium saucepan and prepare an ice bath. Add salt, let the water return to a full boil, and add the beans. Cook for 2 minutes. Drain the beans and plunge them into the ice bath. Drain the beans again, place them in a salad bowl, and set them aside.

4. Place the pancetta in a small skillet and cook over medium-low heat, stirring occasionally, until the fat has rendered and the pancetta is crispy, about 6 minutes. Remove the pan from heat and set it aside.

5. Gently smash the potatoes to flatten them and pat them completely dry with paper towels. Add the pancetta to the salad bowl.

6. Add canola oil to a large, deep cast-iron skillet until it is about ½ inch deep and warm it to 325°F. Working in batches to avoid crowding the pot, gently slip the smashed potatoes into the hot oil and fry on each side until the potatoes are golden brown, turning them as necessary.

7. Remove the lightly fried potatoes from the oil and add them to the salad bowl. Add the vinegar, season with salt and pepper, toss to combine, and transfer them to a serving dish. Top the dish with the Parmesan and serve.

INGREDIENTS:

1½ LBS. BABY POTATOES

SALT AND PEPPER, TO TASTE

5 GARLIC CLOVES, SMASHED

3 SPRIGS OF FRESH THYME

1 TABLESPOON BLACK PEPPERCORNS

½ LB. SUMMER BEANS, TRIMMED AND CUT INTO THIRDS

4 OZ. PANCETTA, DICED

CANOLA OIL, AS NEEDED

2 TABLESPOONS CHAMPAGNE VINEGAR

½ CUP GRATED PARMESAN CHEESE

KING TRUMPET, PARSNIP & BRUSSELS SPROUT SALAD

YIELD: 4 SERVINGS / **ACTIVE TIME:** 30 MINUTES / **TOTAL TIME:** 1 HOUR

This hearty vegetarian salad is a surefire hit once the weather turns cooler.

1. Preheat the oven to 400°F. Place the parsnips in a mixing bowl, add the olive oil, season with salt and pepper, and toss to combine. Place the parsnips on a baking sheet and place them in the oven.

2. Roast the parsnips until they are tender, 10 to 15 minutes. Remove the parsnips from the oven and set them aside. Leave the oven on.

3. Place 3 tablespoons of the canola oil in a large cast-iron skillet and warm it over medium-high heat. Season the king trumpet mushrooms with salt and pepper and place them in the pan, cut side down. Cook until the edges begin to brown and then place the pan in the oven. Roast the mushrooms until they are tender, 5 to 8 minutes.

4. Remove the mushrooms from the oven and add half of the vinegar. Toss to coat the mushrooms and place them in a salad bowl.

5. Place the remaining canola oil in a large skillet and warm it over medium-high heat. Add the shiitake mushrooms, season with salt and pepper, and cook until they are golden brown and crispy, about 8 minutes, stirring occasionally.

6. Add the garlic and shallot and cook, stirring continually, for 1 minute. Add the butter and stir until the mushrooms are coated. Deglaze the pan with the remaining vinegar, scraping any browned bits up from the bottom.

7. Add the spinach, Brussels sprout leaves, and roasted parsnips to the pan and season with salt and pepper. Cook until the spinach and Brussels sprout leaves have wilted. Transfer the mixture to the salad bowl.

8. Add the parsley, stir to combine, and serve.

INGREDIENTS:

- 2 **CUPS CHOPPED PARSNIPS**
- 2 **TABLESPOONS EXTRA-VIRGIN OLIVE OIL**
- **SALT AND PEPPER, TO TASTE**
- 5 **TABLESPOONS CANOLA OIL**
- 10 **LARGE KING TRUMPET MUSHROOMS, STEMS, REMOVED, HALVED AND SCORED**
- 4 **TEASPOONS SHERRY VINEGAR**
- 4 **CUPS SHIITAKE MUSHROOMS, SLICED**
- 4 **GARLIC CLOVES, MINCED**
- 1 **SHALLOT, MINCED**
- 1 **TABLESPOON UNSALTED BUTTER**
- 4 **CUPS SPINACH**
- 2 **CUPS BRUSSELS SPROUT LEAVES**
- 2 **TABLESPOONS CHOPPED FRESH PARSLEY**

ROASTED BEET SALAD

Contrary to what you may think at first glance, beets' earthy character makes them a brilliant match for strawberries.

1. Preheat the oven to 400°F. Group the beets according to color and place each group in a separate aluminum foil pouch. Divide the thyme, garlic, olive oil, soy sauce, and water between the pouches, seal them, and place them in a baking dish.

2. Place the pouches in the oven and roast the beets until a knife inserted into them passes easily to their centers, 45 minutes to 1 hour.

3. Remove the beets from the oven and let them cool.

4. When the beets are cool enough to handle, peel them and cut them into bite-size pieces. Place the beets in a salad bowl and let them cool completely.

5. Place the frisée and strawberries in a mixing bowl and toss to combine. Set the mixture aside.

6. Add some of the vinaigrette to the salad bowl, season with salt and pepper, and toss to combine. Layer the frisée mixture over the top and top the salad with the goat cheese and Candied Walnuts. Serve with any remaining vinaigrette.

INGREDIENTS:

3	RED BEETS
3	GOLDEN BEETS
3	PINK BABY BEETS
6	SPRIGS OF FRESH THYME
6	GARLIC CLOVES
3	TABLESPOONS EXTRA-VIRGIN OLIVE OIL
3	TABLESPOONS SOY SAUCE
6	TABLESPOONS WATER
2	OZ. FRISÉE
8	STRAWBERRIES, HALVED
	CHAMPAGNE VINAIGRETTE (SEE PAGE 592)
	SALT AND PEPPER, TO TASTE
4	OZ. GOAT CHEESE, CRUMBLED
1	CUP CANDIED WALNUTS (SEE PAGE 653)

RAW BEET SALAD WITH
BLOOD ORANGE, JALAPEÑO & BRIE

YIELD: 4 TO 6 SERVINGS / **ACTIVE TIME:** 30 MINUTES / **TOTAL TIME:** 24 HOURS

This salad riffs on the traditional beet-and-goat cheese combo by switching out the goat cheese for creamy, subtle Brie, which allows all of the other flavors present here to shine.

1. Place the beet stems and greens in a bowl of ice water to remove any dirt.

2. Place the grated beets and the jalapeño in a salad bowl. Remove the beet stems and greens from the ice water and dice the stems. Set the greens aside. Add the beet stems, blood orange, and salt to the salad bowl and stir to combine.

3. Place the olive oil, honey, and vinegar in a small bowl and whisk to combine. Pour the mixture over the salad, toss to coat, and cover the salad bowl with plastic wrap. Let the salad sit in the refrigerator overnight.

4. Combine the beet greens with the arugula and place them in the salad bowl. Toss to combine, top the salad with the Brie, and serve.

INGREDIENTS:

6   RED BEETS, PEELED AND GRATED, STEMS AND GREENS RESERVED

1   JALAPEÑO CHILE PEPPER, STEMMED, SEEDED, AND MINCED

1   BLOOD ORANGE, SUPREMED (SEE PAGE 92)

½   TEASPOON KOSHER SALT

3   TABLESPOONS EXTRA-VIRGIN OLIVE OIL

3   TABLESPOONS HONEY

1   TABLESPOON RICE VINEGAR

2   LBS. ARUGULA

½   LB. BRIE CHEESE, SLICED AND SOFTENED

BABY BEET, RADISH & APPLE SALAD
WITH BLUE CHEESE MOUSSE

YIELD: 4 TO 6 SERVINGS / **ACTIVE TIME:** 30 MINUTES / **TOTAL TIME:** 1 HOUR AND 20 MINUTES

Baby beets are picked in the spring to thin the field and leave room for other beets to grow, an early harvest that results in a rich and delicate flavor.

1. Preheat the oven to 400°F. Form three sheets of aluminum foil into pouches. Group the beets according to color and place each group into a pouch. Drizzle the olive oil over each and sprinkle the salt over them. Divide the whole sprigs of thyme, garlic, and water between the pouches and seal them.

2. Place the pouches in a baking dish, place it in the oven, and cook until the beets are fork-tender, 45 minutes to 1 hour.

3. Remove the baking dish from the oven and let the beets cool. When they are cool enough to handle, peel the beets, cut them into bite-size pieces, and set them aside.

4. Bring water to a boil in a large pot and prepare an ice bath. Add salt, let the water return to a full boil, and add the radishes and radish greens. Cook for 1 minute, drain, and add the radishes and radish greens to the ice bath. Drain them again and place them in a salad bowl.

5. Place the blue cheese, heavy cream, ricotta, and thyme leaves in a food processor and blitz until smooth. Set the mousse aside.

6. Place the beets and apples in the salad bowl and toss to combine. Add half of the vinaigrette, season with salt and pepper, and toss to coat.

7. Spread the mousse over the serving plates. Top each portion with the salad, garnish with the honeycomb, and serve with the remaining vinaigrette.

INGREDIENTS:

3	RED BABY BEETS
3	GOLDEN BABY BEETS
3	PINK BABY BEETS
3	TABLESPOONS EXTRA-VIRGIN OLIVE OIL
1	TABLESPOON KOSHER SALT, PLUS MORE TO TASTE
9	SPRIGS OF FRESH THYME, 6 LEFT WHOLE, LEAVES FROM 3
6	GARLIC CLOVES
6	TABLESPOONS WATER
8	RADISHES, DICED, GREENS RESERVED
¾	CUP BLUE CHEESE, SOFTENED
½	CUP HEAVY CREAM
½	CUP RICOTTA CHEESE
2	APPLES, PEELED, CORED, AND DICED
¼	CUP HONEY MUSTARD VINAIGRETTE (SEE PAGE 557)
	BLACK PEPPER, TO TASTE
2	OZ. HONEYCOMB, FOR GARNISH

EASY DETOX SALAD

YIELD: 4 SERVINGS / **ACTIVE TIME:** 20 MINUTES / **TOTAL TIME:** 30 MINUTES

For those days where you're tired of takeout and just want something quick and nourishing.

1. Bring water to a boil in a large saucepan. Add the beets and cook until they are just tender, 10 to 15 minutes. Drain the beets and add them to a salad bowl.

2. Add all of the remaining ingredients, except for the vinaigrette and sunflower seeds, to the salad bowl and toss to combine. Add the vinaigrette and toss to coat.

3. Divide the salad among the serving plates, top each portion with some of the sunflower seeds, and serve.

INGREDIENTS:

1   CUP FINELY DICED BEETS

2   CUPS FINELY DICED CUCUMBERS

1   RED ONION, CHOPPED

1   RED BELL PEPPER, STEMMED, SEEDED, AND CHOPPED

1   CUP CHERRY TOMATOES, HALVED

1   LARGE CARROT, PEELED AND CHOPPED

¼   CUP ROASTED PEANUTS

2   CUPS CHOPPED LETTUCE

2   TABLESPOONS CHOPPED FRESH CILANTRO

WHITE WINE VINAIGRETTE (SEE PAGE 540)

¼   CUP ROASTED SUNFLOWER SEEDS

ZUCCHINI & RADICCHIO SALAD WITH OVEN-ROASTED STILTON

YIELD: 4 SERVINGS / **ACTIVE TIME:** 30 MINUTES / **TOTAL TIME:** 40 MINUTES

This recipe turns the concept of a salad on its head. Each element is cooked separately and then assembled at room temperature for an ideal light supper.

1. Bring water to a boil in a large pot. Add salt and let the water return to a boil. Trim both ends from each zucchini. Using the julienne attachment of a mandoline or a vegetable spiralizer, carefully slice the zucchini into long, thin strips.

2. Add the zucchini to the boiling water and cook for 2 minutes. Drain, rinse the zucchini under cold water, and let it drain again.

3. Place the pine nuts in a small skillet and toast them over medium heat, about 2 minutes, shaking the pan frequently. Remove the pine nuts from the pan.

4. Place the pine nuts, basil, and lemon juice in a food processor and puree until smooth. Transfer the mixture to a large bowl, add the olive oil, season with salt and pepper, and whisk to combine. Add the zucchini and toss to coat.

5. Set the oven's broiler to high and line a baking sheet with parchment paper. Place the Stilton, lemon zest, and honey in a small bowl, season with salt and pepper, and toss to combine. Transfer the mixture to the baking sheet, place it under the broiler, and broil until the top of the mixture has browned, 2 to 3 minutes. Remove the mixture from the oven and let it cool for 2 minutes.

6. Arrange the radicchio in a serving dish, top it with the zucchini mixture, peach wedges, roasted cheese mixture, and cranberries, and serve.

INGREDIENTS:

	SALT AND PEPPER, TO TASTE
4	ZUCCHINI
⅓	CUP PINE NUTS
2	HANDFULS OF FRESH BASIL
	ZEST AND JUICE OF 1 LEMON
2	TABLESPOONS EXTRA-VIRGIN OLIVE OIL
4	OZ. STILTON CHEESE, CRUMBLED
1½	TABLESPOONS HONEY
2	CUPS SHREDDED RADICCHIO
1	PEACH, HALVED, PITTED, AND CUT INTO WEDGES
1	TABLESPOON DRIED CRANBERRIES

MIDSUMMER CORN & BEAN SALAD

YIELD: 4 TO 6 SERVINGS / **ACTIVE TIME:** 15 MINUTES / **TOTAL TIME:** 24 HOURS

This is a great make-ahead recipe when the local corn becomes ripe. In fact, if it is *really* fresh with great flavor, you can skip the cooking part altogether and use the raw kernels.

1. Place the olive oil in a large skillet and warm it over medium heat. Add the corn and cook, stirring occasionally, until it starts to brown, about 5 minutes. Remove the pan from heat and let the corn cool.

2. Drain the beans and place them in a saucepan. Cover with cold water and bring to a boil. Reduce the heat so that the beans simmer and cook until they are tender, about 45 minutes. Drain and let the beans cool completely.

3. Place the beans, corn, and all of the remaining ingredients in a salad bowl, toss to combine, and chill the salad in the refrigerator for 2 hours.

4. Taste, adjust the seasoning as necessary, and serve.

INGREDIENTS:

1   TABLESPOON EXTRA-VIRGIN OLIVE OIL

4   CUPS CORN KERNELS

½   CUP DRIED BEANS, SOAKED OVERNIGHT

1   SMALL RED BELL PEPPER, STEMMED, SEEDED, AND DICED

1   SMALL GREEN BELL PEPPER, STEMMED, SEEDED, AND DICED

½   RED ONION, DICED

   JUICE OF ½ LIME

1   TEASPOON CUMIN

   TABASCO, TO TASTE

3   TABLESPOONS CHOPPED FRESH CILANTRO

1   TABLESPOON MAPLE SYRUP PLUS MORE TO TASTE

   SALT AND PEPPER, TO TASTE

CAULIFLOWER, NECTARINE & BROCCOLINI SALAD

YIELD: 4 SERVINGS / **ACTIVE TIME:** 20 MINUTES / **TOTAL TIME:** 1 HOUR

The neutral flavor of both cauliflower and halloumi allow the nectarines to shine.

1. Bring water to a boil in a large pot.

2. Preheat the oven to 375°F. Place the cauliflower in a baking dish, drizzle the olive oil over it, and season with salt and pepper. Toss to combine, place the dish in the oven, and roast until the cauliflower is browned and tender, about 35 minutes, stirring occasionally.

3. Prepare a gas or charcoal grill for medium-high heat (about 450°F). Place the halloumi on the grill and cook until it is lightly charred on both sides, 6 to 8 minutes, turning it over once. Remove the halloumi from the grill and let it cool.

4. Add salt to the boiling water, let it return to a full boil, and add the corn. Cook until it is just tender, 6 to 8 minutes. Using tongs, remove the corn from the pot and let it drain in a colander.

5. Add the broccolini to the boiling water and cook until it is just tender, 2 to 3 minutes. Drain the broccolini, rinse it under cold water, and let it drain again.

6. Remove the cauliflower from the oven and let it cool.

7. When the corn is cool enough to handle, cut all the kernels off of the cobs and place the kernels in a salad bowl. When the broccolini is cool enough to handle, chop it into bite-size pieces. Chop the halloumi into bite-size pieces.

8. Add the cauliflower, halloumi, broccolini, and nectarines to the salad bowl and toss to combine. Add half of the vinaigrette and toss to coat.

9. Top the salad with the pistachios, garnish with lemon slices, and serve with the remaining vinaigrette.

INGREDIENTS:

1	HEAD OF CAULIFLOWER, CUT INTO FLORETS
2	TABLESPOONS EXTRA-VIRGIN OLIVE OIL
	SALT AND PEPPER, TO TASTE
4	OZ. HALLOUMI CHEESE, SLICED
2	EARS OF CORN, HUSKED
4	OZ. BROCCOLINI
2	NECTARINES, PITTED AND SLICED THIN
	SPICY HONEY VINAIGRETTE (SEE PAGE 585)
½	CUP ROASTED PISTACHIOS
	LEMON SLICES, FOR GARNISH

BLISTERED CORN & GREEN BEAN SALAD
WITH POPPY SEED VINAIGRETTE

YIELD: 4 SERVINGS / ACTIVE TIME: 20 MINUTES / TOTAL TIME: 30 MINUTES

If the weather won't allow you to cook on the grill, stick the corn and green beans in a cast-iron skillet and toss the pan beneath the broiler for a few minutes. The result won't be quite the same, but it's close enough.

1. Prepare a gas or charcoal grill for medium-high heat (about 450°F). Bring water to a boil in a large pot. Add salt, let the water return to a full boil, and add the corn. Cook until it is just tender, 6 to 8 minutes. Using tongs, remove the corn from the pot and let it drain in a colander.

2. Place the green beans in a large cast-iron skillet, add the olive oil, and toss to coat. Place the pan on the grill and cook, stirring occasionally, until the green beans are tender and lightly charred, 8 to 10 minutes.

3. Pat the corn dry and place it on the grill. Cook until it is lightly charred all over, about 8 minutes, turning it as necessary.

4. Remove the corn and green beans from the grill and let them cool slightly.

5. When the corn is cool enough to handle, cut all the kernels off of the cobs and place the kernels in a salad bowl. Add the green beans and salad greens and toss to combine. Add the vinaigrette, season with salt and pepper, toss to coat, and serve.

INGREDIENTS:

SALT AND PEPPER, TO TASTE

6 EARS OF CORN, HUSKED

4 OZ. GREEN BEANS

2 TABLESPOONS EXTRA-VIRGIN OLIVE OIL

5 OZ. SALAD GREENS

POPPY SEED VINAIGRETTE (SEE PAGE 626)

ROASTED CARROT SALAD
WITH LABNEH & GRANOLA

YIELD: 4 SERVINGS / **ACTIVE TIME:** 10 MINUTES / **TOTAL TIME:** 45 MINUTES

Aim for the spring with this preparation, as the young carrots available then will be at the height of their sweetness.

1. Preheat the oven to 375°F. Place the carrots on a baking sheet, drizzle half of the olive oil over them, and season with salt and pepper. Toss to combine, place the carrots in the oven, and roast until they are tender, 30 to 35 minutes, stirring occasionally. Remove the carrots from the oven and set them aside.

2. Spread the Labneh over the serving plates, distribute the carrots on top, and drizzle some of the remaining olive oil over each dish. Sprinkle some of the pomegranate arils, granola, and sumac over each portion, garnish with orange zest and fresh herbs, and serve.

INGREDIENTS:

1   LB. CARROTS, RINSED WELL

¼   CUP EXTRA-VIRGIN OLIVE OIL

    SALT AND PEPPER, TO TASTE

1   CUP LABNEH (SEE PAGE 653)

½   CUP POMEGRANATE ARILS

½   CUP GRANOLA

1½ TABLESPOONS SUMAC

    ORANGE ZEST, FOR GARNISH

    FRESH HERBS, CHOPPED, FOR GARNISH

BEAN SALAD
WITH GOOSEBERRY VINAIGRETTE

YIELD: 6 SERVINGS / **ACTIVE TIME:** 30 MINUTES / **TOTAL TIME:** 2 DAYS

Slow cooking the beans in chicken stock provides a lovely, savory counter to the sweet and tangy dressing. This salad features the all-stars of the bean world, but you can use any beans you find appealing.

1. Drain and rinse the beans and peas and transfer them to a slow cooker. Add the stock, granulated garlic, bay leaves, red pepper flakes, and salt and cook on low for 8 hours, or until the beans are tender. Turn off the slow cooker and let the beans come to room temperature. Place the beans in the refrigerator overnight.

2. Place all of the remaining ingredients, except for the vinaigrette, in a large salad bowl and toss to combine.

3. Drain the beans. Place the beans in the salad bowl, add half of the vinaigrette, and toss to coat. Serve with the remaining vinaigrette.

INGREDIENTS:

¼   **LB. KIDNEY BEANS, SOAKED OVERNIGHT**

¼   **LB. CANNELLINI BEANS, SOAKED OVERNIGHT**

¼   **LB. PINK BEANS, SOAKED OVERNIGHT**

¼   **LB. PINTO BEANS, SOAKED OVERNIGHT**

¼   **LB. DRIED GREEN PEAS, SOAKED OVERNIGHT**

4–6   **CUPS CHICKEN STOCK (SEE PAGE 663)**

2   **TABLESPOONS GRANULATED GARLIC**

2   **BAY LEAVES**

  PINCH OF RED PEPPER FLAKES

1½   **TABLESPOONS KOSHER SALT**

2   **CUPS MINCED CELERY**

2   **LARGE RED RADISHES, GRATED**

1   **PARSNIP, PEELED AND MINCED**

½   **CUP CHOPPED FRESH PARSLEY**

1   **CUP CHOPPED SCALLIONS**

  JUICE OF ½ LEMON

  GOOSEBERRY VINAIGRETTE (SEE PAGE 564)

KALE, PLUM & HUSK CHERRY SALAD

YIELD: 4 SERVINGS / **ACTIVE TIME:** 20 MINUTES / **TOTAL TIME:** 20 MINUTES

Husk cherries, also known as ground cherries, possess a slightly sweet, fresh, tangy flavor, plus an irresistible texture. They are also quite lovely on a fall charcuterie board.

1. Bring water to a boil in a large pot. Add salt, let the water return to a full boil, and add the kale. Cook until it is just tender, 2 to 4 minutes, drain, and rinse the kale under cold water. Place the kale on paper towels to dry.

2. Place the kale, plums, onion, husk cherries, and grapes in a salad bowl and toss to combine. Add half of the vinaigrette, season with salt and pepper, and toss to coat.

3. Top the salad with the pistachios and serve with the remaining vinaigrette.

INGREDIENTS:

SALT AND PEPPER, TO TASTE

½ LB. KALE, STEMMED

3 PLUMS, PITTED AND SLICED

¼ RED ONION, SLICED VERY THIN

1 CUP HUSK CHERRIES

1 CUP SEEDLESS RED GRAPES

GARLIC, LEMON & OREGANO VINAIGRETTE (SEE PAGE 515)

½ CUP PISTACHIOS, CHOPPED

Kale, Plum & Husk Cherry Salad, *see page 377*

KALE & PERSIMMON SALAD

YIELD: 4 SERVINGS / ACTIVE TIME: 20 MINUTES / TOTAL TIME: 30 MINUTES

Batavia lettuce, known as Summer Crisp lettuce in some corners, will supply the crunch you're after here.

1. Bring water to a boil in a large pot.

2. Preheat the oven to 375°F. Place the buckwheat groats and pepitas on a baking sheet, drizzle the olive oil over them, and season with salt. Toss to combine, place the pan in the oven, and roast until the buckwheat groats and pepitas are toasted, 8 to 10 minutes, shaking the pan occasionally. Remove them from the oven and let them cool.

3. Add salt to the boiling water, let it return to a full boil, and add the kale. Cook until it is just tender, 2 to 4 minutes, drain, and rinse the kale under cold water. Place the kale on paper towels to dry.

4. Place the kale, lettuce, and persimmons in a salad bowl and toss to combine. Add half of the vinaigrette and toss to coat.

5. Top the salad with the pomegranate arils, pepitas, and buckwheat groats and serve with the remaining vinaigrette.

INGREDIENTS:

½   CUP BUCKWHEAT GROATS

¼   CUP PEPITAS

2   TABLESPOONS EXTRA-VIRGIN OLIVE OIL

    SALT, TO TASTE

4   OZ. KALE, STEMMED AND CHOPPED

4   OZ. LETTUCE, CHOPPED

2   PERSIMMONS, PEELED, SEEDED, AND SLICED THIN

    LEMON VINAIGRETTE (SEE PAGE 619)

½   CUP POMEGRANATE ARILS

KALE & PUMPKIN SALAD

YIELD: 4 SERVINGS / ACTIVE TIME: 20 MINUTES / TOTAL TIME: 1 HOUR AND 30 MINUTES

A perfect salad to pair with a dinner of roasted pork.

1. Preheat the oven to 375°F. Place the pumpkin in a baking dish, drizzle the olive oil over it, and season with salt and pepper. Cover the dish with aluminum foil, place it in the oven, and roast until the pumpkin is fork-tender, about 40 minutes.

2. Bring water to a boil in a large pot. Add salt to the boiling water, let it return to a full boil, and add the kale. Cook until it is just tender, 2 to 4 minutes, drain, and rinse the kale under cold water. Place the kale on paper towels to dry.

3. Remove the pumpkin from the oven and let it cool.

4. Place the pumpkin, kale, apples, and feta in a salad bowl and toss to combine. Add the dressing and toss to coat.

5. Top the salad with the walnuts and serve.

INGREDIENTS:

1 SMALL PUMPKIN, PEELED, SEEDED, AND DICED

2 TABLESPOONS EXTRA-VIRGIN OLIVE OIL

SALT AND PEPPER, TO TASTE

5 OZ. KALE, STEMMED AND CHOPPED

2 APPLES, CORED AND DICED

4 OZ. FETA CHEESE, CUBED

SUNFLOWER SEED DRESSING (SEE PAGE 642)

1 CUP WALNUTS, CHOPPED

CARROT & SPICY CHICKPEA SALAD

YIELD: 4 SERVINGS / **ACTIVE TIME:** 20 MINUTES / **TOTAL TIME:** 1 HOUR

A salad that provides a strong argument for always having a container of the Spicy Chickpeas at hand.

1. Preheat the oven to 375°F. Place the carrots in a baking dish, drizzle 2 tablespoons of olive oil over them, and season with salt and pepper. Toss to coat, place the carrots in the oven, and cook until they are browned and tender, about 30 minutes, stirring occasionally.

2. Remove the carrots from the oven and let them cool.

3. Place the carrots, chickpeas, and salad greens in a salad bowl and toss to combine. Add the lemon juice and remaining olive oil, season with salt and pepper, and toss to coat.

4. Top the salad with the sesame seeds and serve.

INGREDIENTS:

1	LB. RAINBOW CARROTS
3	TABLESPOONS EXTRA-VIRGIN OLIVE OIL
	SALT AND PEPPER, TO TASTE
2	CUPS SPICY CHICKPEAS (SEE PAGE 676)
5	OZ. SALAD GREENS
1½	TABLESPOONS FRESH LEMON JUICE
2	TABLESPOONS SESAME SEEDS

RAINBOW SALAD

YIELD: 4 SERVINGS / **ACTIVE TIME:** 15 MINUTES / **TOTAL TIME:** 15 MINUTES

The wonderful array of colors and flavors in this salad provides plenty of appeal, but added to how energized and satisfied you'll feel afterward, it's safe to say that it'l become a weeknight staple.

1. Place the salad greens, zucchini, cucumber, celery, carrot, mango, cabbage, berries, watermelon, and tomato in a salad bowl and toss to combine.

2. Drizzle the lime juice and agave nectar over the salad, season with salt, and toss to coat.

3. Top the salad with the sesame seeds and coconut, garnish with edible flowers, and serve.

INGREDIENTS:

4	OZ SALAD GREENS
1	ZUCCHINI, CUT INTO LONG, THIN STRIPS
1	CUCUMBER, CUT INTO LONG, THIN STRIPS
1	CELERY RIB, CUT INTO LONG, THIN STRIPS
1	CARROT, CUT INTO LONG, THIN STRIPS
	FLESH OF 1 MANGO, CUT INTO LONG, THIN STRIPS
2	OZ. RED CABBAGE, SHREDDED
1	CUP BLACKBERRIES
1	CUP BLUEBERRIES
1	CUP HULLED AND SLICED STRAWBERRIES
2	CUPS CHOPPED WATERMELON
1	TOMATO, CHOPPED
2	TABLESPOONS FRESH LIME JUICE
1	TABLESPOON AGAVE NECTAR
	SALT, TO TASTE
2	TABLESPOONS SESAME SEEDS
¼	CUP SHREDDED COCONUT
	EDIBLE FLOWERS, FOR GARNISH

SALADS WITH PASTA & GRAINS

From light and fluffy grain salads that will soak up whatever dressing is applied to pasta and bread salads that offer plenty of nooks and crannies for flavor to find a home in, these recipes are guaranteed to provide bite after bite that is positively packed with pleasantness.

There are also a number of wonderful recipes where the odds and ends in your kitchen can find a home. Whether it's leftover rice and pasta or day-old bread, many of the salads in this chapter are wonderful for those who are anxious about wasting food, but aren't always quite sure what to do with their leftovers.

ORECCHIETTE, SHRIMP & GREEN BEAN SALAD

YIELD: 4 SERVINGS / ACTIVE TIME: 20 MINUTES / TOTAL TIME: 30 MINUTES

Orecchiette owes its name to the way it is shaped, as it resembles "little ears," orecchie in Italian.

1. Bring water to a boil in two large pots.

2. Add salt to one pot, let the water return to a full boil, and add the pasta. Cook until it is al dente, 8 to 10 minutes. Drain the pasta and let it cool.

3. Add salt to the other pot of boiling water, let it return to a full boil, and add the beans. Cook until they are just tender, 3 to 5 minutes. Drain the beans, rinse them under cold water, and let them drain again.

4. Place 1 tablespoon of the olive oil in a large skillet and warm it over medium heat. Add the garlic and cook until it is fragrant, 1 to 2 minutes. Add the shrimp, season it with salt and pepper, and cook until they turn pink and are cooked through, 2 to 4 minutes, turning them over just once. Transfer the mixture to a salad bowl.

5. Add the pasta, beans, and Parmesan to the salad bowl and toss to combine. Add the lemon juice and remaining olive oil, season with salt and pepper, and toss to coat.

6. Garnish with fresh herbs and serve with lemon wedges.

INGREDIENTS:

	SALT AND PEPPER, TO TASTE
¾	LB. ORECCHIETTE
3	OZ. GREEN BEANS, CHOPPED
3	OZ. WAX BEANS, CHOPPED
3	TABLESPOONS EXTRA-VIRGIN OLIVE OIL
3	GARLIC CLOVES, MINCED
1	LB. SHRIMP, SHELLED AND DEVEINED
2	OZ. PARMESAN CHEESE, GRATED
1½	TABLESPOONS FRESH LEMON JUICE
	FRESH HERBS, CHOPPED, FOR GARNISH
	LEMON WEDGES, FOR SERVING

CELLOPHANE NOODLE SALAD WITH SHIITAKES & WATERMELON

YIELD: 4 SERVINGS / ACTIVE TIME: 20 MINUTES / TOTAL TIME: 45 MINUTES

A salad that is fresh, earthy, and filled with a number of delightful textures.

1. Bring water to a boil in a large pot. Place the noodles in a baking dish, cover them with warm water, and let them soak for 20 minutes.

2. Place the olive oil in a large skillet and warm it over medium heat. Add the mushrooms, season with salt and pepper, and cook until they start to brown, stirring occasionally, 8 to 10 minutes. Remove the mushrooms from the pan and let them cool.

3. Add salt to the boiling water, let it return to a full boil, and add the noodles. Cook until they are al dente, 2 to 3 minutes. Drain the noodles, rinse them under cold water, and let them drain again.

4. Place the noodles, mushrooms, and watermelon in a salad bowl and toss to combine. Add the soy sauce and vinegar, season with salt and pepper, and toss to coat.

5. Top the salad with the pickled ginger, peanuts, and sesame seeds, garnish with scallions, and serve.

INGREDIENTS:

½	LB. CELLOPHANE NOODLES
2	TABLESPOONS EXTRA-VIRGIN OLIVE OIL
6	OZ. SHIITAKE MUSHROOMS, STEMMED
	SALT AND PEPPER, TO TASTE
3	CUPS DICED WATERMELON
2	TABLESPOONS SOY SAUCE
1	TABLESPOON RICE VINEGAR
¼	CUP PICKLED GINGER
½	CUP CHOPPED PEANUTS
2	TABLESPOONS SESAME SEEDS
	SCALLIONS, CHOPPED, FOR GARNISH

RICE NOODLE & VEGETABLE SALAD

YIELD: 4 SERVINGS / **ACTIVE TIME:** 20 MINUTES / **TOTAL TIME:** 50 MINUTES

Tamarind's beguiling flavor, moving from sour to buttery to sweet as it passes over the palate, is all it takes to make this straightforward salad memorable.

1. Preheat the oven to 375°F. Place the cauliflower in a baking dish, drizzle the olive oil over it, and season with salt, pepper, the turmeric, and paprika. Toss to combine, place the dish in the oven, and roast until the cauliflower is golden brown and tender, 35 to 45 minutes.

2. Bring water to a boil in a large pot. Add salt, let the water return to a full boil, and add the noodles. Cook until they are al dente, 6 to 8 minutes. Drain the noodles, rinse them under cold water, and let them drain again.

3. Remove the cauliflower from the oven and let it cool.

4. Place the cauliflower, noodles, lettuce, cucumbers, and tomatoes in a salad bowl and toss to combine. Add half of the dressing and toss to coat.

5. Garnish with scallions and serve with the remaining dressing.

INGREDIENTS:

1	HEAD OF CAULIFLOWER, CUT INTO FLORETS
2	TABLESPOONS EXTRA-VIRGIN OLIVE OIL
	SALT AND PEPPER, TO TASTE
1	TEASPOON TURMERIC
1	TEASPOON PAPRIKA
6	OZ. RICE NOODLES
3	OZ. LETTUCE
2	CUCUMBERS, SLICED VERY THIN
2	TOMATOES, DICED
	TAMARIND DRESSING (SEE PAGE 516)
	SCALLIONS, CHOPPED, FOR GARNISH

ORZO SALAD

YIELD: 4 SERVINGS / ACTIVE TIME: 20 MINUTES / TOTAL TIME: 50 MINUTES

Orzo, the rice-shaped pasta, was made to provide the foundation for a summery salad.

1. Preheat the oven to 375°F. Place the Roma tomatoes in a baking dish, drizzle the olive oil over them, and season with salt and pepper. Toss to combine, place the tomatoes in the oven, and roast until they start to collapse, 20 to 30 minutes.

2. Bring water to a boil in a large pot. Add salt, let the water return to a full boil, and add the orzo. Cook until it is al dente, 8 to 10 minutes. Drain the orzo, rinse it under cold water, and let it drain again.

3. Remove the tomatoes from the oven and let them cool slightly.

4. Place the pine nuts in a dry skillet and toast over medium heat until they are golden brown, shaking the pan frequently. Transfer the toasted pine nuts to a salad bowl.

5. Add the orzo, roasted tomatoes, cherry tomatoes, and feta to the salad bowl and toss to combine. Add the lemon zest and lemon juice, season with salt and pepper, and toss to coat.

6. Top the salad with the pomegranate arils, garnish with basil, and serve.

INGREDIENTS:

- 2 ROMA TOMATOES, CHOPPED
- 2 TABLESPOONS EXTRA-VIRGIN OLIVE OIL
- SALT AND PEPPER, TO TASTE
- 2 CUPS ORZO
- 1 CUP PINE NUTS
- 1½ CUPS CHERRY TOMATOES, QUARTERED
- 4 OZ. FETA CHEESE, CRUMBLED
- 1 TABLESPOON LEMON ZEST
- 1½ TABLESPOONS FRESH LEMON JUICE
- 1 CUP POMEGRANATE ARILS
- FRESH BASIL, CHOPPED, FOR GARNISH

ORZO SALAD WITH
GRILLED PEACHES & LIME VINAIGRETTE

YIELD: 4 SERVINGS / **ACTIVE TIME:** 20 MINUTES / **TOTAL TIME:** 30 MINUTES

Pick up a few extra peaches, grill them with those that are going into the salad, and serve them with vanilla ice cream for dessert.

1. Prepare a gas or charcoal grill for medium-high heat (about 450°F).

2. Bring water to a boil in a large pot. Add salt, let the water return to a full boil, and add the orzo. Cook until it is al dente, 8 to 10 minutes. Drain the orzo, rinse it under cold water, and let it drain again.

3. Place the peaches on the grill, cut sides down, and cook until they are lightly charred, about 6 minutes. Turn them over and cook until they are just tender, about 5 minutes. Remove the peaches from the grill and let them cool slightly. When the peaches are cool enough to handle, chop them.

4. Place the orzo, peaches, cucumbers, onion, chiles, and olives in a salad bowl and toss to combine. Add the vinaigrette, season with salt and pepper, and toss to coat.

5. Top the salad with the feta, garnish with mint and dill, and serve.

INGREDIENTS:

  SALT AND PEPPER, TO TASTE

2 CUPS ORZO

4 PEACHES, HALVED AND PITTED

1½ CUCUMBERS, SLICED VERY THIN

1 RED ONION, SLICED THIN

2 JALAPEÑO CHILE PEPPERS, STEMMED, SEEDED, AND SLICED THIN

1½ CUPS PITTED AND HALVED KALAMATA OLIVES

  LIME VINAIGRETTE (SEE PAGE 603)

4 OZ. FETA CHEESE, CRUMBLED

  FRESH MINT, CHOPPED, FOR GARNISH

  FRESH DILL, FOR GARNISH

CONCHIGLIONE SALAD WITH FIGS & OLIVES

YIELD: 4 SERVINGS / ACTIVE TIME: 20 MINUTES / TOTAL TIME: 30 MINUTES

Using a large-format pasta such as conchiglione may be unorthodox, but we can guarantee it will raise no protests.

1. Bring water to a boil in a large pot. Add salt, let the water return to a full boil, and add the pasta. Cook until it is al dente, 8 to 10 minutes. Drain the pasta, rinse it under cold water, and let it drain again.

2. Place the pasta, figs, tomatoes, olives, cucumber, and onion in a salad bowl and toss to combine. Add half of the dressing, season with salt and pepper, and toss to coat.

3. Garnish with parsley and serve with the remaining dressing.

INGREDIENTS:

SALT AND PEPPER, TO TASTE

¾ LB. CONCHIGLIONE

8 FIGS, QUARTERED

1½ CUPS CHERRY TOMATOES, QUARTERED

1½ CUPS KALAMATA OLIVES, PITTED

1 CUCUMBER, DICED

¼ RED ONION, FINELY DICED

ROASTED SCALLION & FETA DRESSING (SEE PAGE 646)

FRESH PARSLEY, CHOPPED, FOR GARNISH

FREEKEH & HAZELNUT SALAD

YIELD: 4 SERVINGS / ACTIVE TIME: 20 MINUTES / TOTAL TIME: 1 HOUR

As the freekeh will keep for three or four days in the fridge, this salad is a great option when you know you're going to have a busy week and are planning out your menu.

1. Preheat the oven to 375°F.

2. Place the freekeh in a large skillet and toast it for 2 minutes, shaking the pan frequently. Add 2 cups water and some salt and bring to a boil. Reduce the heat to low, cover the pan, and cook until the freekeh is tender and has absorbed all of the water, 20 to 25 minutes.

3. Place the pine nuts and hazelnuts on a baking sheet, place them in the oven, and toast until they are golden brown, 8 to 10 minutes, stirring occasionally. Remove the hazelnuts and pine nuts from the oven and let them cool.

4. Remove the freekeh from heat and uncover it. Cover it with a kitchen towel and let it sit for 15 minutes. Uncover the freekeh and let it sit for 15 minutes.

5. Place the freekeh, salad greens, pine nuts, and hazelnuts in a salad bowl and toss to combine. Add the vinaigrette and toss to coat.

6. Garnish with lemon slices and dill and serve.

INGREDIENTS:

1½ CUPS FREEKEH

SALT, TO TASTE

1½ CUPS PINE NUTS

1½ CUPS CHOPPED HAZELNUTS

5 OZ. SALAD GREENS

TARRAGON VINAIGRETTE (SEE PAGE 614)

FRESH LEMON, SLICED THIN, FOR GARNISH

FRESH DILL, CHOPPED, FOR GARNISH

TORTELLINI SALAD WITH PAN-FRIED RADISHES

YIELD: 4 SERVINGS / ACTIVE TIME: 20 MINUTES / TOTAL TIME: 20 MINUTES

There's plenty of indulgent cheesiness here, which makes the bold flavor of arugula and fresh taste of snow peas essential inclusions.

1. Bring water to a boil in a large saucepan. Add salt, let the water return to a full boil, and add the tortellini. Cook until it is al dente, 8 to 10 minutes. Drain the tortellini, rinse it under cold water, and let it cool.

2. Place the olive oil in a large skillet and warm it over medium heat. Add the radishes, cut side down, and cook until they have softened slightly and are browned all over, 6 to 8 minutes, turning them as necessary. Transfer the radishes to a salad bowl.

3. Add the tortellini, arugula, and snow peas to the salad bowl and toss to combine. Add the dressing, season with salt and pepper, and toss to coat.

4. Top the salad with the feta and serve.

INGREDIENTS:

SALT AND PEPPER, TO TASTE

¾ LB. TORTELLINI

2 TABLESPOONS EXTRA-VIRGIN OLIVE OIL

4 OZ. RADISHES, QUARTERED

3 OZ. ARUGULA

4 OZ. SNOW PEAS

LEMON RICOTTA DRESSING (SEE PAGE 657)

2 OZ. FETA CHEESE, CRUMBLED

BREAD SALAD WITH LENTILS & MOZZARELLA

YIELD: 4 SERVINGS / **ACTIVE TIME:** 20 MINUTES / **TOTAL TIME:** 40 MINUTES

A good salad for bakers, as it makes wonderful use of any leftover bread.

1. Preheat the oven to 375°F. Bring water to a boil in a large pot and add the lentils. Cook until they are tender, 20 to 25 minutes.

2. Place the bread in a mixing bowl, drizzle the olive oil over it, and season with salt and pepper. Toss to coat and place the bread on a baking sheet in an even layer. Place the bread in the oven and toast until it is golden brown, 10 to 15 minutes, stirring occasionally. Remove the bread from the oven and let it cool slightly.

3. Drain the lentils, spread them on a baking sheet in an even layer, season with salt, and let them cool completely.

4. Place the lentils, bread, salad greens, endive, orange, and mozzarella in a salad bowl and toss to combine. Add half of the vinaigrette and toss to coat.

5. Garnish with sesame seeds and serve with the remaining vinaigrette.

INGREDIENTS:

1½ CUPS LENTILS

2 CUPS DAY-OLD CRUSTY BREAD PIECES (½-INCH CUBES)

2 TABLESPOONS EXTRA-VIRGIN OLIVE OIL

SALT AND PEPPER, TO TASTE

3 OZ. SALAD GREENS

1 ENDIVE, LEAVES SEPARATED

1 ORANGE, SUPREMED (SEE PAGE 92) AND CHOPPED

2 OZ. MOZZARELLA CHEESE, CUBED

CHAMPAGNE & HERB VINAIGRETTE (SEE PAGE 647)

SESAME SEEDS, FOR GARNISH

COUSCOUS SALAD WITH CORN & BELL PEPPERS

YIELD: 4 SERVINGS / ACTIVE TIME: 20 MINUTES / TOTAL TIME: 35 MINUTES

The Red Onion Vinaigrette supplies the needed oomph to this salad, which is a collection of powerfully fresh ingredients.

1. Cook the couscous according to the directions on the package. Spread it evenly on a baking sheet and let it cool completely.

2. Place the couscous, corn, peas, pepper, scallions, mozzarella, and cashews in a salad bowl and toss to combine. Add half of the vinaigrette, toss to coat, and serve with the remaining vinaigrette.

INGREDIENTS:

⅔ CUP COUSCOUS

1 CUP CANNED CORN, DRAINED

4 OZ. SNOW PEAS, CHOPPED

1 RED BELL PEPPER, STEMMED, SEEDED, AND DICED

6 SCALLIONS, TRIMMED AND CHOPPED

6 OZ. MOZZARELLA CHEESE, CHOPPED

1 CUP CHOPPED CASHEWS

RED ONION VINAIGRETTE (SEE PAGE 524)

PEARL COUSCOUS, BLUEBERRY & HARICOT VERT SALAD

YIELD: 4 SERVINGS / **ACTIVE TIME:** 20 MINUTES / **TOTAL TIME:** 30 MINUTES

Fava beans are a strong substitution idea for the edamame, and arugula would be a good choice if you wanted something other than watercress.

1. Bring water to a boil in a large pot.

2. Cook the couscous according to the directions on the package. Spread it evenly on a baking sheet and let it cool completely.

3. Add salt to the boiling water, let it return to a full boil, and add the green beans and edamame. Cook until they are just tender, 4 to 6 minutes. Drain the vegetables, rinse them under cold water, and let them drain again.

4. Place the couscous, green beans, edamame, watercress, onion, and blueberries in a salad bowl and toss to combine. Add the lemon juice, season with salt and pepper, and toss to coat.

5. Top the salad with the cashews and sesame seeds and divide it among the serving plates. Top each portion with dollops of the yogurt and serve.

INGREDIENTS:

2	CUPS PEARL COUSCOUS
	SALT AND PEPPER, TO TASTE
4	OZ. HARICOTS VERTS
1	CUP SHELLED EDAMAME
2	OZ. WATERCRESS
¼	RED ONION, FINELY DICED
1	CUP BLUEBERRIES
2	TABLESPOONS FRESH LEMON JUICE
1	CUP CHOPPED CASHEWS
1	TABLESPOON BLACK SESAME SEEDS
1	CUP GREEK YOGURT

RED RICE SALAD WITH
RED CABBAGE & CLEMENTINES

YIELD: 4 SERVINGS / ACTIVE TIME: 20 MINUTES / TOTAL TIME: 30 MINUTES

Red rice, long a popular grain in the Southeastern US, has the highest protein content of any variety of rice.

1. Cook the rice according to the directions on the package. Fluff the rice with a fork, cover it, and let it cool.

2. Place the rice, cabbage, radicchio, celery, clementines, and feta in a salad bowl and toss to combine. Add the Leek Oil, season with salt and pepper, and toss to coat.

3. Garnish with parsley and serve.

INGREDIENTS:

⅔ CUP RED RICE

3 OZ. RED CABBAGE, SHREDDED

2 OZ. RADICCHIO, CHOPPED

2 CELERY STALKS, SLICED

3 CLEMENTINES, SUPREMED (SEE PAGE 92)

4 OZ. FETA CHEESE, DICED

LEEK OIL (SEE PAGE 545)

SALT AND PEPPER, TO TASTE

FRESH PARSLEY, CHOPPED, FOR GARNISH

CARROT, CHICKPEA & QUINOA SALAD

YIELD: 4 SERVINGS / **ACTIVE TIME:** 20 MINUTES / **TOTAL TIME:** 30 MINUTES

Consider utilizing the Spicy Chickpeas on page 676 for an added burst of flavor in this salad.

1. Cook the quinoa according to the directions on the package. Spread it in an even layer on a baking sheet and let it cool completely.

2. Place the quinoa, spinach, chickpeas, and carrots in a salad bowl and toss to combine. Add the lemon juice and olive oil, season with salt and pepper, and toss to coat.

3. Serve with lemon wedges.

INGREDIENTS:

⅔ CUP QUINOA

5 OZ. BABY SPINACH

2 CUPS CANNED CHICKPEAS, DRAINED

2 CARROTS, PEELED AND SHREDDED

2 TABLESPOONS FRESH LEMON JUICE

2 TABLESPOONS EXTRA-VIRGIN OLIVE OIL

SALT AND PEPPER, TO TASTE

LEMON WEDGES, FOR SERVING

SPICY TOFU & RICE SALAD

YIELD: 4 SERVINGS / ACTIVE TIME: 15 MINUTES / TOTAL TIMES: 25 MINUTES

Chili paneer, the classic Indo-Chinese dish, is the inspiration behind this light but flavorful salad.

1. Cook the rice according to the directions on the package. Fluff it, cover it, and set the rice aside.

2. Pat the tofu dry with paper towels and cut it into cubes. Place the cornstarch and salt in a shallow bowl, add the tofu, and toss to coat.

3. Place 1 tablespoon of avocado oil in a large skillet and warm it over medium heat. Add the tofu and cook until it is well browned, about 8 minutes.

4. Place the sriracha, vinegar, ketchup, garlic, soy sauce, and remaining avocado oil in a bowl and whisk to combine.

5. Add the sauce to the skillet along with the onion, pepper, and cabbage and gently stir to combine. Cook for 2 to 3 minutes, until the sauce is warmed through.

6. Place the rice in a salad bowl, add the tofu mixture, and gently toss to combine. Garnish with scallions and serve.

INGREDIENTS:

- ⅔ CUP RICE
- 14 OZ. EXTRA-FIRM TOFU, DRAINED
- 2 TABLESPOONS CORNSTARCH
- SALT, TO TASTE
- 3 TABLESPOONS AVOCADO OIL
- ¼ CUP SRIRACHA
- 1 TABLESPOON WHITE VINEGAR
- 2 TABLESPOONS KETCHUP
- 2 GARLIC CLOVES, MINCED
- ¼ CUP SOY SAUCE
- 1 LARGE RED ONION, DICED
- 1 LARGE BELL PEPPER, STEMMED, SEEDED, AND DICED
- 1 CUP SHREDDED RED CABBAGE
- SCALLIONS, CHOPPED, FOR GARNISH

QUINOA, CAULIFLOWER & SWEET POTATO SALAD

YIELD: 4 SERVINGS / **ACTIVE TIME:** 20 MINUTES / **TOTAL TIME:** 40 MINUTES

If you find that you're looking for a bit more from this salad, try an herb-and-garlic goat cheese.

1. Preheat the oven to 425°F. Place the olive oil, chili powder, garlic powder, onion powder, cumin, and salt in a bowl and whisk to combine.

2. Add the cauliflower and sweet potato and toss to combine. Place the vegetables on a baking sheet in an even layer, place the pan in the oven, and roast until the vegetables are golden brown and tender, 25 to 30 minutes, stirring halfway through.

3. Cook the quinoa according to the directions on the package. Fluff it with a fork, cover it, and set it aside.

4. Remove the roasted vegetables from the oven and let them cool slightly.

5. Place the quinoa, roasted vegetables, spinach, avocados, goat cheese, and almonds in a salad bowl and toss to combine. Add half of the dressing and toss to coat.

6. Garnish with cilantro and serve with the remaining dressing.

INGREDIENTS:

3	TABLESPOONS EXTRA-VIRGIN OLIVE OIL
½	TEASPOON CHILI POWDER
1	TEASPOON GARLIC POWDER
1	TEASPOON ONION POWDER
1	TEASPOON CUMIN
1	TEASPOON KOSHER SALT
1	HEAD OF CAULIFLOWER, CUT INTO FLORETS
1	SWEET POTATO, PEELED AND DICED
1	CUP QUINOA
4	CUPS BABY SPINACH
	FLESH OF 2 AVOCADOS, SLICED
½	CUP CRUMBLED GOAT CHEESE
¼	CUP SLICED ALMONDS
	SPICY ALMOND & TAHINI DRESSING (SEE PAGE 564)
	FRESH CILANTRO, CHOPPED, FOR GARNISH

WHEAT BERRY & GRILLED CAULIFLOWER SALAD

YIELD: 4 SERVINGS / ACTIVE TIME: 20 MINUTES / TOTAL TIME: 1 HOUR

Mixing grilled cauliflower with a tahini dressing is a brilliant move, as the flavor of each enhances the other wonderfully.

1. Prepare a gas or charcoal grill for medium heat (about 400°F). Cook the wheat berries according to the directions on the package. Rinse them under cold water and let them drain.

2. Brush both sides of the cauliflower steaks with the olive oil. Place them on the grill and cook until they are tender and lightly charred, 10 to 15 minutes, turning them over halfway through.

3. Remove the cauliflower steaks from the grill and let them cool. When they are cool enough to handle, chop them into bite-size pieces.

4. Place the cauliflower, wheat berries, and arugula in a salad bowl and toss to combine. Add the dressing, season with salt and pepper, and toss to coat.

5. Top the salad with the avocado and serve.

INGREDIENTS:

½   CUP KAMUT WHEAT BERRIES

2   HEADS OF CAULIFLOWER, CUT INTO STEAKS

2   TABLESPOONS EXTRA-VIRGIN OLIVE OIL

4   OZ. BABY ARUGULA

     TAHINI DRESSING (SEE PAGE 565)

     SALT AND PEPPER, TO TASTE

     FLESH FROM 1 AVOCADO, SLICED THIN

FARRO SALAD WITH OLIVE & WHOLE LEMON VINAIGRETTE

YIELD: 8 SERVINGS / **ACTIVE TIME:** 15 MINUTES / **TOTAL TIME:** 1 HOUR

Look for Castelvetrano olives for this recipe; their buttery flesh and mild flavor will convert even the most olive averse.

1. Place the farro in a large, wide saucepan and toast it over medium heat, stirring frequently, until it is golden brown and fragrant, about 4 minutes. Remove the pan from heat, cover the farro by 1 inch with cold water, and add a generous handful of salt.

2. Place the pan over medium-high heat and bring to a boil. Reduce the heat and simmer the farro, skimming any foam from the surface, until it is tender but still has some bite, 25 to 35 minutes. Drain and transfer the farro to a large bowl.

3. Crush the olives to break them up into large, craggy pieces. Place the olives in a bowl.

4. Halve the lemon, remove the seeds, and finely dice the entire lemon, peel and all. Add the lemon and shallots to the olives, toss to combine, and season with salt and pepper. Let the mixture sit for 5 minutes to allow the flavors to meld.

5. Place the olive oil in a small saucepan and warm it over medium heat. Add the olive mixture and cook, swirling the pan occasionally, until it is warmed through and the shallots have softened slightly, about 4 minutes.

6. Add the dressing to the farro and toss to combine. Taste and season with salt, pepper, and lemon juice. Add the fresh herbs, fold to incorporate them, and serve.

INGREDIENTS:

2	CUPS FARRO
	SALT AND PEPPER, TO TASTE
2	CUPS GREEN OLIVES, PITTED
1	LEMON
2	SHALLOTS, MINCED
½	CUP EXTRA-VIRGIN OLIVE OIL
	FRESH LEMON JUICE, TO TASTE
2	CUPS CHOPPED FRESH MINT OR CILANTRO
2	CUPS CHOPPED FRESH PARSLEY

RICE & TOFU SALAD
WITH BENIHANA'S GINGER DRESSING

YIELD: 4 SERVINGS / **ACTIVE TIME:** 15 MINUTES / **TOTAL TIME:** 15 MINUTES

If tofu is not your crew's thing, any protein, even fried eggs, will work in its place.

1. Place the sesame oil in a large skillet and warm it over medium-high heat. Add the tofu and cook until it is browned all over, about 8 minutes, turning it as necessary. Remove the pan from heat.

2. Place the rice, carrots, sprouts, corn, edamame, avocados, and tofu in a salad bowl and toss to combine. Add the dressing, season with salt, and toss to coat.

3. Garnish with sesame seeds and serve.

INGREDIENTS:

- 1 TABLESPOON SESAME OIL
- 1 LB. EXTRA-FIRM TOFU, DRAINED AND CHOPPED
- 2 CUPS LEFTOVER WHITE RICE, AT ROOM TEMPERATURE
- 2 CARROTS, PEELED AND GRATED
- 1 CUP BROCCOLI SPROUTS
- 1 CUP CANNED CORN, DRAINED
- 1 CUP SHELLED, COOKED EDAMAME

    FLESH FROM 2 AVOCADOS, SLICED THIN

    BENIHANA'S GINGER DRESSING (SEE PAGE 557)

    SALT, TO TASTE

    SESAME SEEDS, FOR GARNISH

TOASTED FARRO SALAD WITH
KALE, SWEET POTATO & PARSNIPS

YIELD: 4 TO 6 SERVINGS / **ACTIVE TIME:** 30 MINUTES / **TOTAL TIME:** 2 HOURS

An elaborate-looking salad that is actually very easy to prepare. Sweet, tart, nutty, and earthy, it's more than hearty enough to work as a main.

1. Preheat the oven to 400°F. Place 2 tablespoons of the olive oil in a medium saucepan and warm it over medium heat. Add the farro and toast it, shaking the pan occasionally, until it gives off a nutty aroma.

2. Season the farro with salt, add the water, and bring to a boil. Reduce the heat and simmer the farro until it has absorbed the water and is al dente, 25 to 40 minutes. Spread the farro on a baking sheet in an even layer and let it cool completely.

3. Line two baking sheets with parchment paper. Place the kale in a mixing bowl, add 1 tablespoon of the remaining olive oil, and season with salt and pepper. Toss to combine and place the kale on half of one of the baking sheets. Place the sunflower seeds on the other half of the baking sheet.

4. Place the pan in the oven and roast until the kale is crispy and the sunflower seeds are toasted, 8 to 10 minutes. Remove the pan from the oven and set it aside.

5. Place the sweet potato and parsnips in a mixing bowl, add 1 tablespoon of the remaining olive oil, and season with salt and pepper. Toss to combine and place the sweet potato and parsnips on the other baking sheet.

6. Place the pan in the oven and roast until the vegetables are tender, 20 to 30 minutes. Remove the vegetables from the oven and let them cool completely.

7. Place the remaining olive oil, the vinegar, mustard, chives, parsley, and shallot in a bowl, season with salt and pepper, and whisk to combine. Set the dressing aside.

8. Place the farro, roasted vegetables, toasted sunflower seeds, and dried cranberries in a mixing bowl, add the dressing, and toss to combine. Serve immediately.

INGREDIENTS:

½	CUP EXTRA-VIRGIN OLIVE OIL
2	CUPS FARRO
	SALT AND PEPPER, TO TASTE
5	CUPS WATER
½	BUNCH OF KALE, STEMS REMOVED, LEAVES TORN
½	CUP SUNFLOWER SEEDS
1	LARGE SWEET POTATO, PEELED AND DICED
2	PARSNIPS, TRIMMED AND DICED
¼	CUP APPLE CIDER VINEGAR
1	TEASPOON DIJON MUSTARD
2	TABLESPOONS SLICED FRESH CHIVES
2	TABLESPOONS CHOPPED FRESH PARSLEY
1	TABLESPOON DICED SHALLOT
½	CUP DRIED CRANBERRIES

VIETNAMESE NOODLE SALAD

YIELD: 6 SERVINGS / **ACTIVE TIME:** 25 MINUTES / **TOTAL TIME:** 45 MINUTES

If you like things spicy, a few finely chopped chile peppers would be welcome in this salad.

1. Pat the tofu dry with paper towels and dice it. Set the tofu aside.

2. Bring water to a boil in a large saucepan. Place the bean sprouts in a bowl of cold water and discard any hulls that float to the top. Rinse the remaining sprouts under cold water, add them to the boiling water, and cook for 1 minute. Remove them with a strainer, rinse them under cold water, and let them drain again.

3. Add the noodles to the boiling water and cook until they are al dente, 2 to 3 minutes. Drain, rinse the noodles under cold water, and let them drain again. Set the noodles aside.

4. Place the peanut oil in a large skillet and warm it over medium-high heat. Season the tofu with salt, add it to the pan, and cook until it is browned all over, about 8 minutes, turning it as necessary. Transfer the tofu to a paper towel–lined plate to drain.

5. Chop the bean sprouts and place them in a salad bowl. Add the noodles, lettuce, fresh herbs, cucumbers, and tofu and toss to combine. Add the Nuoc Cham and toss to coat.

6. Garnish with the peanuts and serve.

INGREDIENTS:

1　LB. EXTRA-FIRM TOFU, DRAINED AND CUT INTO ½-INCH STRIPS

2　CUPS MUNG BEAN SPROUTS, PICKED OVER

½　LB. RICE STICK NOODLES

¼　CUP PEANUT OIL

　　SALT, TO TASTE

2½　CUPS SHREDDED ROMAINE LETTUCE

2　HANDFULS OF MIXED FRESH HERBS, CHOPPED (MINT, CILANTRO, AND BASIL RECOMMENDED)

2　SMALL CUCUMBERS, PEELED AND JULIENNED

　　NUOC CHAM (SEE PAGE 623)

2　TABLESPOONS SALTED, ROASTED PEANUTS, CHOPPED, FOR GARNISH

SLOW VEGETABLE & QUINOA SALAD

YIELD: 4 SERVINGS / **ACTIVE TIME:** 15 MINUTES / **TOTAL TIME:** 4 HOURS AND 15 MINUTES

A quick sofrito keys this easy and comforting dish.

1. Dice one of the poblanos, half of the bell peppers, and half of the onion. Place the diced vegetables to the side. Place the remaining ingredients, except for the quinoa and pepitas, in a food processor and blitz until smooth.

2. Place the diced vegetables, the puree, and the quinoa in a slow cooker and cook on low until the quinoa is tender, about 4 hours.

3. Fluff the quinoa with a fork, garnish with the pepitas, and serve.

INGREDIENTS:

2	POBLANO CHILE PEPPERS, STEMMED AND SEEDED
1	RED BELL PEPPER, STEMMED AND SEEDED
1	GREEN BELL PEPPER, STEMMED AND SEEDED
1	WHITE ONION, PEELED AND QUARTERED
3	PLUM TOMATOES
2	GARLIC CLOVES, PEELED
1	TABLESPOON CUMIN
2	TABLESPOONS ADOBO SEASONING
1½	CUPS QUINOA, RINSED WELL
	PEPITAS, TOASTED, FOR GARNISH

Slow Vegetable & Quinoa Salad, see page 429

QUINOA SALAD WITH SPICY PEANUT DRESSING

YIELD: 4 SERVINGS / **ACTIVE TIME:** 10 MINUTES / **TOTAL TIME:** 25 MINUTES

The dressing is the star here, as pairing a bit of spice with peanut butter produces something absolutely irresistible.

1. Cook the quinoa according to the directions on the package. Fluff it and transfer it to a salad bowl.

2. Add the cucumbers, pepper, edamame, cabbage, scallions, and carrot to the salad bowl and toss to combine. Add the dressing and toss to coat.

3. Garnish with the peanuts and cilantro and serve with lime wedges.

INGREDIENTS:

1	CUP QUINOA
2	CUPS CHOPPED CUCUMBERS
1	RED BELL PEPPER, STEMMED, SEEDED, AND CHOPPED
2	CUPS SHELLED, COOKED EDAMAME
1	CUP SHREDDED RED CABBAGE
¼	CUP CHOPPED SCALLIONS
1	CUP DICED CARROT
	SPICY PEANUT DRESSING (SEE PAGE 638)
⅓	CUP CRUSHED ROASTED PEANUTS, FOR GARNISH
	FRESH CILANTRO, CHOPPED, FOR GARNISH
	LIME WEDGES, FOR SERVING

COLD NOODLE SALAD

YIELD: 4 SERVINGS / ACTIVE TIME: 25 MINUTES / TOTAL TIME: 40 MINUTES

The chicken is not essential here, included only to provide some protein. So if you feel like something vegetarian, this salad is a flavorful option.

1. Bring water to a boil in a large pot. Add the noodles and cook until they are al dente, 6 to 8 minutes. Drain the noodles, rinse them under cold water, and let them drain again.

2. Place the olive oil in a skillet and warm it over medium heat. Season the chicken with the garlic powder and salt, add it to the pan, and cook until it is browned on both sides and cooked through (the interior is 165°F), about 10 minutes, turning it over halfway through. Remove the chicken from the pan and let it cool. When it is cool enough to handle, slice the chicken and set it aside.

3. Place the noodles, cucumbers, carrot, cabbage, edamame, bell pepper, peanuts, scallions, and chicken in a salad bowl and toss to combine. Add the dressing and toss to coat.

4. Garnish with cilantro, Crispy Wonton Strips, and additional peanuts and serve with lime wedges.

INGREDIENTS:

½ LB. RICE NOODLES

1 TABLESPOON EXTRA-VIRGIN OLIVE OIL

1 LARGE BONELESS, SKINLESS CHICKEN BREAST, POUNDED THIN

½ TEASPOON GARLIC POWDER

PINCH OF KOSHER SALT

6 PERSIAN CUCUMBERS, FINELY DICED

1 LARGE CARROT, PEELED AND DICED

1 CUP CHOPPED RED CABBAGE

1 CUP SHELLED, COOKED EDAMAME

1 RED BELL PEPPER, STEMMED, SEEDED, AND DICED

¼ CUP ROASTED PEANUTS, PLUS MORE FOR GARNISH

1 CUP CHOPPED SCALLIONS

SWEET & SPICY PEANUT DRESSING (SEE PAGE 639)

FRESH CILANTRO, CHOPPED, FOR GARNISH

CRISPY WONTON STRIPS (SEE PAGE 672), FOR GARNISH

LIME WEDGES, FOR SERVING

SUMMER PASTA SALAD

YIELD: 4 SERVINGS / ACTIVE TIME: 25 MINUTES / TOTAL TIME: 50 MINUTES

Thanks to its valleys for the vinaigrette and feta crumbles to settle in, fusilli is by far the best shape for a pasta-centered salad.

1. Bring water to a boil in a large pot. Add salt, let the water return to a full boil, and add the pasta. Cook until it is al dente, 10 to 12 minutes. Drain the pasta, rinse it under cold water, and let it drain again.

2. Place the pasta, cucumbers, tomatoes, onion, jalapeños, and salami in a salad bowl and toss to combine. Add the dressing and toss to coat.

3. Top the salad with the feta and parsley. Cover the salad bowl with plastic wrap and chill the salad in the refrigerator for 15 minutes before serving.

INGREDIENTS:

	SALT TO TASTE
1	LB. FUSILLI
1½	CUPS DICED CUCUMBERS
2	CUPS CHERRY TOMATOES, HALVED
1	RED ONION, SLICED THIN
2	TABLESPOONS CHOPPED PICKLED JALAPEÑO CHILE PEPPERS
1	LB. SALAMI, CHOPPED
	OREGANO VINAIGRETTE (SEE PAGE 535)
1	CUP CRUMBLED FETA CHEESE
½	CUP CHOPPED FRESH PARSLEY

THAI QUINOA SALAD

YIELD: 4 SERVINGS / **ACTIVE TIME:** 20 MINUTES / **TOTAL TIME:** 40 MINUTES

Though red-veined dock can be tough to find, its tart flavor is capable of transforming a salad.

1. Cook the quinoa according to the directions on the package. Spread it in an even layer on a baking sheet and let it cool completely.

2. Place the quinoa, dock, cabbage, carrot, and radish in a salad bowl and toss to combine. Add the dressing and lime juice and toss to coat.

3. Top the salad with the pomegranate arils, cashews, and peanuts and serve.

INGREDIENTS:

1	CUP QUINOA
2	OZ. YOUNG RED-VEINED DOCK OR SPINACH
¼	HEAD OF PURPLE CABBAGE, SLICED THIN
1	CARROT, PEELED AND SLICED VERY THIN
1	DAIKON RADISH, PEELED AND SLICED VERY THIN
	THAI CHILE DRESSING (SEE PAGE 553)
1	TABLESPOON FRESH LIME JUICE
½	CUP POMEGRANATE ARILS
1	CUP ROASTED CASHEWS
½	CUP ROASTED PEANUTS

PANZANELLA SALAD

YIELD: 4 SERVINGS / ACTIVE TIME: 30 MINUTES / TOTAL TIME: 1 HOUR

The toothsome texture that the dressing lends the bread has made this salad a classic.

1. Preheat the oven to 375°F. Place the bread and olive oil in a mixing bowl, season with salt and pepper, and toss to coat. Place the bread on a baking sheet, place it in the oven, and toast until it is golden brown, 8 to 10 minutes, stirring occasionally. Remove the bread from the oven and let it cool.

2. Place the dressing in a salad bowl, add the tomatoes, beans, and onion, and toss to coat.

3. Add the bread and arugula, toss to combine, and season the salad with salt and pepper. Garnish with Parmesan and enjoy.

INGREDIENTS:

- 4 CUPS DAY-OLD CRUSTY BREAD PIECES
- 2 TABLESPOONS EXTRA-VIRGIN OLIVE OIL
- SALT AND PEPPER, TO TASTE
- PANZANELLA DRESSING (SEE PAGE 589)
- 1 LB. CHERRY TOMATOES, HALVED
- 1 (14 OZ.) CAN OF CANNELLINI BEANS, DRAINED AND RINSED
- ½ RED ONION, SLICED THIN
- 4 CUPS BABY ARUGULA
- PARMESAN CHEESE, SHAVED, FOR GARNISH

BREAD SALAD WITH TOMATOES & OLIVES

YIELD: 4 SERVINGS / **ACTIVE TIME:** 20 MINUTES / **TOTAL TIME:** 35 MINUTES

If you'd like a little more acid in this salad, use some Pickled Red Onion (see page 671) in place of the red onion listed here.

1. Preheat the oven to 375°F. Place the bread in a mixing bowl, drizzle half of the olive oil over it, and season with salt and pepper. Toss to coat and transfer the bread to two baking sheets, making sure it is in an even layer on both.

2. Place the bread in the oven and toast until it is golden brown, 10 to 15 minutes, stirring occasionally. Remove the bread from the oven and let it cool slightly.

3. Place the bread in a salad bowl, add the tomatoes, olives, red onion, and garlic, and toss to combine. Add the vinegar and remaining olive oil, season with salt and pepper, and toss to coat.

4. Garnish with basil and serve.

INGREDIENTS:

4 CUPS DAY-OLD CRUSTY BREAD PIECES (1-INCH CUBES)

¼ CUP EXTRA-VIRGIN OLIVE OIL

SALT AND PEPPER, TO TASTE

2 PLUM TOMATOES, CHOPPED

1½ CUPS OLIVES, PITTED

¼ RED ONION, SLICED

3 GARLIC CLOVES, GRATED

1 TABLESPOON RED WINE VINEGAR

FRESH BASIL, SHREDDED, FOR GARNISH

GREEK RICE SALAD

YIELD: 4 SERVINGS / ACTIVE TIME: 20 MINUTES / TOTAL TIME: 40 MINUTES

If you have a little time and want to ramp up the flavor here, consider roasting the pepper and tomatoes on the grill or in the oven.

1. Cook the rice according to the directions on the package. Fluff it, cover it, and let it cool.

2. Place the tuna and half of the olive oil in a salad bowl, season with salt and pepper, and work the mixture with a fork, breaking up the tuna.

3. Add the rice, tomatoes, bell pepper, cucumber, olives, and feta and toss to combine. Add the remaining olive oil, season with salt and pepper, and toss to coat.

4. Garnish with parsley and serve.

INGREDIENTS:

1	CUP RICE
10	OZ. CANNED TUNA, DRAINED
¼	CUP EXTRA-VIRGIN OLIVE OIL
	SALT AND PEPPER, TO TASTE
1	CUP CHERRY TOMATOES, QUARTERED
1	YELLOW BELL PEPPER, SLICED VERY THIN
1	CUCUMBER, RIBBONED
1	CUP KALAMATA OLIVES, PITTED
4	OZ. FETA CHEESE, CRUMBLED
	FRESH PARSLEY, CHOPPED, FOR GARNISH

THAI NOODLE SALAD

A double dose of cabbage, plus the carrot, pepper, and peanuts supply this salad with a surplus of pleasant crunchiness.

1. Bring water to a boil in a large pot. Add salt, let the water return to a full boil, and add the noodles. Cook until they are al dente, 6 to 8 minutes. Drain the noodles, rinse them under cold water, and let them drain again.

2. Place the noodles, pepper, cabbages, sprouts, and carrot in a salad bowl and toss to combine. Add the dressing, season with salt, and toss to coat.

3. Top the salad with the peanuts, garnish with scallions, and serve.

INGREDIENTS:

SALT, TO TASTE

½ LB. RICE NOODLES

1 RED BELL PEPPER, STEMMED, SEEDED, AND SLICED THIN

¼ HEAD OF GREEN CABBAGE, SHREDDED

¼ HEAD OF PURPLE CABBAGE, SHREDDED

2 OZ. BEAN SPROUTS

1 CARROT, PEELED AND GRATED

THAI CHILE DRESSING (SEE PAGE 53)

1 CUP CHOPPED PEANUTS

SCALLIONS, CHOPPED, FOR GARNISH

Thai Noodle Salad, see page 445

RICE SALAD WITH SUGAR SNAP PEAS, CARROTS, KOHLRABI & SHRIMP

YIELD: 4 SERVINGS / ACTIVE TIME: 10 MINUTES / TOTAL TIME: 40 MINUTES

White rice works perfectly well here, but don't be afraid to experiment with one of the many varieties available, such as bamboo rice or forbidden rice.

1. Cook the rice according to the directions on the package. Fluff it, cover it, and let it cool.

2. Place the rice, peas, carrots, kohlrabi, and shrimp in a salad bowl and toss to combine.

3. Serve with the vinaigrette.

INGREDIENTS:

1   CUP RICE

2   HANDFULS OF SUGAR SNAP PEAS, TRIMMED AND SLICED

3   CARROTS, PEELED AND GRATED

1   KOHLRABI, PEELED AND FINELY DICED

12 COOKED SHRIMP, CHILLED

    BASIL & CILANTRO VINAIGRETTE (SEE PAGE 568), FOR SERVING

MILLET SALAD

YIELD: 4 SERVINGS / ACTIVE TIME: 20 MINUTES / TOTAL TIME: 40 MINUTES

Grassy and nutty with a subtle sweetness, millet is always a great option when you're looking for a grain-centric salad.

1. Place the millet in a medium pot, season with salt, and cover with water by 1 inch. Bring to a boil, reduce the heat so that the millet simmers, and cook, stirring occasionally, until the millet is tender, 20 to 30 minutes. If any water remains, drain the millet. Spread it evenly on a baking sheet and let it cool completely.

2. Place the millet, cucumbers, tomatoes, and olives in a salad bowl and toss to combine. Add the olive oil, season with salt and pepper, and toss to coat.

3. Top the salad with the feta, garnish with parsley, and serve.

INGREDIENTS:

1	CUP MILLET
	SALT AND PEPPER, TO TASTE
2	CUCUMBERS, SLICED THIN
2	TOMATOES, CHOPPED
1	CUP GREEN OLIVES, PITTED
¼	CUP EXTRA-VIRGIN OLIVE OIL
4	OZ. FETA CHEESE, CRUMBLED
	FRESH PARSLEY, CHOPPED, FOR GARNISH

Millet Salad, see page 449

RICE NOODLE SALAD WITH PORK & PEPPERS

YIELD: 4 SERVINGS / ACTIVE TIME: 20 MINUTES / TOTAL TIME: 50 MINUTES

The pork supplies a comforting richness, and the peppers, peas, and Miso Dressing grant the dish the lightness you want in a salad.

1. Bring water to a boil in a large pot.

2. Place the sesame oil in a large skillet and warm it over medium heat. Add the pork, season with salt and pepper, and cook until it is browned and cooked through, about 10 minutes, breaking it up with a wooden spoon as it cooks. Remove the pan from heat and let the pork cool.

3. Add salt to the boiling water, let the water return to a full boil, and add the noodles. Cook until they are al dente, 6 to 8 minutes. Drain the noodles, rinse them under cold water, and let them drain again.

4. Place the pork, noodles, bell peppers, chile, bean sprouts, and peas in a salad bowl and toss to combine. Add half of the dressing and toss to coat.

5. Top the salad with the peanuts, garnish with fresh herbs, and serve with lime wedges and the remaining dressing.

INGREDIENTS:

- 1 TABLESPOON SESAME OIL
- 1 LB GROUND PORK
- SALT AND PEPPER, TO TASTE
- ½ LB RICE NOODLES
- 1 RED BELL PEPPER, STEMMED, SEEDED, AND SLICED
- 1 YELLOW BELL PEPPER, STEMMED, SEEDED, AND SLICED
- 1 RED CHILE PEPPER, STEMMED AND SLICED THIN
- 2 OZ. BEAN SPROUTS
- 2 OZ. SNOW PEAS
- MISO DRESSING (SEE PAGE 571)
- ½ CUP PEANUTS, CHOPPED
- FRESH HERBS, CHOPPED, FOR GARNISH
- LIME WEDGES, FOR SERVING

FRUITY QUINOA SALAD

YIELD: 4 SERVINGS / **ACTIVE TIME:** 20 MINUTES / **TOTAL TIME:** 40 MINUTES

Any variety of apple will work here, but do give Granny Smith apples a try—their tartness will amplify that quality in the raspberries and grant this salad a unique flavor.

1. Cook the quinoa according to the directions on the package. Spread it in an even layer on a baking sheet and let it cool completely.

2. Place the lemon juice and agave nectar in a small bowl and stir to combine.

3. Place the quinoa, zucchini, apples, raspberries, tomatoes, mango, snow peas, and chia seeds in a salad bowl and toss to combine. Add the dressing, toss to coat, and serve.

INGREDIENTS:

⅔ CUP QUINOA

1 TABLESPOON FRESH LEMON JUICE

2 TABLESPOONS AGAVE NECTAR

1 ZUCCHINI, JULIENNED

2 APPLES, CORED AND SLICED THIN

2 CUPS RASPBERRIES

1 CUP CHERRY TOMATOES, HALVED

FLESH OF 1 MANGO, FINELY DICED

2 OZ. SNOW PEAS

2 TABLESPOONS CHIA SEEDS

COUSCOUS SALAD WITH POACHED EGGS

YIELD: 4 SERVINGS / ACTIVE TIME: 20 MINUTES / TOTAL TIME: 40 MINUTES

You could forgo the vinaigrette and simply double up on the poached eggs here, as their runny yolks will function as a type of dressing.

1. Bring water to a boil in a medium pot.

2. Cook the couscous according to the directions on the package. Spread it in an even layer on a baking sheet and let it cool completely.

3. Add salt and the vinegar to the boiling water. Working with one egg at a time, crack it into a shallow bowl and gently slip it into the boiling water. Poach the eggs until the whites are set. Remove the eggs with a slotted spoon and gently transfer them to a plate.

4. Place the couscous, tomatoes, chickpeas, and pine nuts in a salad bowl and toss to combine. Add the vinaigrette and toss to coat.

5. Divide the salad among the serving plates and top each portion with a poached egg. Garnish with parsley and serve.

INGREDIENTS:

- 1 CUP COUSCOUS
- SALT, TO TASTE
- 1 TEASPOON WHITE VINEGAR
- 4 EGGS, WHOLE
- 3 CUPS CHERRY TOMATOES, HALVED
- 1 CUP SUN-DRIED TOMATOES IN OLIVE OIL, DRAINED AND CHOPPED
- 2 CUPS CANNED CHICKPEAS, DRAINED
- ½ CUP PINE NUTS
- HONEY VINAIGRETTE (SEE PAGE 524)
- FRESH PARSLEY, CHOPPED, FOR GARNISH

RICE, TEMPEH & LENTIL SALAD

YIELD: 4 SERVINGS / **ACTIVE TIME:** 20 MINUTES / **TOTAL TIME:** 50 MINUTES

This protein-packed vegan salad has the power to provide a week's worth of lunches.

1. Bring water to a boil in a large pot.

2. Cook the rice according to the directions on the package. Fluff the rice, cover it, and let it cool.

3. Add the lentils to the boiling water and cook until they are tender, 20 to 25 minutes. Drain the lentils, spread them on a baking sheet in an even layer, season with salt, and let them cool completely.

4. Place the olive oil in a large skillet and warm it over medium heat. Season the tempeh with salt and pepper, place it in the pan, and cook until it is browned on both sides, 8 to 10 minutes, turning it over halfway through. Remove the pan from heat.

5. Place the rice, lentils, tempeh, and scallions in a salad bowl and toss to combine. Add the vinaigrette and toss to coat.

6. Garnish with fresh herbs and serve.

INGREDIENTS:

2	CUPS RICE
1	CUP LENTILS
	SALT AND PEPPER, TO TASTE
2	TABLESPOONS EXTRA-VIRGIN OLIVE OIL
½	LB. TEMPEH
8	SCALLIONS, TRIMMED AND CHOPPED
	BASIL & CILANTRO VINAIGRETTE (SEE PAGE 568)
	FRESH HERBS, CHOPPED, FOR GARNISH

SALADA DE FEIJÃO VERDE

YIELD: 4 SERVINGS / **ACTIVE TIME:** 20 MINUTES / **TOTAL TIME:** 40 MINUTES

This is a popular salad in Brazil, keyed by the beloved pigeon pea.

1. Bring water to a boil in a large pot.

2. Cook the rice according to the directions on the package. Fluff the rice, cover it, and let it cool.

3. Add salt to the boiling water, let it return to a full boil, and add the kale. Cook until it is just tender, 4 to 6 minutes. Drain the kale, rinse it under cold water, and let it drain again.

4. Place the rice, kale, carrot, bell pepper, olives, peas, and eggs in a salad bowl and toss to combine. Add the olive oil, season with salt and pepper, and toss to coat.

5. Garnish with parsley and serve with lime wedges.

INGREDIENTS:

⅔ CUP RICE

SALT AND PEPPER, TO TASTE

4 OZ. KALE, STEMMED AND CHOPPED

1 CARROT, PEELED AND JULIENNED

1 BELL PEPPER, STEMMED, SEEDED, AND SLICED THIN

1 CUP BLACK OLIVES, PITTED

2 CUPS CANNED PIGEON PEAS, DRAINED

2 HARD-BOILED EGGS (SEE PAGE 667), QUARTERED

2 TABLESPOONS EXTRA-VIRGIN OLIVE OIL

FRESH PARSLEY, CHOPPED, FOR GARNISH

LIME WEDGES, FOR SERVING

ARUGULA, NECTARINE, FARRO & GOAT CHEESE SALAD

YIELD: 2 SERVINGS / **ACTIVE TIME:** 10 MINUTES / **TOTAL TIME:** 30 MINUTES

Arugula pairs beautifully with sweet fruit, and what better choice than the honey-sweet nectarine?

1. Bring 2 cups of water to a boil in a medium pot, add the farro, and reduce the heat. Simmer the farro until it has absorbed all of the water, about 15 minutes. Remove the pan from heat and let the farro cool.

2. Place the farro, nectarine, goat cheese, cashews, and arugula in a salad bowl and toss to combine. Add half of the vinaigrette, season with salt and pepper, toss to coat, and serve with the remaining vinaigrette.

INGREDIENTS:

1	CUP FARRO
1	RIPE NECTARINE, PITTED AND DICED
2	OZ. GOAT CHEESE, CRUMBLED
¼	CUP CHOPPED CASHEWS
2	HANDFULS OF ARUGULA
	WHITE BALSAMIC VINAIGRETTE (SEE PAGE 565)
	SALT AND PEPPER, TO TASTE

KISIR

This substantial salad is a foundational preparation in Turkish cuisine.

1. Place the bulgur wheat in a heatproof bowl, season with salt, and add 2 cups boiling water. Let the bulgur wheat sit until it has absorbed most of the water, 20 to 25 minutes. Drain the bulgur wheat, pressing it against the side of the strainer to remove any excess liquid.

2. Place the bulgur wheat, cucumber, tomato, and pomegranate arils in a salad bowl and toss to combine. Add the Aleppo pepper, lemon juice, and olive oil and toss to coat.

3. Garnish with parsley and mint and serve with lemon wedges.

INGREDIENTS:

1	CUP BULGUR WHEAT
	SALT, TO TASTE
1	CUCUMBER, FINELY DICED
1	TOMATO, FINELY DICED
¼	CUP POMEGRANATE ARILS
1	TABLESPOON ALEPPO PEPPER
2	TABLESPOONS FRESH LEMON JUICE
2	TABLESPOONS EXTRA-VIRGIN OLIVE OIL
	FRESH PARSLEY, CHOPPED, FOR GARNISH
	FRESH MINT, CHOPPED, FOR GARNISH
	LEMON WEDGES, FOR SERVING

Kisir, see page 463

SOBA NOODLE SALAD

YIELD: 4 SERVINGS / **ACTIVE TIME:** 20 MINUTES / **TOTAL TIME:** 30 MINUTES

The pleasant chewiness of the soba noodles makes them a wonderful choice for a salad, adding an element not often seen in this space.

1. Bring water to a boil in a large pot and a medium pot.

2. Add salt to the boiling water in the large pot, let the water return to a full boil, and add the noodles. Cook until they are al dente, 5 to 8 minutes. Drain the noodles, rinse them under cold water, and let them drain again.

3. Add the edamame to the boiling water in the medium pot and cook until it is just tender, 4 to 5 minutes. Drain the edamame, rinse it under cold water, and let it drain again.

4. Place the noodles, edamame, peppers, and peanuts in a salad bowl and toss to combine. Add the Rayu and toss to coat.

5. Top the salad with the Crispy Wonton Strips and sesame seeds and serve.

INGREDIENTS:

SALT, TO TASTE

¾ LB. SOBA NOODLES

2 CUPS SHELLED EDAMAME

2 RED BELL PEPPERS, STEMMED, SEEDED, AND SLICED

½ CUP CHOPPED PEANUTS

RAYU (SEE PAGE 520)

½ CUP CRISPY WONTON STRIPS (SEE PAGE 672)

2 TABLESPOONS BLACK SESAME SEEDS

RATATOUILLE SALAD

YIELD: 4 SERVINGS / ACTIVE TIME: 20 MINUTES / TOTAL TIME: 40 MINUTES

The classic French dish gets repurposed as a salad, to stunning effect.

1. Preheat the oven to 375°F. Place the eggplant in a colander, season with salt, and toss to coat. Let the eggplant drain.

2. Place the bread in a mixing bowl, drizzle half of the olive oil over it, and season with salt and pepper. Toss to coat and transfer the bread to a baking sheet, making sure it is in an even layer.

3. Place the bread in the oven and toast until it is golden brown, 8 to 10 minutes, stirring occasionally. Remove the bread from the oven and let it cool.

4. Place the remaining olive oil in a large skillet and warm it over medium heat. Add the eggplant and zucchini, season with salt and pepper, and cook, stirring occasionally, until they are browned and tender, 8 to 10 minutes.

5. Stir in the onion, garlic, and bell pepper and cook, stirring occasionally, until the pepper has softened, about 5 minutes. Remove the pan from heat and let the vegetables cool.

6. Place the bread, zucchini mixture, olives, and beans in a salad bowl and toss to combine. Add the vinaigrette and toss to coat.

7. Garnish with parsley and serve.

INGREDIENTS:

1   EGGPLANT, PEELED AND
        CHOPPED

        SALT AND PEPPER, TO
        TASTE

3   CUPS DAY-OLD BREAD
        PIECES (1-INCH CUBES)

¼   CUP EXTRA-VIRGIN OLIVE
        OIL

1   ZUCCHINI, SLICED AND
        CHOPPED

½   ONION, SLICED THIN

3   GARLIC CLOVES, MINCED

1   RED BELL PEPPER,
        STEMMED, SEEDED, AND
        SLICED VERY THIN

2   TOMATOES, SLICED

1   CUP GREEN OLIVES,
        PITTED

2   CUPS CANNED CANNELLINI
        BEANS, DRAINED

        BALSAMIC VINAIGRETTE
        (SEE PAGE 573)

        FRESH PARSLEY, CHOPPED,
        FOR GARNISH

PEARL BARLEY & PEAR SALAD

YIELD: 4 SERVINGS / **ACTIVE TIME:** 20 MINUTES / **TOTAL TIME:** 50 MINUTES

Who would have ever thought that barley could be at the center of such a beautiful preparation?

1. Bring water to a boil in a medium pot. Add salt and the barley, reduce the heat so that the barley simmers, and cook until it is al dente, about 20 minutes. Drain the barley, rinse it under cold water, and let it drain again.

2. Place the barley, pears, cucumber, and watercress in a salad bowl and toss to combine. Add the vinaigrette and toss to coat.

3. Garnish with fresh herbs and serve.

INGREDIENTS:

SALT, TO TASTE

1 CUP PEARL BARLEY

1½ PEARS, CORED AND FINELY DICED

1 CUCUMBER, FINELY DICED

4 OZ. WATERCRESS

CITRUS VINAIGRETTE (SEE PAGE 610)

FRESH HERBS, CHOPPED, FOR GARNISH

FRUIT SALADS

While previous chapters contain plenty of instances where the unique flavors of fruits are smartly deployed along with other ingredients, they are not quite fruit-forward enough to fit the bill of a "fruit salad."

Instead, recipes that fit neatly into this category can be found here. Capable of serving as a needed source of lightness at a barbecue or a dessert that will dazzle the taste buds, these unique preparations are guaranteed to lift every occasion where they make an appearance.

ORANGE & GRAPEFRUIT SALAD WITH WALNUTS

YIELD: 4 SERVINGS / **ACTIVE TIME:** 20 MINUTES / **TOTAL TIME:** 20 MINUTES

This lovely salad can awaken the palate as a first course, or serve as the foundation of the main course, with a grilled protein placed on top.

1. Place the all of the ingredients, except for the vinaigrette, in a salad bowl and toss to combine.

2. Add the vinaigrette, season with salt and pepper, toss to coat, and serve.

INGREDIENTS:

2   OZ. BABY SPINACH

2   ORANGES, SUPREMED (SEE PAGE 92)

2   GRAPEFRUIT, SUPREMED

     FLESH OF 2 AVOCADOS, SLICED THIN

1   RED ONION, SLICED VERY THIN

     SALT AND PEPPER, TO TASTE

1   CUP WALNUTS

2   CUPS BLUEBERRIES

1   CUP POMEGRANATE ARILS

     CHAMPAGNE VINAIGRETTE (SEE PAGE 592)

BERRY & GRILLED APRICOT SALAD

YIELD: 4 SERVINGS / ACTIVE TIME: 20 MINUTES / TOTAL TIME: 30 MINUTES

A sweet, tart, and luscious salad that cries out for an accompaniment of proteins grilled over charcoal.

1. Prepare a gas or charcoal grill for medium-high heat (about 450°F).

2. Place the apricots on the grill, cut sides down, and cook until they are lightly charred, about 6 minutes. Turn them over and cook until they are tender, about 5 minutes. Remove the apricots from the grill and let them cool slightly.

3. When the apricots are cool enough to handle, chop them into bite-size pieces.

4. Place the apricots, strawberries, cherries, raspberries, blueberries, and currants in a salad bowl and toss to combine. Add the lemon juice and honey and toss to coat.

5. Divide the salad among the serving plates and top each portion with some of the burrata. Garnish with fresh herbs and serve.

INGREDIENTS:

- 4 APRICOTS, HALVED AND PITTED
- 2 CUPS HALVED STRAWBERRIES
- 2 CUPS CHERRIES, PITTED AND HALVED
- 2 CUPS RASPBERRIES
- 2 CUPS BLUEBERRIES
- 1 CUP CURRANTS
- 2 TABLESPOONS FRESH LEMON JUICE
- 1 TABLESPOON HONEY
- 4 OZ. BURRATA CHEESE

  FRESH HERBS, FOR GARNISH

PERSIMMON & BLOOD ORANGE SALAD
WITH CHICKPEAS

YIELD: 4 SERVINGS / **ACTIVE TIME:** 20 MINUTES / **TOTAL TIME:** 20 MINUTES

Make sure that you're working with perfectly ripe persimmons here—anything else will be too difficult to chew and severely lacking in terms of flavor.

1. Place the cabbage, persimmons, blood oranges, avocados, chickpeas, and lamb's lettuce in a salad bowl and toss to combine. Add half of the vinaigrette and toss to coat.

2. Top the salad with the walnuts, pomegranate arils, and sesame seeds and serve with the remaining vinaigrette.

INGREDIENTS:

¼ HEAD OF PURPLE CABBAGE, CHOPPED

2 PERSIMMONS, PEELED AND SLICED

2 BLOOD ORANGES, HALVED AND SLICED THIN

FLESH OF 2 AVOCADOS, SLICED

2 CUPS CANNED CHICKPEAS, DRAINED

2 OZ. LAMB'S LETTUCE

WHITE WINE VINAIGRETTE (SEE PAGE 540)

1 CUP WALNUTS, CHOPPED

1 CUP POMEGRANATE ARILS

2 TABLESPOONS SESAME SEEDS

BLOOD ORANGE SALAD
WITH GORGONZOLA & CAPER BERRIES

YIELD: 4 SERVINGS / ACTIVE TIME: 20 MINUTES / TOTAL TIME: 20 MINUTES

The blood oranges and caper berries are the perfect contrast to the rich Gorgonzola.

1. Place the lamb's lettuce, blood oranges, caper berries, Gorgonzola, and walnuts in a salad bowl and toss to combine. Add half of the vinaigrette and toss to coat.

2. Garnish with microgreens and edible flowers and serve with the remaining vinaigrette.

INGREDIENTS:

5 OZ. LAMB'S LETTUCE

3 BLOOD ORANGES, SUPREMED (SEE PAGE 92)

½ CUP CAPER BERRIES

4 OZ. GORGONZOLA CHEESE, CRUMBLED

1 CUP WALNUTS

MUSTARD VINAIGRETTE (SEE PAGE 549)

MICROGREENS, FOR GARNISH

EDIBLE FLOWERS, FOR GARNISH

MELON & MOZZARELLA SALAD
WITH SPICY CHICKPEAS

YIELD: 4 SERVINGS / **ACTIVE TIME:** 20 MINUTES / **TOTAL TIME:** 20 MINUTES

Any type of pepper will work here, but Aleppo pepper, with its mild spice and fruity character, is the ideal.

1. Place the chickpeas, watermelon, honeydew melon, and mozzarella in a salad bowl and toss to combine. Add the Pesto, season with Aleppo pepper, and toss to coat.

2. Garnish with mint and edible flowers and serve.

INGREDIENTS:

SPICY CHICKPEAS (SEE PAGE 676)

4 OZ. WATERMELON BALLS

4 OZ. HONEYDEW MELON BALLS

5 OZ. FRESH MOZZARELLA CHEESE, DRAINED AND CHOPPED

PESTO (SEE PAGE 603)

ALEPPO PEPPER, TO TASTE

FRESH MINT, FOR GARNISH

EDIBLE FLOWERS, FOR GARNISH

MANGO & PAPAYA SALAD

YIELD: 4 SERVINGS / ACTIVE TIME: 20 MINUTES / TOTAL TIME: 20 MINUTES

The flavors and textures of Southeast Asia are available in this light, flavorful salad.

1. Place the mangoes, carrots, cucumber, papaya, and red onion in a salad bowl and toss to combine. Add the lime juice and toss to coat.

2. Garnish with cilantro and serve.

INGREDIENTS:

FLESH OF 2 MANGOES, CHOPPED

1½ CARROTS, PEELED AND JULIENNED

1 CUCUMBER, JULIENNED

1 GREEN PAPAYA, JULIENNED

¼ RED ONION, FINELY CHOPPED

2 TABLESPOONS FRESH LIME JUICE

FRESH CILANTRO, CHOPPED, FOR GARNISH

TROPICAL FRUIT SALAD

YIELD: 4 SERVINGS / **ACTIVE TIME:** 20 MINUTES / **TOTAL TIME:** 20 MINUTES

You can only resist the tropical fruit display at the grocery store for so long. When it finally breaks you down, utilize your bounty in this salad.

1. Place all of the fruits in a salad bowl and toss to combine. Add the lime juice and agave nectar and toss to coat.

2. Garnish with edible flowers and serve.

INGREDIENTS:

2	OZ. STAR FRUIT, SLICED
2	OZ. DRAGON FRUIT BALLS
2	OZ. WATERMELON
2	OZ. PAPAYA
2	OZ. TAMARILLO
2	OZ. PASSION FRUIT
2	TABLESPOONS FRESH LIME JUICE
2	TABLESPOONS AGAVE NECTAR
	EDIBLE FLOWERS, FOR GARNISH

CITRUS & PASSION FRUIT SALAD

YIELD: 4 SERVINGS / **ACTIVE TIME:** 20 MINUTES / **TOTAL TIME:** 20 MINUTES

Passion fruit's rich, tropically tinged tartness actually provides a nice counter to the sharp, zesty, sour taste of the citrus.

1. Place the grapefruit, oranges, and passion fruits in a salad bowl and toss to combine. Add the agave nectar and toss to coat.

2. Garnish with lemon verbena and serve.

INGREDIENTS:

4   GRAPEFRUIT, SUPREMED
      (SEE PAGE 92)

4   ORANGES, SUPREMED

      PULP OF 2 PASSION FRUITS

1   TABLESPOON AGAVE
      NECTAR

      FRESH LEMON VERBENA,
      FOR GARNISH

CRUNCHY POMEGRANATE SALAD

YIELD: 4 TO 6 SERVINGS / **ACTIVE TIME:** 30 MINUTES / **TOTAL TIME:** 30 MINUTES

The pop of each pomegranate seed when bitten into, followed by the mouth-puckering tartness, is an experience that simply can't be recreated by any other ingredient.

1. Place the cream in the work bowl of a stand mixer fitted with the whisk attachment and whip until it starts to thicken.

2. Add the sugar and vanilla and beat until the mixture holds stiff peaks.

3. Fold in the pomegranate seeds and apples, sprinkle the pecans over the top, and serve.

INGREDIENTS:

- 2 CUPS HEAVY CREAM
- ¼ CUP SUGAR
- 2 TEASPOONS PURE VANILLA EXTRACT
- 2½ CUPS POMEGRANATE SEEDS
- 2 APPLES, PEELED, CORED, AND CUBED
- 1 CUP CHOPPED PECANS, TOASTED

WATERMELON, GRAPE & MANGO SALAD

YIELD: 4 SERVINGS / **ACTIVE TIME:** 20 MINUTES / **TOTAL TIME:** 20 MINUTES

Jalapeño and scallions add depth and intrigue to what is otherwise a straightforward fruit salad.

1. Place the watermelon, melon, mango, grapes, blueberries, bell pepper, and chile in a salad bowl and toss to combine.

2. Place the lime juice and agave nectar in a small bowl and stir to combine.

3. Add the dressing to the salad bowl and toss to coat.

4. Garnish with scallions and serve.

INGREDIENTS:

2	CUPS DICED WATERMELON
2	CUPS DICED MELON
1	CUP DICED MANGO
4	OZ. SEEDLESS GRAPES, HALVED
½	CUP BLUEBERRIES
1	RED BELL PEPPER, STEMMED, SEEDED, AND DICED
1	JALAPEÑO CHILE PEPPER, STEMMED, SEEDED, AND DICED
2	TABLESPOONS FRESH LIME JUICE
2	TABLESPOONS AGAVE NECTAR
	SCALLIONS, CHOPPED, FOR GARNISH

PLUM, FIG & BEET SALAD

YIELD: 4 SERVINGS / ACTIVE TIME: 20 MINUTES / TOTAL TIME: 2 HOURS

The versatility of both plums and figs is on full display here.

1. Preheat the oven to 375°F. Place the beets in a baking dish, drizzle the olive oil over them, and sprinkle the rosemary and fennel seeds over the top. Season with salt and pepper, toss to combine, and cover the dish with aluminum foil. Place the beets in the oven and roast until a knife inserted into them passes easily to their centers, 45 minutes to 1 hour.

2. Remove the beets from the oven and let them cool. When they are cool enough to handle, peel the beets.

3. Prepare a gas or charcoal grill for medium-high heat (about 450°F).

4. Place the plums and beets on the grill, cut sides down, and cook until they are lightly charred, about 6 minutes. Turn them over and cook until the plums are just tender, about 5 minutes. Remove the beets and plums from the grill and let them cool slightly.

5. Arrange the grilled plums and beets in a serving dish, add the strawberries and figs, and toss to combine.

6. Drizzle the crème fraîche over the salad, garnish with red currants, and serve.

INGREDIENTS:

3	BEETS, HALVED
2	TABLESPOONS EXTRA-VIRGIN OLIVE OIL
2	TABLESPOONS FRESH ROSEMARY
2	TEASPOONS FENNEL SEEDS
	SALT AND PEPPER, TO TASTE
2	PLUMS, HALVED AND PITTED
1	CUP STRAWBERRIES, HULLED AND HALVED
6	FIGS, HALVED
½	CUP CRÈME FRAÎCHE
	RED CURRANTS, FOR GARNISH

TROPICAL FRUIT SALAD
WITH MINT-INFUSED SUGAR

YIELD: 6 SERVINGS / **ACTIVE TIME:** 10 MINUTES / **TOTAL TIME:** 30 MINUTES

When you grind the mint and sugar with a mortar and pestle, the former's aromatic oils will transform the latter.

1. Using a mortar and pestle, work the mint into the sugar. Set the mixture aside.

2. Place the watermelon, mangoes, pineapple, kiwis, and red grapes in a salad bowl and toss to combine.

3. Add the mint-infused sugar and lime juice to the salad bowl and toss to coat. Let the salad macerate in the refrigerator for 15 minutes before serving.

INGREDIENTS:

2	TABLESPOONS FINELY CHOPPED FRESH MINT
¼	CUP SUGAR
3	CUPS DICED WATERMELON
2	CUPS DICED MANGOES
2	CUPS DICED PINEAPPLE
3	KIWIS, PEELED AND DICED
2	CUPS SEEDLESS RED GRAPES
1	TABLESPOON FRESH LIME JUICE

STRAWBERRY, ORANGE & BANANA SALAD

YIELD: 4 SERVINGS / **ACTIVE TIME:** 20 MINUTES / **TOTAL TIME:** 35 MINUTES

While any orange liqueur will work, Cointreau or Grand Marnier will provide the very best results.

1. Place the brown sugar and orange liqueur in a small bowl and stir to combine.

2. Place the bananas and lemon juice in a separate small bowl and stir to combine.

3. Place the bananas, strawberries, and oranges in a salad bowl and toss to combine.

4. Add the liqueur mixture, toss to coat, and let the salad macerate in the refrigerator for 15 minutes before serving.

INGREDIENTS:

- 2 TABLESPOONS BROWN SUGAR
- 2 TABLESPOONS ORANGE LIQUEUR
- 2 CUPS DICED BANANAS
- 2 TABLESPOONS FRESH LEMON JUICE
- 2 CUPS DICED STRAWBERRIES
- 2 CUPS CHOPPED ORANGES

STONE FRUIT SALAD WITH TAHINI & LABNEH

YIELD: 4 SERVINGS / **ACTIVE TIME:** 20 MINUTES / **TOTAL TIME:** 20 MINUTES

Rainier cherries, another stone fruit, are an addition worth considering here.

1. Place the tahini and Labneh in a small bowl and stir to combine, adding water as necessary to get the desired texture.

2. Place the peaches, nectarines, and apples in a salad bowl and toss to combine. Add the lemon juice and honey and toss to coat.

3. Top the salad with the Labneh mixture, garnish with sesame seeds and mint, and serve.

INGREDIENTS:

2   TABLESPOONS TAHINI PASTE

1   CUP LABNEH (SEE PAGE 653)

2   PEACHES, PITTED AND SLICED

2   NECTARINES, PITTED AND SLICED

2   APPLES, CORED AND SLICED

2   TABLESPOONS FRESH LEMON JUICE

2   TABLESPOONS HONEY

    SESAME SEEDS, FOR GARNISH

    FRESH MINT, FOR GARNISH

SPICY FRUIT SALAD

YIELD: 4 SERVINGS / **ACTIVE TIME:** 20 MINUTES / **TOTAL TIME:** 20 MINUTES

If you can stand the heat, add as much chili-garlic paste as you'd like—the salad improves the spicier it is.

1. Place the lime juice, agave nectar, and chili-garlic paste in a small bowl, season with salt, and stir to combine.

2. Place the bananas, apples, mangoes, and melon in a salad bowl and toss to combine. Add the dressing, toss to coat, and serve.

INGREDIENTS:

2   TABLESPOONS FRESH LIME JUICE

2   TABLESPOONS AGAVE NECTAR

1   TABLESPOON CHILI-GARLIC PASTE

    SALT, TO TASTE

2   BANANAS, SLICED THIN

3   CUPS DICED GREEN APPLES

3   CUPS DICED MANGOES

3   CUPS DICED MELON

AVOCADO & BERRY SALAD

YIELD: 4 SERVINGS / ACTIVE TIME: 20 MINUTES / TOTAL TIME: 20 MINUTES

If you're looking for another texture to incorporate here, consider chopping up some pistachios and topping each serving with some of them.

1. Place the avocados, grapes, berries, watermelon, and pineapple in a salad bowl and toss to combine. Add the lime juice and agave nectar and toss to coat.

2. Garnish with mint and serve.

INGREDIENTS:

	FLESH OF 2 AVOCADOS, DICED
1	CUP HALVED RED GRAPES
1	CUP HALVED GREEN GRAPES
1	CUP BLUEBERRIES
1	CUP RASPBERRIES
1½	CUPS HULLED AND HALVED STRAWBERRIES
1	CUP DICED WATERMELON
1	CUP DICED PINEAPPLE
2	TABLESPOONS FRESH LIME JUICE
2	TABLESPOONS AGAVE NECTAR
	FRESH MINT, FINELY CHOPPED, FOR GARNISH

PEACH, RASPBERRY & TOMATO SALAD

YIELD: 4 SERVINGS / **ACTIVE TIME:** 10 MINUTES / **TOTAL TIME:** 20 MINUTES

The perfect salad to celebrate the height of summer, that brief window when the main players here are all in season.

1. Place 1 cup of raspberries and the lemon juice in a small bowl and mash to combine. Let the mixture macerate for 10 minutes.

2. Place the remaining raspberries, the tomatoes, and peaches in a salad bowl and toss to combine. Add the mashed raspberry mixture and toss to coat.

3. Divide the salad among the serving plates and top each portion with some of the burrata. Garnish with mint and thyme and serve.

INGREDIENTS:

3 CUPS RASPBERRIES

2 TABLESPOONS FRESH LEMON JUICE

1 PLUM TOMATO, SLICED THIN

1 CUP CHERRY TOMATOES, QUARTERED

2 PEACHES, PITTED AND SLICED THIN

4 OZ. BURRATA CHEESE

FRESH MINT, FOR GARNISH

FRESH THYME, FOR GARNISH

DRESSINGS, SAUCES & CONDIMENTS

There is a reason that each and every time you order a salad at a restaurant, the server immediately responds with "And what dressing would you like with that?" Salads, for all of their wonderful qualities, are rarely complete without an accompaniment, something that can either counter the flavors present, or amplify them.

While many of the recipes here are already called out in the previous chapters, many more are included for you to experiment with, making it easy to ensure that each and every salad you prepare is tailored perfectly to both the ingredients present and your own palate.

CILANTRO PESTO

YIELD: 1½ CUPS / ACTIVE TIME: 5 MINUTES / TOTAL TIME: 5 MINUTES

1. Place all of the ingredients in a food processor and blitz until emulsified and smooth. Use immediately or store in the refrigerator.

INGREDIENTS:

1   CUP FRESH CILANTRO

1   GARLIC CLOVE

¼   CUP ROASTED AND SHELLED SUNFLOWER SEEDS

¼   CUP SHREDDED QUESO ENCHILADO

¼   CUP EXTRA-VIRGIN OLIVE OIL

1   TEASPOON FRESH LEMON JUICE

    SALT AND PEPPER, TO TASTE

BALSAMIC GLAZE

YIELD: ½ CUP / **ACTIVE TIME:** 10 MINUTES / **TOTAL TIME:** 25 MINUTES

1. Place the vinegar and brown sugar in a small saucepan and bring the mixture to a boil.

2. Reduce the heat to medium-low and simmer for 8 to 10 minutes, stirring frequently, until the mixture has thickened.

3. Remove the pan from heat and let the glaze cool for 15 minutes before using.

INGREDIENTS:

1   CUP BALSAMIC VINEGAR

¼   CUP BROWN SUGAR

PASSION FRUIT EMULSION

YIELD: 1 CUP / ACTIVE TIME: 5 MINUTES / TOTAL TIME: 5 MINUTES

1. Place the shallot and passion fruit puree in a blender and puree on medium until the mixture is smooth.

2. Reduce the speed to low and slowly drizzle in the canola oil until it has emulsified. Use immediately or store in the refrigerator.

INGREDIENTS:

1	SHALLOT, CHOPPED
1	CUP PASSION FRUIT PUREE
1	CUP CANOLA OIL

TAMARIND DRESSING

YIELD: 1½ CUPS / ACTIVE TIME: 5 MINUTES / TOTAL TIME: 5 MINUTES

1. Place all of the ingredients, except for the sesame oil, in a blender and puree until smooth.

2. With the blender running on low, slowly drizzle in the sesame oil until it has emulsified. Use as desired.

INGREDIENTS:

3	TABLESPOONS RICE VINEGAR
¼	CUP PURE MAPLE SYRUP
2	TABLESPOONS TAMARIND CONCENTRATE
3	GARLIC CLOVES, GRATED
6	TABLESPOONS FRESH LIME JUICE
1	TABLESPOON FINE SEA SALT
¾	CUP SESAME OIL

SEA BUCKTHORN DRESSING

YIELD: 1 CUP / **ACTIVE TIME:** 15 MINUTES / **TOTAL TIME:** 30 MINUTES

1. Place the berries, honey, oranges, ginger, and water in a small saucepan, bring to a simmer, and cover the pan. Cook until the berries start to pop, 5 to 10 minutes.

2. Strain the mixture into a clean saucepan through a fine-mesh sieve, pressing down on the solids to extract as much liquid as possible.

3. Add the lemon juice and sugar to the saucepan and warm the mixture over medium-low heat, stirring to dissolve the sugar. When the sugar has dissolved, pour the dressing into a container and let it cool before using.

INGREDIENTS:

- ½ LB. SEA BUCKTHORN BERRIES
- 2 TEASPOONS HONEY
- ZEST OF 2 ORANGES
- 1-INCH PIECE OF FRESH GINGER, PEELED AND GRATED
- ¼ CUP WATER
- 2 TABLESPOONS FRESH LEMON JUICE
- 2 TABLESPOONS DEMERARA SUGAR

SALSA VERDE, MEDITERRANEAN STYLE

YIELD: 3 CUPS / **ACTIVE TIME:** 20 MINUTES / **TOTAL TIME:** 45 MINUTES

1. Pluck the leaves from the basil and the leaves and tender stems from the cilantro and parsley. You should have about 2 cups of each herb.

2. Place the basil, cilantro, and parsley in a food processor and pulse until finely chopped. Add the olive oil, vinegar, red pepper flakes, and salt and pulse until the mixture is a thick, slightly textured sauce. Use immediately or store in the refrigerator until needed.

INGREDIENTS:

- 1 BUNCH OF FRESH BASIL
- 1 BUNCH OF FRESH CILANTRO
- 1 BUNCH OF FRESH PARSLEY
- 1¼ CUPS EXTRA-VIRGIN OLIVE OIL
- ½ CUP SHERRY OR RED WINE VINEGAR
- 1 TEASPOON RED PEPPER FLAKES
- 2½ TEASPOONS KOSHER SALT

Salsa Verde, Mediterranean Style, see page 517

RAYU

YIELD: ½ CUP / **ACTIVE TIME:** 15 MINUTES / **TOTAL TIME:** 1 HOUR

1. Place ¼ cup of sesame oil, the garlic, ginger, and scallions in a saucepan and cook over medium heat, stirring frequently, until the sesame oil starts to shimmer. Reduce the heat to medium-low and cook, stirring occasionally, for another 3 minutes. Remove the pan from heat and transfer the mixture to a heatproof bowl.

2. Add the togarashi and cayenne, stir to combine, and let the mixture cool to room temperature.

3. Stir in the remaining sesame oil and strain the rayu. Use immediately or store in the refrigerator.

INGREDIENTS:

½ CUP SESAME OIL

3 GARLIC CLOVES, MINCED

1 TABLESPOON MINCED FRESH GINGER

1 TABLESPOON MINCED SCALLION WHITES

1 TABLESPOON SHICHIMI TOGARASHI (SEE PAGE 666)

1½ TEASPOONS CAYENNE PEPPER

HARISSA SAUCE

YIELD: 1 CUP / **ACTIVE TIME:** 20 MINUTES / **TOTAL TIME:** 1 HOUR

1. Preheat the oven to 400°F. Place the garlic in a piece of aluminum foil, drizzle half of the olive oil over it, and seal the foil closed.

2. Place the garlic on a baking sheet with the bell peppers and place it in the oven. Roast until the garlic is very tender and the peppers are charred all over. Remove them from the oven and let them cool.

3. While the garlic and peppers are cooling, place the coriander seeds in a dry skillet and toast them over medium heat, shaking the pan frequently. Transfer the coriander seeds to a blender along with the remaining ingredients, including the remaining olive oil.

4. Squeeze the roasted garlic cloves into the blender. Remove the skin, seeds, and stems from the roasted peppers and place the flesh in the blender.

5. Puree until the harissa paste has the desired texture and use immediately or store it in the refrigerator.

INGREDIENTS:

1	HEAD OF GARLIC, HALVED AT THE EQUATOR
2	TABLESPOONS EXTRA-VIRGIN OLIVE OIL
2	BELL PEPPERS
2	TABLESPOONS CORIANDER SEEDS
6	CHILES DE ÁRBOL
3	PASILLA CHILE PEPPERS
2	SHALLOTS, HALVED
2	TEASPOONS KOSHER SALT

RED ONION VINAIGRETTE

YIELD: ¾ CUP / **ACTIVE TIME:** 5 MINUTES / **TOTAL TIME:** 15 MINUTES

1. Place the red onion in a bowl, cover it with water, and let it soak for 5 to 7 minutes to diminish its sharp bite.

2. Drain the onion, chop it, and place it in a container. Add the remaining ingredients and whisk to combine. Use immediately or store in the refrigerator.

INGREDIENTS:

1	RED ONION, SLICED THIN
½	CUP PLUS 2 TEASPOONS EXTRA-VIRGIN OLIVE OIL
1	GARLIC CLOVE, MINCED
½	TEASPOON FRESH THYME
¼	CUP APPLE CIDER VINEGAR
2	TABLESPOONS WHITE BALSAMIC VINEGAR
4	TEASPOONS HONEY
1	TEASPOON KOSHER SALT
1	TEASPOON BLACK PEPPER

HONEY VINAIGRETTE

YIELD: ¾ CUP / **ACTIVE TIME:** 5 MINUTES / **TOTAL TIME:** 5 MINUTES

1. Place all of the ingredients, except for the olive oil, in a blender and puree until smooth.

2. With the blender running on low, slowly drizzle in the olive oil until it has emulsified. Use immediately or store in the refrigerator.

INGREDIENTS:

1	TEASPOON KOSHER SALT
¼	CUP SHERRY VINEGAR
1	TABLESPOON HONEY
1	TEASPOON FRESH THYME
6	TABLESPOONS EXTRA-VIRGIN OLIVE OIL

MINT VINAIGRETTE

YIELD: ¾ CUP / ACTIVE TIME: 5 MINUTES / TOTAL TIME: 5 MINUTES

1. Place all of the ingredients, except for the olive oil, in a food processor and blitz until smooth.

2. With the food processor running on low, add the olive oil in a slow stream until it has emulsified. Use immediately or store in the refrigerator.

INGREDIENTS:

3	TABLESPOONS CHOPPED FRESH MINT
3	TABLESPOONS APPLE CIDER VINEGAR
1	TABLESPOON HONEY
2	TEASPOONS DICED SHALLOT
1	TEASPOON KOSHER SALT
¼	TEASPOON BLACK PEPPER
¼	CUP EXTRA-VIRGIN OLIVE OIL

SPICY GREEN CHUTNEY

YIELD: 1¼ CUPS / ACTIVE TIME: 5 MINUTES / TOTAL TIME: 5 MINUTES

1. Place all of the ingredients in a blender and puree until smooth. Use immediately or store in the refrigerator.

INGREDIENTS:

½	CUP FRESH CILANTRO
½	CUP FRESH MINT
1	TABLESPOON PEANUTS
½	TEASPOON CUMIN
½	TEASPOON KASHMIRI CHILI POWDER
¼	TEASPOON KOSHER SALT
	PINCH OF SUGAR
1	GARLIC CLOVE, GRATED
	JUICE OF ½ LEMON

Spicy Green Chutney, see page 525

RED CURRANT DRESSING

1. Place all of the ingredients, except for the olive oil, in a food processor and blitz until smooth.

2. With the food processor running on low, add the olive oil in a slow stream until it has emulsified. Use immediately or store in the refrigerator.

INGREDIENTS:

3½	OZ. RED CURRANTS
¼	CUP RED WINE VINEGAR
¼	CUP HONEY
¼	CUP YOGURT
1	TABLESPOON KOSHER SALT
½	CUP EXTRA-VIRGIN OLIVE OIL

TAHINI & LEMON DRESSING

YIELD: 1 CUP / **ACTIVE TIME:** 5 MINUTES / **TOTAL TIME:** 5 MINUTES

1. Place the yogurt, garlic, tahini, lemon juice, and cumin in a small bowl and whisk to combine.

2. Season the dressing with salt and pepper, add the sesame seeds and olive oil, and whisk to combine. Use immediately or store in the refrigerator.

INGREDIENTS:

¾ CUP FULL-FAT GREEK YOGURT

1 GARLIC CLOVE, MINCED

2 TABLESPOONS TAHINI PASTE

JUICE OF 1 LEMON

½ TEASPOON CUMIN

SALT AND PEPPER, TO TASTE

1 TABLESPOON BLACK SESAME SEEDS

1 TABLESPOON EXTRA-VIRGIN OLIVE OIL

BALSAMIC RANCH DRESSING

YIELD: 2 CUPS / **ACTIVE TIME:** 5 MINUTES / **TOTAL TIME:** 5 MINUTES

1. Place all of the ingredients in a bowl and whisk until well combined.

2. Taste, adjust the seasoning as necessary, and use immediately or store in the refrigerator.

INGREDIENTS:

½	CUP MAYONNAISE
½	CUP SOUR CREAM
½	CUP BUTTERMILK
3	TABLESPOONS BALSAMIC VINEGAR
¼	TEASPOON ONION POWDER
½	TEASPOON GARLIC POWDER
2	TEASPOONS CHOPPED FRESH PARSLEY

RED PLUM–INFUSED VINEGAR

YIELD: 2 CUPS / **ACTIVE TIME**: 15 MINUTES / **TOTAL TIME**: 2 HOURS AND 30 MINUTES

1. Place the ingredients in a small saucepan and cook the mixture over the lowest possible heat until the liquid has reduced by one-third, about 30 minutes.

2. Remove the pan from heat and let the mixture cool completely.

3. Strain the vinegar into a mason jar and use immediately or store in the refrigerator.

INGREDIENTS:

3	CUPS BLACK VINEGAR
8	DRIED RED PLUMS

CHILE & CURRY DRESSING

YIELD: 1½ CUPS / **ACTIVE TIME**: 5 MINUTES / **TOTAL TIME**: 5 MINUTES

1. Place all of the ingredients in a food processor, blitz until smooth, and use immediately or store in the refrigerator.

INGREDIENTS:

2	BIRD'S EYE CHILE PEPPERS, STEMMED AND SEEDED
½	CUP SOY SAUCE
½	CUP SAMBAL OELEK
	JUICE OF 3 LIMES
¼	CUP BROWN SUGAR
1	TABLESPOON GRATED FRESH GINGER
2	TABLESPOONS RED CURRY PASTE

OREGANO VINAIGRETTE

YIELD: 1 CUP / **ACTIVE TIME:** 5 MINUTES / **TOTAL TIME:** 5 MINUTES

1. Place all of the ingredients, except for the olive oil, in a food processor and blitz until smooth.

2. With the food processor running on low, slowly drizzle in the olive oil until it has emulsified. Use immediately or store in an airtight container.

INGREDIENTS

¼	CUP CHAMPAGNE VINEGAR
½	SHALLOT, CHOPPED
1	TEASPOON DIJON MUSTARD
2	TABLESPOONS HONEY
1	TEASPOON KOSHER SALT
¼	TEASPOON BLACK PEPPER
1	TABLESPOON CHOPPED FRESH OREGANO
¾	CUP EXTRA-VIRGIN OLIVE OIL

AVOCADO & LIME YOGURT DRESSING

YIELD: 1½ CUPS / **ACTIVE TIME:** 5 MINUTES / **TOTAL TIME:** 5 MINUTES

1. Place all of the ingredients in a food processor, blitz until smooth, and use immediately or store in the refrigerator.

INGREDIENTS:

	FLESH OF 1 AVOCADO
1	CUP FULL-FAT GREEK YOGURT
	ZEST AND JUICE OF 1 LIME
	PINCH OF CAYENNE PEPPER
1	TABLESPOON FINELY CHOPPED FRESH CILANTRO

Avocado & Lime Yogurt Dressing, see page 535

GREEN GODDESS DRESSING

YIELD: 1½ CUPS / **ACTIVE TIME:** 5 MINUTES / **TOTAL TIME:** 5 MINUTES

1. Place all of the ingredients in a food processor, blitz until smooth, and use immediately or store in the refrigerator.

INGREDIENTS:

½   CUP MAYONNAISE

⅔   CUP BUTTERMILK

1   TABLESPOON FRESH
    LEMON JUICE

2   TABLESPOONS FINELY
    CHOPPED CELERY LEAVES

2   TABLESPOONS FINELY
    CHOPPED FRESH PARSLEY

2   TABLESPOONS FINELY
    CHOPPED FRESH
    TARRAGON

2   TABLESPOONS SLICED
    FRESH CHIVES

2   TEASPOONS KOSHER SALT

1   TEASPOON BLACK PEPPER

SPICY GARLIC OIL

YIELD: ½ CUP / **ACTIVE TIME:** 10 MINUTES / **TOTAL TIME:** 1 HOUR

1. Place the olive oil in a saucepan and warm it over low heat for 2 minutes.

2. Add the garlic and red pepper flakes and cook for 2 minutes.

3. Remove the pan from heat and let the mixture cool completely.

4. Season the infused oil with soy sauce, stir to combine, and use immediately or store in an airtight container.

INGREDIENTS:

½ CUP EXTRA-VIRGIN OLIVE OIL

6 GARLIC CLOVES, MINCED

2 TEASPOONS RED PEPPER FLAKES

SOY SAUCE, TO TASTE

WHITE WINE VINAIGRETTE

YIELD: 1 CUP / **ACTIVE TIME:** 5 MINUTES / **TOTAL TIME:** 5 MINUTES

1. Place all of the ingredients, except for the olive oil, in a food processor and blitz until smooth.

2. With the food processor running, slowly drizzle in the olive oil until it has emulsified. Use immediately or store in an airtight container.

INGREDIENTS:

¼ CUP WHITE WINE VINEGAR

4 TEASPOONS WHOLE-GRAIN MUSTARD

2 TABLESPOONS HONEY

2 TABLESPOONS FINELY CHOPPED FRESH CHIVES

4 TEASPOONS FRESH THYME

4 TEASPOONS KOSHER SALT

½ CUP EXTRA-VIRGIN OLIVE OIL

PARSLEY & LEMON OIL

YIELD: 1¼ CUPS / **ACTIVE TIME:** 15 MINUTES / **TOTAL TIME:** 1 HOUR AND 15 MINUTES

1. Place the olive oil in a saucepan and warm it over medium heat.

2. Add the shallot and cook until it has softened, about 5 minutes.

3. Remove the pan from heat, stir in the lemon zest, and let the mixture steep for 1 hour.

4. Stir in the lemon juice and parsley and use immediately or store in the refrigerator.

INGREDIENTS:

1	CUP EXTRA-VIRGIN OLIVE OIL
1	SHALLOT, MINCED
	ZEST AND JUICE OF 1 LEMON
2	TABLESPOONS FINELY CHOPPED FRESH PARSLEY

COCONUT & POPPY SEED DRESSING

YIELD: 1½ CUPS / **ACTIVE TIME:** 5 MINUTES / **TOTAL TIME:** 2 HOURS

1. Place all of the ingredients in a mixing bowl, stir to combine, and chill in the refrigerator for 2 hours.

2. Place the mixture in a blender and pulse until it is just combined. Use immediately or store in the refrigerator.

INGREDIENTS:

7	OZ. COCONUT MILK
1¾	OZ. GRATED FRESH GINGER
7	TABLESPOONS FRESH LEMON JUICE
¾	TEASPOONS KOSHER SALT
2½	TEASPOONS CASTER (SUPERFINE) SUGAR
1½	TABLESPOONS POPPY SEEDS

Coconut & Poppy Seed Dressing, see page 541

HORSERADISH OIL

YIELD: 1 CUP / **ACTIVE TIME:** 10 MINUTES / **TOTAL TIME:** 1 HOUR AND 15 MINUTES

1. Place the ingredients in a saucepan and warm the mixture over medium heat for 5 minutes.

2. Remove the pan from heat and let the mixture steep for 1 hour.

3. Strain the oil through a fine-mesh sieve and use immediately or store in an airtight container.

INGREDIENTS:

½   CUP PEELED AND GRATED FRESH HORSERADISH

     ZEST OF ½ LEMON

1   CUP EXTRA-VIRGIN OLIVE OIL

SICHUAN PEPPERCORN & CHILE OIL

YIELD: 1¾ CUPS / **ACTIVE TIME:** 5 MINUTES / **TOTAL TIME:** 5 MINUTES

1. Place the canola oil in a saucepan and warm it over low heat for 2 minutes.

2. Add the star anise, cinnamon stick, bay leaves, and peppercorns and reduce the heat to the lowest-possible setting. Cook for 20 minutes, stirring occasionally.

3. Place the red pepper flakes in a small bowl and strain the warm oil over the flakes. Let the oil cool completely.

4. Stir in the salt and use immediately or store in an airtight container.

INGREDIENTS:

1½   CUPS CANOLA OIL

5   STAR ANISE PODS

1   CINNAMON STICK

2   BAY LEAVES

3   TABLESPOONS SICHUAN PEPPERCORNS

⅓   CUP RED PEPPER FLAKES

1   TEASPOON KOSHER SALT

LEEK OIL

YIELD: 1 CUP / ACTIVE TIME: 15 MINUTES / TOTAL TIME: 1 HOUR AND 15 MINUTES

1. Bring water to a boil in a small saucepan. Prepare an ice bath.

2. Add the leeks and spinach to the pan and cook for 1 minute. Drain the mixture, plunge it into the ice bath until it is cool, and then drain the mixture again.

3. Place the mixture in a food processor, add the olive oil, and blitz until smooth, about 3 minutes.

4. Strain the oil through a fine-mesh sieve and use immediately or store in an airtight container.

INGREDIENTS:

1	CUP CHOPPED LEEKS, GREEN PARTS ONLY
1	CUP SPINACH
1	CUP EXTRA-VIRGIN OLIVE OIL

PRESERVED LEMON VINAIGRETTE

YIELD: 1¼ CUPS / ACTIVE TIME: 5 MINUTES / TOTAL TIME: 1 HOUR

1. Place all of the ingredients in a bowl, whisk to combine, and let the mixture steep for 1 hour before serving.

INGREDIENTS:

2	TABLESPOONS MINCED PRESERVED LEMON
¾	CUP EXTRA-VIRGIN OLIVE OIL
¼	CUP FRESH LEMON JUICE
½	TEASPOON RED PEPPER FLAKES
2	TEASPOONS FRESH THYME
	PINCH OF KOSHER SALT

Preserved Lemon Vinaigrette, see page 545

CHORIZO OIL

YIELD: ¼ CUP / **ACTIVE TIME:** 10 MINUTES / **TOTAL TIME:** 1 HOUR

1. Place the olive oil in a saucepan and warm it over medium heat.

2. Add the chorizo and garlic and cook, stirring continually, for 2 minutes.

3. Remove the pan from heat and let the mixture cool completely.

4. Strain the oil through a fine-mesh sieve and use immediately or store in an airtight container.

INGREDIENTS:

¼   CUP EXTRA-VIRGIN OLIVE OIL

2   TABLESPOONS CHOPPED CHORIZO

1   GARLIC CLOVE, CHOPPED

BASIL OIL

YIELD: 1 CUP / **ACTIVE TIME:** 15 MINUTES / **TOTAL TIME:** 20 MINUTES

1. Bring water to a boil in a small saucepan. Prepare an ice bath.

2. Add the basil and spinach to the pan and cook for 1 minute. Drain the mixture, plunge it into the ice bath until it is cool, and let it drain again.

3. Place the mixture in a linen towel and wring the towel to remove as much water from it as possible.

4. Place the mixture in a food processor. With the food processor running on low, slowly drizzle in the olive oil and blitz until it has emulsified.

5. Strain the oil through a fine-mesh sieve and use immediately or store in an airtight container.

INGREDIENTS:

1   CUP FRESH BASIL LEAVES

1   CUP BABY SPINACH

1   CUP EXTRA-VIRGIN OLIVE OIL

CHIVE & SHALLOT OIL

YIELD: ⅔ CUP / ACTIVE TIME: 5 MINUTES / TOTAL TIME: 15 MINUTES

1. Place the olive oil in a saucepan and warm it over medium heat.

2. Add the shallot and cook, stirring occasionally, until it has softened, about 5 minutes.

3. Remove the pan from heat, stir in the chives, and use immediately or store in an airtight container.

INGREDIENTS:

- ½   CUP EXTRA-VIRGIN OLIVE OIL
- 1   SHALLOT, MINCED
- 1   TABLESPOON FINELY CHOPPED FRESH CHIVES

MUSTARD VINAIGRETTE

YIELD: 1 CUP / ACTIVE TIME: 5 MINUTES / TOTAL TIME: 15 MINUTES

1. Place the vinegar, mustard, garlic, and olive oil in a large mixing bowl and whisk until well combined. Let the vinaigrette rest for 10 minutes.

2. Add the lemon zest, whisk to incorporate, and use as desired.

INGREDIENTS:

- 6   TABLESPOONS RED WINE VINEGAR
- ¼   CUP DIJON MUSTARD
- 2   GARLIC CLOVES, FINELY GRATED
- ¼   CUP EXTRA-VIRGIN OLIVE OIL, PLUS MORE TO TASTE

     ZEST OF 1 LEMON

Mustard Vinaigrette, see page 549

HARISSA VINAIGRETTE

YIELD: 1½ CUPS / **ACTIVE TIME:** 5 MINUTES / **TOTAL TIME:** 5 MINUTES

1. Place all of the ingredients, except for the olive oil, in a food processor and blitz until smooth.

2. With the food processor running on low, slowly drizzle in the olive oil until it has emulsified. Use immediately or store in the refrigerator.

INGREDIENTS:

3	TABLESPOONS HARISSA PASTE
1	TEASPOON RAS EL HANOUT
⅓	CUP RICE VINEGAR
1	TABLESPOON FRESH LEMON JUICE
3	TABLESPOONS HONEY
2	GARLIC CLOVES
2	TEASPOONS GRATED FRESH GINGER
	SALT, TO TASTE
1	CUP EXTRA-VIRGIN OLIVE OIL

PAPRIKA OIL

YIELD: 2 CUPS / **ACTIVE TIME:** 5 MINUTES / **TOTAL TIME:** 5 MINUTES

1. Place the paprika and avocado oil in a mason jar and shake until thoroughly combined.

2. Store the oil in a dark, dry place and always shake before using.

INGREDIENTS:

½	CUP SWEET PAPRIKA
2	CUPS AVOCADO OIL

THAI CHILE DRESSING

YIELD: 1½ CUPS / ACTIVE TIME: 5 MINUTES / TOTAL TIME: 5 MINUTES

1. Place all of the ingredients, except for the sesame oil, in a food processor and blitz until smooth.

2. With the food processor running on low, slowly drizzle in the sesame oil until it has emulsified. Use immediately or store in the refrigerator.

INGREDIENTS:

2	RED BIRD'S EYE CHILE PEPPERS
½	CUP SOY SAUCE
½	CUP SAMBAL OELEK
	JUICE OF 2 LIMES
¼	CUP BROWN SUGAR
1	TABLESPOON MINCED FRESH GINGER
1	TABLESPOON FISH SAUCE
½	CUP SESAME OIL

CREAMY CILANTRO DRESSING

YIELD: ½ CUP / ACTIVE TIME: 5 MINUTES / TOTAL TIME: 5 MINUTES

1. Place all of the ingredients in a blender and puree until smooth. Use immediately or store in the refrigerator.

INGREDIENTS:

	FLESH OF 1 AVOCADO
1	GARLIC CLOVE
¼	CUP CHOPPED FRESH CILANTRO
	JUICE OF 1 LIME
	SPLASH OF WATER
2	TABLESPOONS CHOPPED ONION
	SALT, TO TASTE
½	JALAPEÑO CHILE PEPPER, CHOPPED

Creamy Cilantro Dressing, see page 553

MAPLE VINAIGRETTE

YIELD: 1½ CUPS / ACTIVE TIME: 5 MINUTES / TOTAL TIME: 5 MINUTES

1. Place all of the ingredients, except for the olive oil, in a food processor and blitz to combine.

2. With the food processor running on low, slowly drizzle in the olive oil until it has emulsified. Taste, adjust the seasoning as necessary, and use immediately or store in the refrigerator.

INGREDIENTS:

¼	CUP APPLE CIDER VINEGAR
¼	CUP MAPLE SYRUP
½	TEASPOON ORANGE ZEST
1	TEASPOON DIJON MUSTARD
1½	TEASPOONS KOSHER SALT
½	TEASPOON BLACK PEPPER
¾	CUP EXTRA-VIRGIN OLIVE OIL

RED WINE & CHILE DRESSING

YIELD: 1 CUP / ACTIVE TIME: 5 MINUTES / TOTAL TIME: 5 MINUTES

1. Place all of the ingredients, except for the olive oil, in a food processor and blitz until smooth.

2. With the food processor running on low, slowly drizzle in the olive oil until it has emulsified. Use immediately or store in the refrigerator.

INGREDIENTS:

½	TEASPOON CHILI POWDER
½	TEASPOON CHIPOTLE CHILE POWDER
½	TEASPOON BLACK PEPPER
½	TEASPOON ONION POWDER
½	TEASPOON GARLIC POWDER
½	TEASPOON PAPRIKA
1	TABLESPOON KOSHER SALT
2	SCALLIONS, SLICED THIN
2	FRESNO CHILE PEPPERS, STEMMED, SEEDED, AND SLICED
3	TABLESPOONS SUGAR
¼	CUP RED WINE VINEGAR
½	CUP EXTRA-VIRGIN OLIVE OIL

BENIHANA'S GINGER DRESSING

1. Place all of the ingredients in a food processor, blitz until smooth, and use immediately or store in the refrigerator.

INGREDIENTS:

¼	CUP CHOPPED WHITE ONION
¼	CUP PEANUT OIL
1	TABLESPOON RICE VINEGAR
1	TABLESPOON MINCED FRESH GINGER
1	TABLESPOON MINCED CELERY
1	TABLESPOON SOY SAUCE
1	TEASPOON TOMATO PASTE
1½	TEASPOONS SUGAR
1	TEASPOON FRESH LEMON JUICE
½	TEASPOON KOSHER SALT
	BLACK PEPPER, TO TASTE

HONEY MUSTARD VINAIGRETTE

1. Place all of the ingredients, except for the olive oil, in a small mixing bowl and whisk to combine.

2. While whisking continually, slowly drizzle in the olive oil until it has emulsified. Use immediately or store in an airtight container.

INGREDIENTS:

¼	CUP HONEY
2	TABLESPOONS WHOLE-GRAIN MUSTARD
3	TABLESPOONS APPLE CIDER VINEGAR
1	TEASPOON KOSHER SALT
½	TEASPOON BLACK PEPPER
⅓	CUP EXTRA-VIRGIN OLIVE OIL

Honey Mustard Vinaigrette *see page 557*

RED WINE & MAPLE VINAIGRETTE

YIELD: ¾ CUP / **ACTIVE TIME:** 5 MINUTES / **TOTAL TIME:** 5 MINUTES

1. Place all of the ingredients, except for the olive oil, in a food processor and blitz until smooth.

2. With the food processor running, add the olive oil in a slow stream until it has emulsified. Use immediately or store in the refrigerator.

INGREDIENTS:

2   TABLESPOONS RED WINE VINEGAR

1   TEASPOON DIJON MUSTARD

1   TEASPOON MAPLE SYRUP

    SALT AND PEPPER, TO TASTE

½   CUP EXTRA-VIRGIN OLIVE OIL

GINGER & LEMON DRESSING

YIELD: 1 CUP / **ACTIVE TIME:** 5 MINUTES / **TOTAL TIME:** 5 MINUTES

1. Place all of the ingredients, except for the oils, in a food processor and blitz to combine.

2. With the food processor running, add the oils in a slow stream until they have emulsified. Use immediately or store in the refrigerator.

INGREDIENTS:

    ZEST AND JUICE OF 1 LEMON

    2-INCH PIECE OF FRESH GINGER, PEELED AND GRATED

¼   CUP SOY SAUCE

¼   CUP RICE VINEGAR

1½ TABLESPOONS HONEY

½   TEASPOON THAI SEASONING BLEND

3   TABLESPOONS EXTRA-VIRGIN OLIVE OIL

2   TEASPOONS TOASTED SESAME OIL

BLOOD ORANGE VINAIGRETTE

YIELD: 1½ CUPS / **ACTIVE TIME:** 5 MINUTES / **TOTAL TIME:** 5 MINUTES

1. Place all of the ingredients, except for the olive oil, in a food processor and blitz until smooth.

2. With the food processor running on low, slowly drizzle in the olive oil until it has emulsified. Use immediately or store in the refrigerator.

INGREDIENTS:

½   CUP FRESH BLOOD ORANGE JUICE (FROM ABOUT 2 BLOOD ORANGES)

½   TEASPOON KOSHER SALT

¼   TEASPOON BLACK PEPPER

1½   TABLESPOONS APPLE CIDER VINEGAR

1   TABLESPOON HONEY

1   CUP EXTRA-VIRGIN OLIVE OIL

APPLE CIDER VINAIGRETTE

YIELD: ¾ CUP / **ACTIVE TIME:** 5 MINUTES / **TOTAL TIME:** 5 MINUTES

1. Place all of the ingredients, except for the olive oil, in a food processor and blitz until smooth.

2. With the food processor running on low, slowly drizzle in the olive oil until it has emulsified. Use immediately or store in an airtight container.

INGREDIENTS:

3   TABLESPOONS APPLE CIDER VINEGAR

½   TEASPOON KOSHER SALT

½   TEASPOON BLACK PEPPER

1   TEASPOON HONEY

½   CUP EXTRA-VIRGIN OLIVE OIL

Apple Cider Vinaigrette, see page 561

SPICY ALMOND & TAHINI DRESSING

YIELD: 1 CUP / **ACTIVE TIME:** 5 MINUTES / **TOTAL TIME:** 5 MINUTES

1. Place all of the ingredients in a food processor and blitz until smooth. Use immediately or store in the refrigerator.

INGREDIENTS:

2	TABLESPOONS ALMOND BUTTER
½	CUP TAHINI PASTE
¼	CUP SRIRACHA
2	TABLESPOONS MAPLE SYRUP
2	TEASPOONS CURRY POWDER
½	TEASPOON KOSHER SALT
2	TABLESPOONS WATER
	JUICE OF 1 LEMON

GOOSEBERRY VINAIGRETTE

YIELD: 1½ CUPS / **ACTIVE TIME:** 5 MINUTES / **TOTAL TIME:** 5 MINUTES

1. Place all of the ingredients, except for the olive oil, in a food processor and blitz until smooth.

2. With the food processor running on low, slowly drizzle in the olive oil until it has emulsified. Use immediately or store in the refrigerator.

INGREDIENTS:

3½	OZ. GOOSEBERRIES, RINSED WELL
¼	CUP RED WINE VINEGAR
¼	CUP HONEY
1	TABLESPOON KOSHER SALT
½	CUP EXTRA-VIRGIN OLIVE OIL

WHITE BALSAMIC VINAIGRETTE

YIELD: 1½ CUPS / **ACTIVE TIME:** 5 MINUTES / **TOTAL TIME:** 5 MINUTES

1. Place all of the ingredients, except for the olive oil, in a food processor and blitz to combine.

2. With the food processor running on low, slowly drizzle in the olive oil until it has emulsified. Use immediately or store in the refrigerator.

INGREDIENTS

- ½ CUP WHITE BALSAMIC VINEGAR
- 2 TABLESPOONS MINCED SHALLOT
- ¼ CUP SLICED SCALLIONS
- 2 TABLESPOONS CHOPPED FRESH PARSLEY
- 2 TEASPOONS KOSHER SALT
- 1 TEASPOON BLACK PEPPER
- ¼ CUP EXTRA-VIRGIN OLIVE OIL

TAHINI DRESSING

YIELD: ¾ CUP / **ACTIVE TIME:** 5 MINUTES / **TOTAL TIME:** 5 MINUTES

1. Place all of the ingredients, except for the water, in a bowl and whisk to combine.

2. Incorporate water 1 tablespoon at a time until the dressing has the desired consistency. Use immediately or store in the refrigerator.

INGREDIENTS:

- ½ CUP TAHINI PASTE
- 2 GARLIC CLOVES, CRUSHED
- ¼ CUP EXTRA-VIRGIN OLIVE OIL
- 2 TEASPOONS HONEY
- JUICE OF 2 LEMONS
- SALT AND PEPPER, TO TASTE
- ICE WATER, AS NEEDED

Tahini Dressing, see page 565

BASIL & CILANTRO VINAIGRETTE

YIELD: 1½ CUPS / **ACTIVE TIME:** 5 MINUTES / **TOTAL TIME:** 5 MINUTES

1. Place all of the ingredients, except for the olive oil, in a food processor and blitz until smooth.

2. With the food processor running on low, slowly drizzle in the olive oil until it has emulsified. Use immediately or store in the refrigerator.

INGREDIENTS:

½   CUP CHOPPED FRESH CILANTRO

½   CUP CHOPPED FRESH BASIL

2   TABLESPOONS CHOPPED FRESH PARSLEY

1   GARLIC CLOVE, MINCED

2   TABLESPOONS MINCED JALAPEÑO PEPPER

2   TABLESPOONS FRESH LIME JUICE

1   TEASPOON BLACK PEPPER

1   TEASPOON KOSHER SALT

⅓   CUP EXTRA-VIRGIN OLIVE OIL

MISO DRESSING

1. Place all of the ingredients in a bowl, whisk to combine, and use immediately or store in the refrigerator.

INGREDIENTS:

¼	CUP WHITE MISO
¼	CUP RICE VINEGAR
4	TEASPOONS SESAME OIL
4	TEASPOONS MINCED FRESH GINGER
4	TEASPOON SOY SAUCE
¾	CUP PEANUT OIL
¼	CUP SESAME SEEDS
4	TEASPOONS MAPLE SYRUP

CILANTRO OIL

YIELD: 1 CUP / ACTIVE TIME: 5 MINUTES / TOTAL TIME: 5 MINUTES

1. Place all of the ingredients, except for the olive oil, in a food processor and blitz to combine.

2. With the food processor running on low, slowly drizzle in the olive oil until it has emulsified. Use immediately or store in the refrigerator.

INGREDIENTS:

2   BUNCHES OF FRESH CILANTRO

2   GARLIC CLOVES, MINCED

     JUICE OF 1 LIME

½   CUP EXTRA-VIRGIN OLIVE OIL

MAPLE & MUSTARD VINAIGRETTE

YIELD: 1 CUP / ACTIVE TIME: 5 MINUTES / TOTAL TIME: 5 MINUTES

1. Place all of the ingredients, except for the olive oil, in a food processor and blitz to combine.

2. With the food processor running on low, slowly drizzle in the olive oil until it has emulsified. Use immediately or store in the refrigerator.

INGREDIENTS:

2   TABLESPOONS DIJON MUSTARD

2   TABLESPOONS MAPLE SYRUP

¼   CUP APPLE CIDER VINEGAR

     SALT AND PEPPER, TO TASTE

½   CUP EXTRA-VIRGIN OLIVE OIL

CHILE & CORIANDER OIL

YIELD: ¾ CUP / **ACTIVE TIME:** 5 MINUTES / **TOTAL TIME:** 5 MINUTES

1. Place the chile peppers in a small saucepan and toast them over medium-high heat until lightly charred, about 3 minutes, shaking the pan occasionally. Remove the chiles from the pan and set them aside.

2. Add the olive oil to the saucepan and warm it over medium heat. Stir in the garlic clove and coriander and cook for 4 minutes.

3. Return the chiles to the pan and cook for another 4 minutes. Remove the pan from heat and let the oil cool.

4. Strain before using or storing in an airtight container.

INGREDIENTS:

- 2 DRIED CHILE PEPPERS, STEMMED AND SEEDED
- ¾ CUP EXTRA-VIRGIN OLIVE OIL
- 1 GARLIC CLOVE, CRUSHED
- 1 TEASPOON CORIANDER SEEDS

BALSAMIC VINAIGRETTE

YIELD: 1½ CUPS / **ACTIVE TIME:** 5 MINUTES / **TOTAL TIME:** 5 MINUTES

1. Place all of the ingredients, except for the olive oil, in a food processor and blitz to combine.

2. With the food processor running on low, slowly drizzle in the olive oil until it has emulsified. Use immediately or store in the refrigerator.

INGREDIENTS:

- ½ CUP BALSAMIC VINEGAR
- 2 TABLESPOONS MINCED SHALLOT
- ¼ CUP SLICED SCALLIONS
- 2 TABLESPOONS CHOPPED FRESH PARSLEY
- 2 TEASPOONS KOSHER SALT
- 1 TEASPOON BLACK PEPPER
- ¼ CUP EXTRA-VIRGIN OLIVE OIL

Balsamic Vinaigrette, see page 573

BAY LEAF OIL

YIELD: ½ CUP / **ACTIVE TIME:** 20 MINUTES / **TOTAL TIME:** 24 HOURS

1. Place the bay leaves and olive oil in a food processor and blitz until smooth, about 5 minutes.

2. Strain the oil into a bowl through a coffee filter and season with salt.

3. Prepare an ice bath and place the bowl containing the oil in it. Transfer the oil to the refrigerator and let it sit overnight.

4. Pour the mixture through a cheesecloth-lined sieve and let it sit until the oil is free of any debris. Use immediately or store in the refrigerator.

INGREDIENTS:

1	OZ. BAY LEAVES
10	TABLESPOONS EXTRA-VIRGIN OLIVE OIL
	SALT, TO TASTE

CUMIN & CILANTRO VINAIGRETTE

YIELD: 2 CUPS / **ACTIVE TIME:** 5 MINUTES / **TOTAL TIME:** 5 MINUTES

1. Place the cumin seeds in a dry skillet and toast them over medium heat until they are fragrant, 1 to 2 minutes, shaking the pan frequently.

2. Place the toasted cumin seeds and all of the remaining ingredients, except for the olive oil, in a food processor and blitz to combine.

3. With the food processor running on low, slowly drizzle in the olive oil until it has emulsified. Use immediately or store in the refrigerator.

INGREDIENTS:

¼	CUP CUMIN SEEDS
¼	CUP BROWN SUGAR
3	EGG YOLKS
⅓	CUP FRESH LIME JUICE
½	CUP WATER
2	CUPS FRESH CILANTRO, CHOPPED
	SALT AND PEPPER, TO TASTE
1½	CUPS EXTRA-VIRGIN OLIVE OIL

SHALLOT, HONEY & HERB VINAIGRETTE

YIELD: 1½ CUPS / ACTIVE TIME: 5 MINUTES / TOTAL TIME: 5 MINUTES

1. Place all of the ingredients, except for the olive oil, in a food processor and blitz to combine.

2. With the food processor running on low, slowly drizzle in the olive oil until it has emulsified. Use immediately or store in the refrigerator.

INGREDIENTS:

- 2 TABLESPOONS SLICED FRESH CHIVES
- 2 TEASPOONS FRESH THYME
- 2 TEASPOONS FINELY CHOPPED FRESH OREGANO
- 2 TABLESPOONS FINELY CHOPPED FRESH PARSLEY
- 6 TABLESPOONS APPLE CIDER VINEGAR
- 2 TABLESPOONS HONEY
- 4 TEASPOONS MINCED SHALLOT
- 2 TEASPOONS KOSHER SALT
- ½ TEASPOON BLACK PEPPER
- ½ CUP EXTRA-VIRGIN OLIVE OIL

MORITA OIL

YIELD: 2 CUPS / ACTIVE TIME: 5 MINUTES / TOTAL TIME: 24 HOURS

1. Place the chiles and olive oil in a food processor and blitz for 7 minutes. Let the mixture sit at room temperature for 24 hours.

2. Strain the oil before using or storing in an airtight container.

INGREDIENTS:

- 3½ OZ CHIPOTLE MORITA CHILE PEPPERS, STEMMED AND SEEDED
- 2 CUPS EXTRA-VIRGIN OLIVE OIL

Morita Oil, *see page 577*

COCONUT DRESSING

YIELD: 3 CUPS / ACTIVE TIME: 15 MINUTES / TOTAL TIME: 45 MINUTES

1. Place all of the ingredients in a mixing bowl, stir to combine, and chill in the refrigerator for 30 minutes.

2. Place the mixture in a blender and puree until emulsified, making sure the mixture does not heat up at all.

3. Strain the dressing through a fine-mesh sieve and use immediately or store in an airtight container.

INGREDIENTS:

1	(14 OZ.) CAN OF COCONUT MILK
3½	OZ. GRATED FRESH GINGER
14	TABLESPOONS FRESH LEMON JUICE
1½	TEASPOONS KOSHER SALT
5	TEASPOONS CASTER (SUPERFINE) SUGAR
1½	CUPS CHOPPED FRESH CILANTRO
1½	TABLESPOONS CRACKED CORIANDER SEEDS

YUZU VINAIGRETTE

YIELD: 1½ CUPS / ACTIVE TIME: 5 MINUTES / TOTAL TIME: 5 MINUTES

1. Place all of the ingredients, except for the canola oil, in a food processor and blitz to combine.

2. With the food processor running on low, slowly drizzle in the canola oil until it has emulsified. Use immediately or store in the refrigerator.

INGREDIENTS:

4	GARLIC CLOVES, MINCED
2	TABLESPOONS YUZU KOSHO
¼	CUP FRESH YUZU JUICE
	SALT AND PEPPER, TO TASTE
¾	CUP CANOLA OIL

POMEGRANATE & MINT VINAIGRETTE

YIELD: 1½ CUPS / **ACTIVE TIME:** 5 MINUTES / **TOTAL TIME:** 5 MINUTES

1. Place all of the ingredients, except for the olive oil, in a food processor and blitz to combine.

2. With the food processor running on low, slowly drizzle in the olive oil until it has emulsified. Use immediately or store in the refrigerator.

INGREDIENTS:

2	TABLESPOONS POMEGRANATE MOLASSES
1	CUP CHOPPED FRESH MINT
1	TEASPOON RAS EL HANOUT
	SALT AND PEPPER, TO TASTE
⅓	CUP EXTRA-VIRGIN OLIVE OIL

GARLIC & MUSTARD VINAIGRETTE

YIELD: 1¾ CUPS / **ACTIVE TIME:** 5 MINUTES / **TOTAL TIME:** 5 MINUTES

1. Place all of the ingredients, except for the olive oil, in a food processor and blitz to combine.

2. With the food processor running on low, slowly drizzle in the olive oil until it has emulsified. Use immediately or store in the refrigerator.

INGREDIENTS:

¾	CUP RED WINE VINEGAR
½	CUP DIJON MUSTARD
4	GARLIC CLOVES, GRATED
	SALT AND PEPPER, TO TASTE
½	CUP EXTRA-VIRGIN OLIVE OIL

Garlic & Mustard Vinaigrette,
see page 581

HARISSA & DIJON VINAIGRETTE

YIELD: 1½ CUPS / **ACTIVE TIME:** 5 MINUTES / **TOTAL TIME:** 5 MINUTES

1. Place all of the ingredients, except for the olive oil, in a food processor and blitz to combine.

2. With the food processor running on low, slowly drizzle in the olive oil until it has emulsified. Use immediately or store in the refrigerator.

INGREDIENTS:

6   TABLESPOONS RED WINE VINEGAR

¼   CUP HARISSA SAUCE (SEE PAGE 523)

1   TABLESPOON DIJON MUSTARD

     SALT AND PEPPER, TO TASTE

⅔   CUP EXTRA-VIRGIN OLIVE OIL

ORANGE VINAIGRETTE

YIELD: 1½ CUPS / **ACTIVE TIME:** 5 MINUTES / **TOTAL TIME:** 5 MINUTES

1. Place all of the ingredients, except for the olive oil and poppy seeds, in a food processor and blitz to combine.

2. With the food processor running on low, slowly drizzle in the olive oil until it has emulsified. Stir in the poppy seeds and use immediately or store in the refrigerator.

INGREDIENTS:

¼   CUP FRESH ORANGE JUICE

2   SHALLOTS, FINELY DICED

2   TABLESPOONS CHAMPAGNE VINEGAR

     SALT AND PEPPER, TO TASTE

     PAPRIKA, TO TASTE

¾   CUP EXTRA-VIRGIN OLIVE OIL

1   TEASPOON POPPY SEEDS

SPICY HONEY VINAIGRETTE

YIELD: 1 CUP / **ACTIVE TIME:** 5 MINUTES / **TOTAL TIME:** 5 MINUTES

1. Place all of the ingredients, except for the olive oil, in a food processor and blitz to combine.

2. With the food processor running on low, slowly drizzle in the olive oil until it has emulsified. Use immediately or store in the refrigerator.

INGREDIENTS:

- 1 TEASPOON CHOPPED FRESH DILL
- 1 TEASPOON CHOPPED FRESH MINT
- 1 TABLESPOON CHOPPED FRESH PARSLEY
- 1 TABLESPOON HONEY
- 3 TABLESPOONS WHITE WINE VINEGAR
- 1 TABLESPOON FRESH GRAPEFRUIT JUICE
- 1 JALAPEÑO CHILE PEPPER, STEMMED, SEEDED, AND SLICED THIN

  SALT AND PEPPER, TO TASTE
- ½ CUP EXTRA-VIRGIN OLIVE OIL

CRANBERRY & ORANGE VINAIGRETTE

YIELD: ¾ CUP / **ACTIVE TIME:** 5 MINUTES / **TOTAL TIME:** 5 MINUTES

1. Place all of the ingredients, except for the canola oil, in a blender and puree on medium until smooth.

2. With the blender running on low, add the canola oil in a slow drizzle until it has emulsified. Taste, adjust the seasoning as necessary, and use as desired.

INGREDIENTS:

- 2 TABLESPOONS APPLE CIDER VINEGAR
- 1 TABLESPOON HONEY
- 1½ TEASPOONS KOSHER SALT

  ZEST OF 1 ORANGE
- ¼ CUP FRESH ORANGE JUICE
- 1½ TEASPOONS DIJON MUSTARD
- ½ CUP FRESH CRANBERRIES
- ½ CUP CANOLA OIL

Cranberry & Orange Vinaigrette,
see page 585

FIG VINAIGRETTE

YIELD: 1½ CUPS / **ACTIVE TIME:** 5 MINUTES / **TOTAL TIME:** 5 MINUTES

1. Place the vinegar, water, jam, mustard, and shallot in a mixing bowl and whisk to combine.

2. While whisking continually, add the olive oil in a slow, steady stream until it has emulsified.

3. Add the figs and chives, whisk to incorporate, and season the vinaigrette with salt and pepper. Use immediately or store in the refrigerator.

INGREDIENTS:

3	TABLESPOONS BALSAMIC VINEGAR
1	TABLESPOON WATER
1	TABLESPOON FIG JAM
1	TABLESPOON DIJON MUSTARD
1	SHALLOT, MINCED
½	CUP EXTRA-VIRGIN OLIVE OIL
½	CUP DICED FIGS
2	TABLESPOONS CHOPPED FRESH CHIVES
	SALT AND PEPPER, TO TASTE

DIJON DRESSING

YIELD: 1 CUP / **ACTIVE TIME:** 5 MINUTES / **TOTAL TIME:** 5 MINUTES

1. Place all of the ingredients, except for the olive oil, in a food processor and blitz to combine.

2. With the food processor running on low, slowly drizzle in the olive oil until it has emulsified. Use immediately or store in the refrigerator.

INGREDIENTS:

	JUICE OF 2 LEMONS
1	TABLESPOON MINCED SHALLOT
1	TABLESPOON CHOPPED FRESH BASIL
2	TEASPOONS FRESH THYME
2	TEASPOONS CHOPPED FRESH OREGANO
2	TEASPOONS DIJON MUSTARD
2	ANCHOVIES IN OLIVE OIL, DRAINED AND FINELY CHOPPED
2	TEASPOONS CAPERS, DRAINED AND CHOPPED
	SALT AND PEPPER, TO TASTE
¾	CUP EXTRA-VIRGIN OLIVE OIL

SOY & SESAME DRESSING

YIELD: ½ CUP / **ACTIVE TIME:** 5 MINUTES / **TOTAL TIME:** 5 MINUTES

1. Place all of the ingredients in a bowl and whisk until thoroughly combined. Use immediately or store in the refrigerator.

INGREDIENTS:

½ CUP SOY SAUCE

2 TABLESPOONS SESAME OIL

1 TEASPOON WASABI

PANZANELLA DRESSING

YIELD: 1½ CUPS / **ACTIVE TIME:** 5 MINUTES / **TOTAL TIME:** 5 MINUTES

1. Place the vinegar in a bowl. While whisking continually, slowly drizzle in the olive oil. As this is a split dressing, the oil will not emulsify.

2. Add the herbs, season the dressing with salt and pepper, and stir to combine. Use immediately or store in an airtight container.

INGREDIENTS

¼ CUP RED WINE VINEGAR

½ CUP EXTRA-VIRGIN OLIVE OIL

2 TABLESPOONS CHOPPED FRESH BASIL

2 TABLESPOONS CHOPPED FRESH OREGANO

SALT AND PEPPER, TO TASTE

Panzanella Dressing, see page 589

POMEGRANATE VINAIGRETTE

YIELD: 2 CUPS / ACTIVE TIME: 30 MINUTES / TOTAL TIME: 30 MINUTES

1. Place the pomegranate juice in a small saucepan and bring it to a boil over medium-high heat. Boil until it has reduced to ¼ cup. Remove the pan from heat and let the reduction cool.

2. Place the pomegranate reduction and the remaining ingredients, except for the olive oil, in a food processor and blitz until smooth.

3. With the food processor running on low, slowly drizzle in the olive oil until it has emulsified. Use immediately or store in the refrigerator.

IINGREDIENTS:

1	CUP POMEGRANATE JUICE
¼	CUP RED WINE VINEGAR
1	TABLESPOON DIJON MUSTARD
1	TABLESPOON HONEY
1½	TEASPOONS ZA'ATAR
1	TEASPOON SUMAC
1	TABLESPOON KOSHER SALT
1½	TEASPOONS BLACK PEPPER
1½	TEASPOONS FINELY CHOPPED FRESH OREGANO
1½	TEASPOONS FINELY CHOPPED FRESH BASIL
1½	TEASPOONS FINELY CHOPPED FRESH MINT
1½	CUPS EXTRA-VIRGIN OLIVE OIL

CHAMPAGNE VINAIGRETTE

YIELD: 2½ CUPS / ACTIVE TIME: 5 MINUTES / TOTAL TIME: 5 MINUTES

1. Place all of the ingredients, except for the olive oil, in a bowl and whisk to combine.

2. While whisking continually, slowly drizzle in the olive oil until it has emulsified. Use immediately or store in an airtight container.

INGREDIENTS:

⅔	CUP CHAMPAGNE VINEGAR
¼	CUP WATER
2	TABLESPOONS DIJON MUSTARD
½	TEASPOON KOSHER SALT
½	TEASPOON BLACK PEPPER
1	TEASPOON FRESH THYME
2	TABLESPOONS HONEY
1½	CUPS EXTRA-VIRGIN OLIVE OIL

RANCH DRESSING

YIELD: 2 CUPS / ACTIVE TIME: 5 MINUTES / TOTAL TIME: 5 MINUTES

1. Place all of the ingredients in a bowl, whisk to combine, and use immediately or store in the refrigerator.

INGREDIENTS:

- 1 CUP MAYONNAISE
- 1 CUP BUTTERMILK
- 1 TEASPOON DRIED PARSLEY
- 1 TEASPOON DRIED DILL
- 1 TABLESPOON ONION POWDER
- 1 TEASPOON GARLIC POWDER
- SALT AND PEPPER, TO TASTE
- ¼ CUP CHOPPED FRESH CHIVES

CLASSIC CAESAR DRESSING

YIELD: 1 CUP / ACTIVE TIME: 15 MINUTES / TOTAL TIME: 25 MINUTES

1. Bring water to a boil in a small saucepan.

2. Rub the inside of a bowl with the garlic and then discard it.

3. Using a needle, pierce a tiny hole in the wide end of each egg. Place them in the water and boil until the insides just begin to firm up, about 1 minute. Remove the eggs from the water, crack them into the salad bowl, making sure to scoop out any of the whites that cling to the shells.

4. While whisking continually, add the lemon juice and then the olive oil in a slow stream. Stir in the anchovies and Worcestershire sauce, season the dressing with salt and pepper, and use immediately.

INGREDIENTS:

- 1 GARLIC CLOVE, HALVED
- 2 EGGS
- 2 TABLESPOONS FRESH LEMON JUICE
- ½ CUP EXTRA-VIRGIN OLIVE OIL
- 3 TABLESPOONS MINCED ANCHOVIES
- DASH OF WORCESTERSHIRE SAUCE
- SALT AND PEPPER, TO TASTE

Classic Caesar Dressing,
see page 593

HONEY MUSTARD & TARRAGON DRESSING

YIELD: 1 CUP / ACTIVE TIME: 5 MINUTES / TOTAL TIME: 5 MINUTES

1. Place the vinegar, lemon juice, mustard, and honey in a food processor and blitz until smooth.

2. With the food processor running, slowly drizzle in the olive oil until it has emulsified.

3. Stir in the shallot and tarragon, season the dressing with salt and pepper, and use immediately or store in the refrigerator.

INGREDIENTS:

2	TABLESPOONS WHITE WINE VINEGAR
1	TABLESPOON FRESH LEMON JUICE
1	TABLESPOON WHOLE-GRAIN MUSTARD
1	TEASPOON HONEY
½	CUP EXTRA-VIRGIN OLIVE OIL
1	SHALLOT, MINCED
2	TEASPOONS CHOPPED FRESH TARRAGON
	SALT AND PEPPER, TO TASTE

BUTTERMILK CAESAR DRESSING

YIELD: 1 CUP / **ACTIVE TIME:** 5 MINUTES / **TOTAL TIME:** 5 MINUTES

1. Place all of the ingredients in a food processor and blitz until smooth.

2. Taste, adjust the seasoning as necessary, and use immediately or store in the refrigerator.

INGREDIENTS:

1	LARGE GARLIC CLOVE, MINCED
1	TEASPOON WHITE MISO
⅔	CUP MAYONNAISE
¼	CUP BUTTERMILK
¼	CUP FRESHLY GRATED PARMESAN CHEESE
	ZEST OF 1 LEMON
1	TEASPOON WORCESTERSHIRE SAUCE
1	TEASPOON KOSHER SALT, PLUS MORE TO TASTE
½	TEASPOON BLACK PEPPER, PLUS MORE TO TASTE

THOUSAND ISLAND DRESSING

YIELD: 1½ CUPS / **ACTIVE TIME:** 5 MINUTES / **TOTAL TIME:** 5 MINUTES

1. Place all of the ingredients in a bowl, stir to combine, and use immediately or store in the refrigerator.

INGREDIENTS:

1	HARD-BOILED EGG (SEE PAGE 667), CHOPPED
1	CUP MAYONNAISE
¼	CUP KETCHUP
2	TABLESPOONS FINELY DICED PIMIENTO-STUFFED GREEN OLIVES
2	TABLESPOONS FINELY DICED SWEET PICKLES
1	TABLESPOON CHOPPED ONION
2	TEASPOONS CHOPPED FRESH PARSLEY
1	TEASPOON FRESH LEMON JUICE
1	TEASPOON SMOKED PAPRIKA
	SALT AND PEPPER, TO TASTE

RED WINE VINAIGRETTE

YIELD: ¾ CUP / ACTIVE TIME: 5 MINUTES / TOTAL TIME: 5 MINUTES

1. Place all of the ingredients, except for the olive oil, in a food processor and blitz to combine.

2. With the food processor running on low, slowly drizzle in the olive oil until it has emulsified. Use immediately or store in the refrigerator.

INGREDIENTS:

3	TABLESPOONS RED WINE VINEGAR
1	TEASPOON WHOLE-GRAIN MUSTARD
1	SHALLOT, MINCED
½	TEASPOON KOSHER SALT
½	TEASPOON BLACK PEPPER
½	CUP EXTRA-VIRGIN OLIVE OIL

HOT HONEY

YIELD: 1 CUP / ACTIVE TIME: 10 MINUTES / TOTAL TIME: 2 HOURS

1. Place the chiles and honey in a saucepan and bring to a very gentle simmer over medium-low heat. Reduce the heat to lowest possible setting and cook for 1 hour.

2. Remove the saucepan from heat and let the mixture infuse for another hour.

3. Remove the chiles. Transfer the honey to a container, cover, and store in the refrigerator.

INGREDIENTS:

4	RED CHILE PEPPERS
1	CUP HONEY

Hot Honey, see page 599

SHERRY VINAIGRETTE

YIELD: ¾ CUP / **ACTIVE TIME:** 5 MINUTES / **TOTAL TIME:** 5 MINUTES

1. Place all of the ingredients, except for the olive oil, in a food processor and blitz to combine.

2. With the food processor running on low, slowly drizzle in the olive oil until it has emulsified. Use immediately or store in the refrigerator.

INGREDIENTS:

3	TABLESPOONS SHERRY VINEGAR
½	TEASPOON KOSHER SALT
½	TEASPOON BLACK PEPPER
½	TEASPOON CASTER (SUPERFINE) SUGAR
½	CUP EXTRA-VIRGIN OLIVE OIL

RICE VINAIGRETTE

YIELD: ¾ CUP / **ACTIVE TIME:** 5 MINUTES / **TOTAL TIME:** 5 MINUTES

1. Place all of the ingredients, except for the canola oil, in a food processor and blitz to combine.

2. With the food processor running on low, slowly drizzle in the canola oil until it has emulsified. Use immediately or store in the refrigerator.

INGREDIENTS:

3	TABLESPOONS RICE VINEGAR
1	TEASPOON KOSHER SALT
1	TEASPOON BLACK PEPPER
1	TEASPOON AGAVE NECTAR
½	CUP CANOLA OIL

LIME VINAIGRETTE

YIELD: ¾ CUP / **ACTIVE TIME:** 5 MINUTES / **TOTAL TIME:** 5 MINUTES

1. Place all of the ingredients, except for the olive oil, in a food processor and blitz to combine.

2. With the food processor running on low, slowly drizzle in the olive oil until it has emulsified. Use immediately or store in the refrigerator.

INGREDIENTS:

3	TABLESPOONS FRESH LIME JUICE
	ZEST OF ½ LIME
½	TEASPOON KOSHER SALT
½	TEASPOON BLACK PEPPER
1	TEASPOON HONEY
½	CUP EXTRA-VIRGIN OLIVE OIL

PESTO

YIELD: 2 CUPS / **ACTIVE TIME:** 10 MINUTES / **TOTAL TIME:** 10 MINUTES

1. Place all the ingredients, except for the olive oil, in a food processor and pulse until pureed.

2. Transfer the puree to a mixing bowl. While whisking continually, slowly drizzle in the olive oil until it has emulsified. Use immediately or store in the refrigerator.

INGREDIENTS:

2	CUPS PACKED FRESH BASIL LEAVES
1	CUP PACKED FRESH BABY SPINACH
2	CUPS FRESHLY GRATED PARMESAN CHEESE
¼	CUP PINE NUTS
1	GARLIC CLOVE
2	TEASPOONS FRESH LEMON JUICE
	SALT AND PEPPER, TO TASTE
½	CUP EXTRA-VIRGIN OLIVE OIL

Pesto, see page 603

STRAWBERRY VINAIGRETTE

YIELD: ¾ CUP / ACTIVE TIME: 5 MINUTES / TOTAL TIME: 5 MINUTES

1. Place all of the ingredients, except for the olive oil, in a food processor and blitz to combine.

2. With the food processor running on low, slowly drizzle in the olive oil until it has emulsified. Use immediately or store in the refrigerator.

INGREDIENTS:

3	TABLESPOONS FRESH LEMON JUICE
½	CUP HULLED STRAWBERRIES
1	TEASPOON KOSHER SALT
1	TEASPOON BLACK PEPPER
1	TEASPOON AGAVE NECTAR
½	CUP EXTRA-VIRGIN OLIVE OIL

LEMON & THYME DRESSING

YIELD: ¾ CUP / ACTIVE TIME: 5 MINUTES / TOTAL TIME: 5 MINUTES

1. Place all of the ingredients, except for the olive oil, in a food processor and blitz to combine.

2. With the food processor running on low, slowly drizzle in the olive oil until it has emulsified. Use immediately or store in the refrigerator.

INGREDIENTS:

3	TABLESPOONS FRESH LEMON JUICE
2	TABLESPOONS FRESH THYME
1	TEASPOON KOSHER SALT
1	TEASPOON BLACK PEPPER
1	TEASPOON LEMON ZEST
½	CUP EXTRA-VIRGIN OLIVE OIL

PARSLEY & MINT VINAIGRETTE

YIELD: 1 CUP / **ACTIVE TIME:** 5 MINUTES / **TOTAL TIME:** 5 MINUTES

1. Place all of the ingredients, except for the olive oil, in a food processor and blitz to combine.

2. With the food processor running on low, slowly drizzle in the olive oil until it has emulsified. Use immediately or store in the refrigerator.

INGREDIENTS:

1	GARLIC CLOVE, MINCED
1	CUP FRESH PARSLEY, FINELY CHOPPED
½	CUP FRESH MINT, FINELY CHOPPED
2	ANCHOVIES IN OLIVE OIL, MINCED
3	TABLESPOONS FRESH LEMON JUICE
1	TEASPOON KOSHER SALT
1	TEASPOON BLACK PEPPER
½	CUP EXTRA-VIRGIN OLIVE OIL

RASPBERRY VINAIGRETTE

YIELD: ¾ CUP / **ACTIVE TIME:** 5 MINUTES / **TOTAL TIME:** 5 MINUTES

1. Place all of the ingredients, except for the olive oil, in a food processor and blitz to combine.

2. With the food processor running on low, slowly drizzle in the olive oil until it has emulsified. Use immediately or store in the refrigerator.

INGREDIENTS:

½	CUP FRESH RASPBERRIES
3	TABLESPOONS CHAMPAGNE VINEGAR
1	TEASPOON KOSHER SALT
1	TEASPOON BLACK PEPPER
1	TEASPOON HONEY
½	CUP EXTRA-VIRGIN OLIVE OIL

Raspberry Vinaigrette, see page 607

CITRUS VINAIGRETTE

YIELD: ¾ CUP / **ACTIVE TIME:** 5 MINUTES / **TOTAL TIME:** 5 MINUTES

1. Place all of the ingredients, except for the olive oil, in a food processor and blitz to combine.

2. With the food processor running on low, slowly drizzle in the olive oil until it has emulsified. Use immediately or store in the refrigerator.

INGREDIENTS:

1	TABLESPOON FRESH LEMON JUICE
1	TABLESPOON FRESH LIME JUICE
1	TABLESPOON FRESH ORANGE JUICE
1	TEASPOON KOSHER SALT
½	TEASPOON BLACK PEPPER
½	TEASPOON LEMON ZEST
½	TEASPOON LIME ZEST
½	TEASPOON ORANGE ZEST
½	CUP EXTRA-VIRGIN OLIVE OIL

BACON VINAIGRETTE

YIELD: ¾ CUP / **ACTIVE TIME:** 5 MINUTES / **TOTAL TIME:** 5 MINUTES

1. Place all of the ingredients, except for the bacon fat and olive oil, in a food processor and blitz to combine.

2. With the food processor running on low, slowly drizzle in the olive oil until it has emulsified. Add the bacon fat and blitz until it has emulsified. Use immediately or store in the refrigerator.

INGREDIENTS:

3	TABLESPOONS APPLE CIDER VINEGAR
1	TABLESPOON DIJON MUSTARD
2	TEASPOONS LIGHT BROWN SUGAR
1	TEASPOON BLACK PEPPER
	SALT, TO TASTE
¼	CUP EXTRA-VIRGIN OLIVE OIL
2	TABLESPOONS RENDERED BACON FAT

ADOBO VINAIGRETTE

YIELD: ¾ CUP / **ACTIVE TIME:** 5 MINUTES / **TOTAL TIME:** 5 MINUTES

1. Place all of the ingredients, except for the canola oil, in a food processor and blitz to combine.

2. With the food processor running on low, slowly drizzle in the canola oil until it has emulsified. Use immediately or store in the refrigerator.

INGREDIENTS

2	TABLESPOONS WHITE WINE VINEGAR
2	CHIPOTLE CHILE PEPPERS IN ADOBO
1	TEASPOON ADOBO SAUCE
½	TEASPOON KOSHER SALT
½	TEASPOON BLACK PEPPER
1	TEASPOON HONEY
1	TEASPOON DIJON MUSTARD
1	TABLESPOON FRESH LIME JUICE
½	CUP CANOLA OIL

PROVENÇAL VINAIGRETTE

YIELD: ¾ CUP / **ACTIVE TIME:** 5 MINUTES / **TOTAL TIME:** 5 MINUTES

1. Place all of the ingredients, except for the olive oil, in a food processor and blitz to combine.

2. With the food processor running on low, slowly drizzle in the olive oil until it has emulsified. Use immediately or store in the refrigerator.

INGREDIENTS

1	TEASPOON DRIED HERBES DE PROVENCE
¼	CUP WHITE WINE VINEGAR
1	GARLIC CLOVE, MINCED
¼	TEASPOON BLACK PEPPER
¼	TEASPOON KOSHER SALT
½	CUP EXTRA-VIRGIN OLIVE OIL

Provençal Vinaigrette, see page 611

PEAR & BALSAMIC VINAIGRETTE

YIELD: 1 CUP / **ACTIVE TIME:** 5 MINUTES / **TOTAL TIME:** 5 MINUTES

1. Place all of the ingredients, except for the olive oil, in a food processor and blitz to combine.

2. With the food processor running on low, slowly drizzle in the olive oil until it has emulsified. Use immediately or store in the refrigerator.

INGREDIENTS:

- 3 TABLESPOONS PEAR NECTAR
- 2 TABLESPOONS WHITE BALSAMIC VINEGAR
- 1½ TEASPOONS FRESH LEMON JUICE
- ¼ TEASPOON DIJON MUSTARD
- ¼ TEASPOON KOSHER SALT
- ¼ TEASPOON BLACK PEPPER
- ½ CUP CRUMBLED GORGONZOLA CHEESE
- ⅓ CUP EXTRA-VIRGIN OLIVE OIL

TARRAGON VINAIGRETTE

YIELD: ¾ CUP / **ACTIVE TIME:** 5 MINUTES / **TOTAL TIME:** 5 MINUTES

1. Place all of the ingredients, except for the olive oil, in a food processor and blitz to combine.

2. With the food processor running on low, slowly drizzle in the olive oil until it has emulsified. Use immediately or store in the refrigerator.

INGREDIENTS:

- 2 GARLIC CLOVES, MINCED
- 1 TEASPOON DIJON MUSTARD
- 3 TABLESPOONS RED WINE VINEGAR
- 1 TABLESPOON FRESH LEMON JUICE
- 2 TABLESPOONS CHOPPED FRESH PARSLEY
- 2 TABLESPOONS FINELY CHOPPED FRESH TARRAGON
- 1 TEASPOON KOSHER SALT
- 1 TEASPOON BLACK PEPPER
- ½ CUP EXTRA-VIRGIN OLIVE OIL

SWEET & SOUR DRESSING

YIELD: ¾ CUP / **ACTIVE TIME:** 5 MINUTES / **TOTAL TIME:** 5 MINUTES

1. Place all of the ingredients in a food processor and blitz to combine. Use immediately or store in the refrigerator.

INGREDIENTS:

1	GARLIC CLOVE, MINCED
¼	CUP FRESH LIME JUICE
2	TABLESPOONS ORANGE JUICE
2	TABLESPOONS FISH SAUCE
2	TEASPOONS RICE VINEGAR
2	TABLESPOONS HONEY
½	TEASPOON SRIRACHA

GARLIC, LEMON & OREGANO VINAIGRETTE

YIELD: ¾ CUP / **ACTIVE TIME:** 5 MINUTES / **TOTAL TIME:** 5 MINUTES

1. Place all of the ingredients, except for the olive oil, in a food processor and blitz to combine.

2. With the food processor running on low, slowly drizzle in the olive oil until it has emulsified. Use immediately or store in the refrigerator.

INGREDIENTS:

2	GARLIC CLOVES, CHOPPED
2	ANCHOVIES IN OLIVE OIL, DRAINED
¾	TEASPOON RED PEPPER FLAKES
2	TABLESPOONS FRESH LEMON JUICE
½	LEMON, MINCED
¼	CUP FRESH OREGANO
	PINCH OF KOSHER SALT
¼	CUP EXTRA-VIRGIN OLIVE OIL

Garlic, Lemon & Oregano Vinaigrette, see page 615

LEMON & DILL VINAIGRETTE

YIELD: ¾ CUP / **ACTIVE TIME:** 5 MINUTES / **TOTAL TIME:** 5 MINUTES

1. Place all of the ingredients, except for the olive oil, in a food processor and blitz to combine.

2. With the food processor running on low, slowly drizzle in the olive oil until it has emulsified. Use immediately or store in the refrigerator.

INGREDIENTS:

3	TABLESPOONS FRESH LEMON JUICE
	ZEST OF ½ LEMON
½	TEASPOON KOSHER SALT
½	TEASPOON BLACK PEPPER
1	TEASPOON HONEY
2	TABLESPOONS FINELY CHOPPED FRESH DILL
½	CUP EXTRA-VIRGIN OLIVE OIL

FENNEL & BLOOD ORANGE VINAIGRETTE

YIELD: ¾ CUP / **ACTIVE TIME:** 5 MINUTES / **TOTAL TIME:** 10 MINUTES

1. Place the fennel seeds in a dry skillet and toast them over medium heat for 1 to 2 minutes, shaking the pan frequently. Remove the fennel seeds from the pan, crush them, and place them in a food processor.

2. Add all of the remaining ingredients, except for the olive oil, in a food processor and blitz to combine.

3. With the food processor running on low, slowly drizzle in the olive oil until it has emulsified. Use immediately or store in the refrigerator.

INGREDIENTS:

2	TEASPOONS FENNEL SEEDS
6	TABLESPOONS FRESH BLOOD ORANGE JUICE
4	TEASPOONS WHITE WINE VINEGAR
½	TEASPOON BLOOD ORANGE ZEST
½	TEASPOON BLACK PEPPER
2	TEASPOONS KOSHER SALT
¼	CUP EXTRA-VIRGIN OLIVE OIL

ROASTED RED PEPPER VINAIGRETTE

YIELD: 1 CUP / **ACTIVE TIME:** 5 MINUTES / **TOTAL TIME:** 35 MINUTES

1. Preheat the oven to 400°F. Place the bell pepper on a baking sheet, place it in the oven, and roast until it is charred all over, 15 to 20 minutes, turning it as necessary. Remove the roasted pepper from the oven, place it in a heatproof bowl, and cover it with a kitchen towel. Let the pepper steam for 10 minutes.

2. Remove the charred skin, stem, and seed pod from the pepper and discard them. Cut the roasted pepper into strips and place it in a food processor.

3. Add all of the remaining ingredients, except for the olive oil, in a food processor and blitz to combine.

4. With the food processor running on low, slowly drizzle in the olive oil until it has emulsified. Use immediately or store in the refrigerator.

INGREDIENTS

1	RED BELL PEPPER
3	TABLESPOONS FRESH LEMON JUICE
	ZEST OF ½ LEMON
½	TEASPOON KOSHER SALT
½	TEASPOON BLACK PEPPER
1	TEASPOON HONEY
1	TEASPOON FINELY CHOPPED FRESH ROSEMARY
½	CUP EXTRA-VIRGIN OLIVE OIL

LEMON VINAIGRETTE

YIELD: ¾ CUP / **ACTIVE TIME:** 5 MINUTES / **TOTAL TIME:** 5 MINUTES

1. Place all of the ingredients, except for the olive oil, in a food processor and blitz to combine.

2. With the food processor running on low, slowly drizzle in the olive oil until it has emulsified. Use immediately or store in the refrigerator.

INGREDIENTS:

3	TABLESPOONS FRESH LEMON JUICE
	ZEST OF ½ LEMON
½	TEASPOON SEA SALT
½	TEASPOON BLACK PEPPER
1	TEASPOON HONEY
2	TABLESPOONS CHOPPED FRESH PARSLEY
½	CUP EXTRA-VIRGIN OLIVE OIL

Lemon Vinaigrette, see page 619

CHIMICHURRI VINAIGRETTE

YIELD: 1 CUP / ACTIVE TIME: 5 MINUTES / TOTAL TIME: 5 MINUTES

1. Place all of the ingredients, except for the olive oil, in a food processor and blitz to combine.

2. With the food processor running on low, slowly drizzle in the olive oil until it has emulsified. Use immediately or store in the refrigerator.

INGREDIENTS:

- ½   CUP RED WINE VINEGAR
- 2   GARLIC CLOVES, MINCED
- 1   SMALL SHALLOT, MINCED
- 1   SCALLION, TRIMMED AND MINCED
- 1   SERRANO CHILE PEPPER, STEMMED, SEEDED, AND MINCED
- 1   TABLESPOON FRESH LIME JUICE
- 1   TEASPOON KOSHER SALT
- ½   CUP FINELY CHOPPED FRESH PARSLEY
- ½   CUP FINELY CHOPPED FRESH CILANTRO
- ¾   CUP EXTRA-VIRGIN OLIVE OIL

BLACK TRUFFLE VINAIGRETTE

YIELD: 1 CUP / ACTIVE TIME: 5 MINUTES / TOTAL TIME: 5 MINUTES

1. Place all of the ingredients, except for the oils, in a food processor and blitz to combine.

2. With the food processor running on low, slowly drizzle in the oils until they have emulsified. Use immediately or store in the refrigerator.

INGREDIENTS:

- 1   TABLESPOON DIJON MUSTARD
- 1   TABLESPOON CHAMPAGNE VINEGAR
- 1   SHALLOT, MINCED
- ½   TEASPOON KOSHER SALT
- 1   TEASPOON BLACK PEPPER
- ¼   CUP BLACK TRUFFLE OIL
- ⅓   CUP EXTRA-VIRGIN OLIVE OIL

MANGO VINAIGRETTE

YIELD: 1 CUP / **ACTIVE TIME:** 5 MINUTES / **TOTAL TIME:** 5 MINUTES

1. Place all of the ingredients, except for the canola oil, in a food processor and blitz to combine.

2. With the food processor running on low, slowly drizzle in the canola oil until it has emulsified. Use immediately or store in the refrigerator.

INGREDIENTS:

¼	CUP MANGO CHUTNEY
¼	CUP FRESH LIME JUICE
1	TEASPOON CUMIN
2	TEASPOONS KOSHER SALT
½	CUP CANOLA OIL

NUOC CHAM

YIELD: 1 CUP / **ACTIVE TIME:** 10 MINUTES / **TOTAL TIME:** 10 MINUTES

1. Place all of the ingredients in a mixing bowl and stir until the sugar has dissolved and the mixture is well combined.

2. Taste, adjust the seasoning as necessary, and use as desired.

INGREDIENTS:

¼	CUP FISH SAUCE
⅓	CUP WATER
2	TABLESPOONS CASTER (SUPERFINE) SUGAR
¼	CUP FRESH LIME JUICE
1	GARLIC CLOVE, MINCED
2	BIRD'S EYE CHILE PEPPERS, STEMMED, SEEDED, AND SLICED THIN
1	TABLESPOON CHILI-GARLIC SAUCE

Nuoc Cham, see page 623

POPPY SEED VINAIGRETTE

YIELD: 1 CUP / ACTIVE TIME: 5 MINUTES / TOTAL TIME: 5 MINUTES

1. Place all of the ingredients, except for the olive oil, in a food processor and blitz to combine.

2. With the food processor running on low, slowly drizzle in the olive oil until it has emulsified. Use immediately or store in the refrigerator.

INGREDIENTS:

1	TABLESPOON POPPY SEEDS
6	TABLESPOONS APPLE CIDER VINEGAR
2	TABLESPOONS HONEY
2	TEASPOONS DIJON MUSTARD
1	TEASPOON KOSHER SALT
⅔	CUP EXTRA-VIRGIN OLIVE OIL

EGGLESS CAESAR DRESSING

YIELD: 1½ CUPS / ACTIVE TIME: 5 MINUTES / TOTAL TIME: 5 MINUTES

1. Place all of the ingredients, except for the olive oil, in a food processor and blitz to combine.

2. With the food processor running on low, slowly drizzle in the olive oil until it has emulsified. Use immediately or store in the refrigerator.

INGREDIENTS:

5	ANCHOVIES IN OLIVE OIL, DRAINED
3	GARLIC CLOVES, CHOPPED
1½	TEASPOONS BLACK PEPPER
¼	CUP FRESH LEMON JUICE
2	TABLESPOONS SHERRY VINEGAR
1	TABLESPOON DIJON MUSTARD
½	CUP GRATED PARMESAN CHEESE
½	CUP EXTRA-VIRGIN OLIVE OIL

CREAMY & LIGHT CAESAR DRESSING

YIELD: 1 CUP / **ACTIVE TIME:** 5 MINUTES / **TOTAL TIME:** 5 MINUTES

1. Place all of the ingredients in a food processor and blitz to combine. Use immediately or store in the refrigerator.

INGREDIENTS:

- ½ CUP NONFAT GREEK YOGURT
- 2 TABLESPOONS GRATED PARMESAN CHEESE
- 1 TABLESPOON EXTRA-VIRGIN OLIVE OIL
- 1 TABLESPOON WATER
- 1 GARLIC CLOVE, CHOPPED
- 3 DASHES OF WORCESTERSHIRE SAUCE
- 4 ANCHOVIES IN OLIVE OIL, DRAINED
- 2 TABLESPOONS FRESH LEMON JUICE

ITALIAN DRESSING

YIELD: 1 CUP / **ACTIVE TIME:** 5 MINUTES / **TOTAL TIME:** 5 MINUTES

1. Place all of the ingredients, except for the olive oil, in a mixing bowl and whisk to combine.

2. While whisking continually, slowly drizzle in the olive oil until it has emulsified. Serve immediately.

INGREDIENTS:

- 3 TABLESPOONS WHITE WINE VINEGAR
- 3 TABLESPOONS FRESH LEMON JUICE
- 1½ TEASPOONS DRIED PARSLEY
- 1½ TEASPOONS HONEY
- 1½ TEASPOONS DRIED OREGANO
- 1 GARLIC CLOVE, GRATED
- ¾ TEASPOON DIJON MUSTARD
- ¾ TEASPOON DRIED THYME
- ¼ TEASPOON KOSHER SALT
- 6 TABLESPOONS EXTRA-VIRGIN OLIVE OIL

Italian Dressing, see page 627

RUSSIAN DRESSING

YIELD: 1½ CUPS / **ACTIVE TIME:** 5 MINUTES / **TOTAL TIME:** 5 MINUTES

1. Place all of the ingredients in a food processor and blitz to combine. Use immediately or store in the refrigerator.

INGREDIENTS:

1	TABLESPOON GRATED ONION
1	CUP MAYONNAISE
¼	CUP KETCHUP
4	TEASPOONS GRATED FRESH HORSERADISH
½	TEASPOON HOT SAUCE
1	TEASPOON DIJON MUSTARD
1	TEASPOON WORCESTERSHIRE SAUCE
¼	TEASPOON SWEET PAPRIKA
1	TEASPOON KOSHER SALT

BLUE CHEESE DRESSING

YIELD: 3 CUPS / **ACTIVE TIME:** 5 MINUTES / **TOTAL TIME:** 5 MINUTES

1. Place all of the ingredients in a mixing bowl and stir to combine. Use immediately or store in the refrigerator.

INGREDIENTS:

- ¾   CUP MAYONNAISE
- ¾   CUP SOUR CREAM
- 2   TABLESPOONS FRESH LEMON JUICE
- 1   TABLESPOON BLACK PEPPER
- 1   TEASPOON KOSHER SALT
- 1   TEASPOON TABASCO
- 1   CUP CRUMBLED GORGONZOLA OR STILTON CHEESE
- 3   DASHES OF WORCESTERSHIRE SAUCE

SMOKY RANCH DRESSING

YIELD: 1½ CUPS / **ACTIVE TIME:** 5 MINUTES / **TOTAL TIME:** 5 MINUTES

1. Place all of the ingredients in a food processor and blitz to combine. Use immediately or store in the refrigerator.

INGREDIENTS:

½	CUP BUTTERMILK
¼	CUP MAYONNAISE
¼	CUP SOUR CREAM
2	TABLESPOONS FRESH LIME JUICE
2	TABLESPOONS MINCED CHIPOTLE CHILE PEPPERS IN ADOBO
2	TABLESPOONS FINELY CHOPPED FRESH CILANTRO
½	TEASPOON HONEY
½	TEASPOON KOSHER SALT
⅛	TEASPOON GARLIC POWDER

GOAT CHEESE DRESSING

YIELD: 1½ CUPS / **ACTIVE TIME:** 5 MINUTES / **TOTAL TIME:** 5 MINUTES

1. Place all of the ingredients, except for the olive oil, in a food processor and blitz to combine.

2. With the food processor running on low, slowly drizzle in the olive oil until it has emulsified. Use immediately or store in the refrigerator.

INGREDIENTS:

¾	CUP CRUMBLED GOAT CHEESE
¼	CUP FRESH LEMON JUICE
1	TEASPOON KOSHER SALT
1	TEASPOON BLACK PEPPER
½	CUP EXTRA-VIRGIN OLIVE OIL

HORSERADISH & MUSTARD DRESSING

YIELD: 1 CUP / ACTIVE TIME: 5 MINUTES / TOTAL TIME: 5 MINUTES

1. Place all of the ingredients, except for the olive oil, in a food processor and blitz to combine.

2. With the food processor running on low, slowly drizzle in the olive oil until it has emulsified. Use immediately or store in the refrigerator.

INGREDIENTS:

1	TEASPOON KOSHER SALT
1	TEASPOON BLACK PEPPER
¼	CUP MAYONNAISE
¼	CUP APPLE CIDER VINEGAR
2	TABLESPOONS PREPARED HORSERADISH
2	TABLESPOONS WHOLE-GRAIN MUSTARD
2	TEASPOONS HONEY
¼	CUP EXTRA-VIRGIN OLIVE OIL

GINGER & TAHINI DRESSING

YIELD: 1 CUP / ACTIVE TIME: 5 MINUTES / TOTAL TIME: 5 MINUTES

1. Place all of the ingredients in a bowl, whisk vigorously to combine, and use immediately or store in the refrigerator.

INGREDIENTS:

3	TABLESPOONS FRESH LEMON JUICE
2	TABLESPOONS SOY SAUCE
2	TABLESPOONS TAHINI PASTE
1	TEASPOON MAPLE SYRUP
1	TEASPOON GRATED FRESH GINGER
1	TEASPOON RICE VINEGAR
1	TEASPOON TOASTED SESAME OIL
½	CUP EXTRA-VIRGIN OLIVE OIL

Ginger & Tahini Dressing, see page 635

CARROT & GINGER DRESSING

YIELD: 1 CUP / **ACTIVE TIME:** 5 MINUTES / **TOTAL TIME:** 5 MINUTES

1. Bring water to a boil in a small saucepan. Add salt, let the water return to a full boil, and add the carrot. Cook until it is tender, 10 to 12 minutes, drain, and place it in a food processor.

2. Add the remaining ingredients and blitz to combine. Use immediately or store in an airtight container.

INGREDIENTS:

1	TEASPOON KOSHER SALT, PLUS MORE TO TASTE
1	CARROT, PEELED AND CHOPPED
2	TABLESPOONS RICE VINEGAR
2	TABLESPOONS GRATED FRESH GINGER
1	TEASPOON SUGAR
1	TEASPOON SOY SAUCE
1	TEASPOON SESAME OIL
1	TEASPOON SALT
1	TEASPOON PEPPER
½	CUP WATER

SPICY PEANUT DRESSING

YIELD: 1 CUP / **ACTIVE TIME:** 5 MINUTES / **TOTAL TIME:** 5 MINUTES

1. Place all of the ingredients in a food processor and blitz to combine. Use immediately or store in the refrigerator.

INGREDIENTS:

⅔	CUP CREAMY PEANUT BUTTER
2	TABLESPOON SOY SAUCE
3	TABLESPOONS SRIRACHA
2	TEASPOONS MAPLE SYRUP
¼	CUP WATER
2	TEASPOONS KOSHER SALT
	JUICE OF 2 LIMES

SWEET & SPICY PEANUT DRESSING

YIELD: 1 CUP / **ACTIVE TIME:** 5 MINUTES / **TOTAL TIME:** 5 MINUTES

1. Place all of the ingredients in a food processor and blitz to combine. Use immediately or store in the refrigerator.

INGREDIENTS:

⅔	CUP PEANUT BUTTER
2	TABLESPOONS MAPLE SYRUP
1	GARLIC CLOVE, GRATED
1	THAI CHILE PEPPER, STEMMED, SEEDED, AND MINCED
2	TABLESPOONS RICE VINEGAR
2	TABLESPOONS SRIRACHA
2	TABLESPOONS SOY SAUCE
¼	CUP WATER
	PINCH OF KOSHER SALT

SESAME & GINGER DRESSING

YIELD: 1 CUP / **ACTIVE TIME:** 5 MINUTES / **TOTAL TIME:** 5 MINUTES

1. Place all of the ingredients, except for the canola oil, in a food processor and blitz to combine.

2. With the food processor running on low, slowly drizzle in the canola oil until it has emulsified. Use immediately or store in the refrigerator.

INGREDIENTS:

¼	CUP APPLE CIDER VINEGAR
2	TABLESPOONS BROWN SUGAR
1	TABLESPOON GRATED FRESH GINGER
6	TABLESPOONS SESAME OIL
½	TEASPOON KOSHER SALT
½	TEASPOON BLACK PEPPER
1	TEASPOON SESAME SEEDS
⅔	CUP CANOLA OIL

Sesame & Ginger Dressing, see page 639

ANCHOVY & MISO DRESSING

YIELD: 1 CUP / **ACTIVE TIME:** 5 MINUTES / **TOTAL TIME:** 5 MINUTES

1. Place all of the ingredients in a food processor and blitz to combine. Use immediately or store in the refrigerator.

INGREDIENTS:

4	ANCHOVIES IN OLIVE OIL, DRAINED
1	TEASPOON LEMON ZEST
2	TABLESPOONS FRESH LEMON JUICE
2	TABLESPOONS RICE VINEGAR
1	TABLESPOON SOY SAUCE
4	TEASPOONS WHITE MISO
¼	TEASPOON SUGAR
1	TABLESPOON CANOLA OIL
½	CUP CELERY LEAVES
2	SCALLIONS, TRIMMED AND MINCED
1	CUP FRESH CILANTRO, FINELY CHOPPED
1	SERRANO CHILE PEPPER, STEMMED, SEEDED, AND MINCED
2	TEASPOONS BLACK SESAME SEEDS
1	TEASPOON KOSHER SALT
1	TEASPOON BLACK PEPPER

SUNFLOWER SEED DRESSING

YIELD: 1 CUP / **ACTIVE TIME:** 5 MINUTES / **TOTAL TIME:** 5 MINUTES

1. Place the sunflower seeds in a dry skillet and toast them over medium heat for 1 to 2 minutes, shaking the pan frequently. Remove the sunflower seeds from the pan and place them in a food processor.

2. Add all of the remaining ingredients, except for the olive oil, in a food processor and blitz to combine.

3. With the food processor running on low, slowly drizzle in the olive oil until it has emulsified. Use immediately or store in the refrigerator.

INGREDIENTS:

1	TABLESPOON SUNFLOWER SEEDS
½	CUP FRESH BASIL
1	TABLESPOON FRESH LIME JUICE
¼	TEASPOON HONEY
¼	TEASPOON KOSHER SALT
½	CUP EXTRA-VIRGIN OLIVE OIL

GREEN CURRY DRESSING

YIELD: 1½ CUPS / ACTIVE TIME: 5 MINUTES / TOTAL TIME: 5 MINUTES

1. Place all of the ingredients, except for the peanut oil, in a food processor and blitz to combine.

2. With the food processor running on low, slowly drizzle in the peanut oil until it has emulsified. Use immediately or store in the refrigerator.

INGREDIENTS:

¾	CUP COCONUT MILK
1	TABLESPOON GREEN CURRY PASTE
1	TABLESPOON SUGAR
2	TABLESPOONS FINELY CHOPPED FRESH CILANTRO
1	TABLESPOON FRESH LIME JUICE
¾	CUP PEANUT OIL

HERB VINAIGRETTE

YIELD: 1 CUP / ACTIVE TIME: 5 MINUTES / TOTAL TIME: 5 MINUTES

1. Place all of the ingredients, except for the olive oil, in a food processor and blitz to combine.

2. With the food processor running on low, slowly drizzle in the olive oil until it has emulsified. Use immediately or store in the refrigerator.

INGREDIENTS:

2	TABLESPOONS SLICED FRESH CHIVES
2	TEASPOONS FRESH THYME
2	TEASPOONS CHOPPED FRESH OREGANO
2	TABLESPOONS CHOPPED FRESH PARSLEY
6	TABLESPOONS APPLE CIDER VINEGAR
2	TABLESPOONS HONEY
4	TEASPOONS DICED SHALLOT
2	TEASPOONS KOSHER SALT
½	TEASPOON FRESHLY GROUND BLACK PEPPER
½	CUP EXTRA-VIRGIN OLIVE OIL

Herb Vinaigrette, see page 643

RED CURRY DRESSING

YIELD: 2 CUPS / ACTIVE TIME: 5 MINUTES / TOTAL TIME: 5 MINUTES

1. Place all of the ingredients in a food processor and blitz to combine. Use immediately or store in the refrigerator.

INGREDIENTS:

1	CUP COCONUT MILK
½	CUP CHICKEN STOCK (SEE PAGE 663)
2	TABLESPOONS PEANUT BUTTER
2	TABLESPOONS RED CURRY PASTE
1½	TABLESPOONS FISH SAUCE
1	TABLESPOON FRESH LIME JUICE
3	TABLESPOONS BROWN SUGAR
⅓	CUP PEANUTS, CRUSHED

ROASTED SCALLION & FETA DRESSING

YIELD: 1½ CUPS / ACTIVE TIME: 5 MINUTES / TOTAL TIME: 25 MINUTES

1. Preheat the oven to 375°F. Place the scallions on a baking sheet, drizzle 1 tablespoon of olive oil over them, and season with the salt and pepper. Toss to combine, place the scallions in the oven, and roast until they are browned all over, stirring occasionally.

2. Remove the scallions from the oven and transfer them to a food processor. Add all of the remaining ingredients, except for the remaining olive oil, and blitz to combine.

3. With the food processor running on low, slowly drizzle in the remaining olive oil until it has emulsified. Use immediately or store in the refrigerator.

INGREDIENTS:

10	SCALLIONS, TRIMMED
½	CUP EXTRA-VIRGIN OLIVE OIL
¼	TEASPOON KOSHER SALT
1	TEASPOON BLACK PEPPER
¾	CUP CRUMBLED FETA CHEESE
3	TABLESPOONS WHOLE MILK
2	TABLESPOONS FRESH LEMON JUICE

SPICY ARUGULA DRESSING

YIELD: 1½ CUPS / **ACTIVE TIME:** 5 MINUTES / **TOTAL TIME:** 5 MINUTES

1. Place all of the ingredients, except for the oils, in a food processor and blitz to combine.

2. With the food processor running on low, slowly drizzle in the oils until they have emulsified. Use immediately or store in the refrigerator.

INGREDIENTS:

- 1   SERRANO CHILE PEPPER, STEMMED, SEEDED, AND CHOPPED
- ½   CUP ARUGULA
- ½   CUP FRESH MINT
- ½   TEASPOON LIME ZEST
- ¼   CUP FRESH LIME JUICE
- ½   TEASPOON CASTER (SUPERFINE) SUGAR
- 1   TEASPOON KOSHER SALT
- 1   TEASPOON BLACK PEPPER
- ¼   CUP EXTRA-VIRGIN OLIVE OIL
- ½   CUP CANOLA OIL

CHAMPAGNE & HERB VINAIGRETTE

YIELD: 2 CUPS / **ACTIVE TIME:** 5 MINUTES / **TOTAL TIME:** 5 MINUTES

1. Place all of the ingredients, except for the olive oil, in a food processor and blitz to combine.

2. With the food processor running on low, slowly drizzle in the olive oil until it has emulsified. Use immediately or store in the refrigerator.

INGREDIENTS:

- 2   SHALLOTS, MINCED
- ½   CUP HONEY
- ¼   CUP CHAMPAGNE VINEGAR
- 1   TABLESPOON DIJON MUSTARD
- ¼   CUP CHOPPED FRESH CHIVES
- 2   TABLESPOONS FRESH THYME
- ¾   CUP EXTRA-VIRGIN OLIVE OIL

Champagne & Herb Vinaigrette,
see page 647

SPICY HONEY MUSTARD DRESSING

YIELD: ¾ CUP / **ACTIVE TIME:** 5 MINUTES / **TOTAL TIME:** 5 MINUTES

1. Place all of the ingredients, except for the olive oil, in a food processor and blitz to combine.

2. With the food processor running on low, slowly drizzle in the olive oil until it has emulsified. Use immediately or store in the refrigerator.

INGREDIENTS:

- 2   TEASPOONS HONEY
- 2   TEASPOONS DIJON MUSTARD
- 2½   TABLESPOONS FRESH LIME JUICE
-      ZEST OF ½ LIME
- 1   TEASPOON KOSHER SALT
- 2   TEASPOONS FRESH LEMON THYME
- 1   FRESH CHILE PEPPER, STEMMED, SEEDED, AND MINCED
-      PINCH OF BLACK PEPPER
- ½   CUP EXTRA-VIRGIN OLIVE OIL

AVOCADO & HABANERO DRESSING

YIELD: 1½ CUPS / **ACTIVE TIME:** 5 MINUTES / **TOTAL TIME:** 5 MINUTES

1. Place all of the ingredients, except for the olive oil, in a food processor and blitz to combine.

2. With the food processor running on low, slowly drizzle in the olive oil until it has emulsified. Use immediately or store in the refrigerator.

INGREDIENTS:

	FLESH OF 1 AVOCADO
½	HABANERO CHILE PEPPER, CHOPPED
1	CUP SOUR CREAM
½	TEASPOON HONEY
1	TEASPOON KOSHER SALT
1	TEASPOON BLACK PEPPER
¼	CUP EXTRA-VIRGIN OLIVE OIL

CHILE & MANGO DRESSING

YIELD: 1 CUP / **ACTIVE TIME:** 5 MINUTES / **TOTAL TIME:** 5 MINUTES

1. Place all of the ingredients, except for the canola oil, in a food processor and blitz to combine.

2. With the food processor running on low, slowly drizzle in the canola oil until it has emulsified. Use immediately or store in the refrigerator.

INGREDIENTS:

	FLESH OF 1 MANGO
1	TEASPOON CHILI POWDER
1	TEASPOON KOSHER SALT
1	TEASPOON BLACK PEPPER
3	TABLESPOONS RICE WINE VINEGAR
¼	CUP CANOLA OIL

GRAPEFRUIT & PAPAYA DRESSING

YIELD: 1½ CUPS / ACTIVE TIME: 5 MINUTES / TOTAL TIME: 5 MINUTES

1. Place all of the ingredients in a food processor and blitz to combine. Use immediately or store in the refrigerator.

INGREDIENTS:

- FLESH OF ½ PAPAYA, DICED
- ½ CUP FRESH GRAPEFRUIT JUICE
- ¼ CUP HONEY
- ¼ CUP WATER
- 1 TEASPOON KOSHER SALT

LABNEH

YIELD: 4 CUPS / ACTIVE TIME: 10 MINUTES / TOTAL TIME: 2 DAYS

1. Place the yogurt in a large bowl and season it with the salt; the salt helps pull out excess whey, giving you a creamier, thicker labneh.

2. Place a fine-mesh strainer on top of a medium-sized bowl. Line the strainer with cheesecloth or a linen towel, letting a few inches hang over the side of the strainer. Spoon the seasoned yogurt into the cheesecloth and gently wrap the sides over the top of the yogurt, protecting it from being exposed to air in the refrigerator.

3. Store everything in the refrigerator for 24 to 48 hours, discarding the whey halfway through if the bowl beneath the strainer becomes too full.

4. Remove the labneh from the cheesecloth and store it in an airtight container.

5. To serve, drizzle the olive oil over the labneh and sprinkle the za'atar on top.

INGREDIENTS:

- 4 CUPS FULL-FAT GREEK YOGURT
- ½ TEASPOON FINE SEA SALT
- 1 TABLESPOON EXTRA-VIRGIN OLIVE OIL
- 2 TEASPOONS ZA'ATAR

Labneh, see page 653

APRICOT & ROSE WATER DRESSING

YIELD: 1 CUP / **ACTIVE TIME:** 5 MINUTES / **TOTAL TIME:** 5 MINUTES

1. Place all of the ingredients, except for the canola oil, in a food processor and blitz to combine.

2. With the food processor running on low, slowly drizzle in the canola oil until it has emulsified. Use immediately or store in the refrigerator.

INGREDIENTS:

¼   **CUP APRICOT PRESERVES**

3   **TABLESPOONS CHAMPAGNE VINEGAR**

2   **TABLESPOONS FRESH LEMON JUICE**

1   **TABLESPOON ROSE WATER**

¼   **TEASPOON KOSHER SALT**

⅔   **CUP CANOLA OIL**

BACON, PEACH & BOURBON DRESSING

YIELD: 1 CUP / **ACTIVE TIME:** 5 MINUTES / **TOTAL TIME:** 5 MINUTES

1. Place the bacon in a skillet and cook over medium heat until it is crispy, 6 to 8 minutes, turning it as necessary. Remove the bacon from the pan and transfer it to a paper towel–lined plate to drain.

2. Place the bacon in a food processor and blitz until it is finely chopped. Add all of the remaining ingredients, except for the olive oil, and blitz to combine.

3. With the food processor running on low, slowly drizzle in the olive oil until it has emulsified. Use immediately or store in the refrigerator.

INGREDIENTS:

3   **STRIPS OF BACON**

½   **PEACH, PITTED AND DICED**

2   **TABLESPOONS BOURBON**

¼   **CUP RED WINE VINEGAR**

1   **TEASPOON HONEY**

1   **TEASPOON DIJON MUSTARD**

½   **CUP EXTRA-VIRGIN OLIVE OIL**

MAPLE & BOURBON DRESSING

YIELD: 1 CUP / **ACTIVE TIME:** 5 MINUTES / **TOTAL TIME:** 25 MINUTES

1. Place the bourbon in a small saucepan and bring to a boil over medium heat. Cook until it has reduced to ⅓ cup. Remove the pan from heat and let the bourbon cool.

2. Place the bourbon and all of the remaining ingredients, except for the canola oil, in a food processor and blitz to combine.

3. With the food processor running on low, slowly drizzle in the canola oil until it has emulsified. Use immediately or store in the refrigerator.

INGREDIENTS:

1	CUP BOURBON
¼	CUP MAPLE SYRUP
¼	CUP APPLE CIDER VINEGAR
1	SMALL SHALLOT, FINELY DICED
½	TEASPOON FRESH THYME
1	TEASPOON KOSHER SALT
3	TABLESPOONS CANOLA OIL

LEMON RICOTTA DRESSING

YIELD: 1 CUP / **ACTIVE TIME:** 5 MINUTES / **TOTAL TIME:** 5 MINUTES

1. Place all of the ingredients, except for the olive oil, in a food processor and blitz to combine.

2. With the food processor running on low, slowly drizzle in the olive oil until it has emulsified. Use immediately or store in the refrigerator.

INGREDIENTS:

¾	CUP WHOLE-MILK RICOTTA CHEESE
3	TABLESPOONS FRESH LEMON JUICE
1	TEASPOON KOSHER SALT
1	TEASPOON BLACK PEPPER
¼	CUP EXTRA-VIRGIN OLIVE OIL

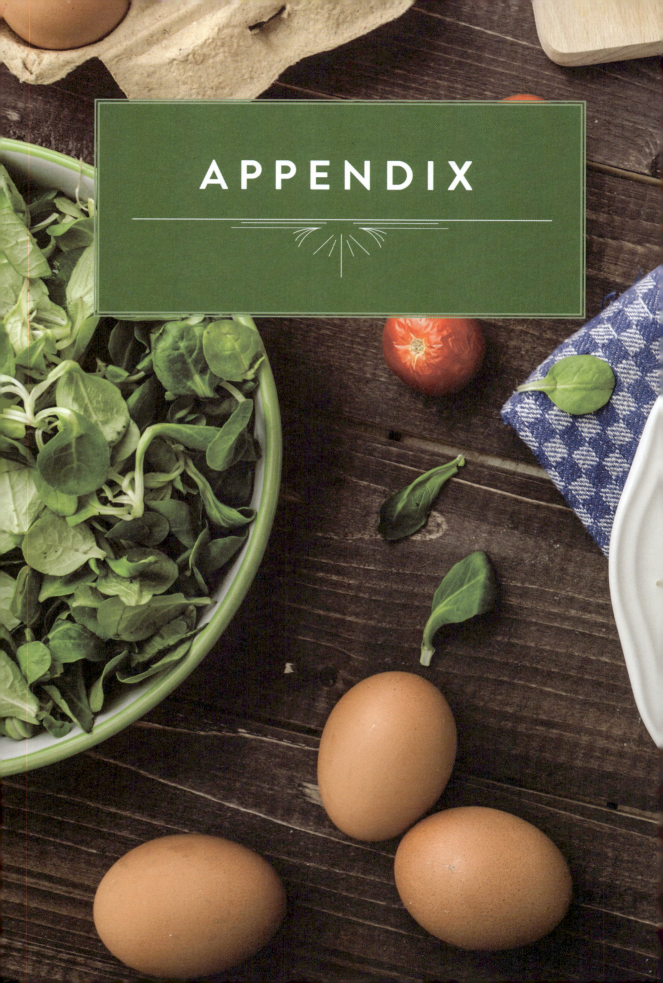

APPENDIX

PITA BREAD

YIELD: 8 SERVINGS / **ACTIVE TIME:** 30 MINUTES / **TOTAL TIME:** 2 HOURS

1. In a large mixing bowl, combine the water, yeast, and sugar. Let the mixture sit until it starts to foam, about 15 minutes.

2. Add the flours and salt and work the mixture until it comes together as a smooth dough. Cover the bowl with a kitchen towel and let it rise for about 15 minutes.

3. Preheat the oven to 500°F and place a baking stone on the floor of the oven.

4. Divide the dough into eight pieces and form them into balls. Place the balls on a flour-dusted work surface, press them down, and roll them until they are about ¼ inch thick.

5. Place one pita on the baking stone and bake until it is puffy and brown, about 8 minutes. Remove the pita from the oven and repeat with the remaining pitas. Serve warm or at room temperature.

INGREDIENTS:

1   CUP LUKEWARM WATER (90°F)

1   TABLESPOON ACTIVE DRY YEAST

1   TABLESPOON SUGAR

1¾   CUPS ALL-PURPOSE FLOUR, PLUS MORE AS NEEDED

1   CUP WHOLE WHEAT FLOUR

1   TABLESPOON KOSHER SALT

CANDIED PECANS

YIELD: 1½ CUPS / **ACTIVE TIME:** 5 MINUTES / **TOTAL TIME:** 25 MINUTES

1. Preheat the oven to 350°F and line a baking sheet with parchment paper. Place the pecans on another baking sheet and place them in the oven. Toast the pecans until they are fragrant, about 6 minutes. Remove the pecans from the oven and set them aside.

2. Place the remaining ingredients in a medium saucepan and bring to a boil, stirring to dissolve the sugar. Cook the syrup until it is 235°F.

3. Add the toasted pecans and stir until they are coated. Place the pecans on the parchment-lined baking sheet and let them cool completely before serving.

INGREDIENTS:

1½	CUPS PECANS
¼	CUP WATER
¾	CUP SUGAR
½	TEASPOON FINE SEA SALT
¾	TEASPOON CINNAMON
¼	TEASPOON GROUND GINGER

AVOCADO PANNA COTTA

YIELD: 4 SERVINGS / **ACTIVE TIME:** 25 MINUTES / **TOTAL TIME:** 24 HOURS

1. Place the sheets of gelatin in a bowl of ice water and let them sit until they have softened, about 20 minutes.

2. Combine the milk, heavy cream, and lemon zest in a medium saucepan and bring to a simmer. Remove the pan from heat and let the mixture steep for 10 minutes.

3. Remove the gelatin from the ice water and squeeze it to remove any excess water. Add it to the cream and stir until the mixture is smooth.

4. Place the avocado in a blender and add half of the milk mixture. Puree until smooth.

5. Stir the puree back into the saucepan. Pour the mixture into the wells of a muffin tin and refrigerate overnight before serving.

INGREDIENTS:

2	SHEETS OF SILVER GELATIN
1	CUP WHOLE MILK
1	CUP HEAVY CREAM
	ZEST OF ½ LEMON
	FLESH OF 1 AVOCADO
	SALT, TO TASTE

CHICKEN STOCK

YIELD: 8 CUPS / ACTIVE TIME: 1 HOUR / TOTAL TIME: 6 HOURS

1. Place the chicken bones in a stockpot and cover them with cold water. Bring to a simmer over medium-high heat and use a ladle to skim off any impurities that rise to the surface.

2. Add the vegetables, thyme, peppercorns, and bay leaf, reduce the heat to low, and simmer for 5 hours, skimming the stock occasionally to remove any impurities that rise to the surface.

3. Strain the stock, let it cool slightly, and transfer it to the refrigerator. Leave the stock uncovered and let it cool completely. Remove the layer of fat and cover. The stock will keep in the refrigerator for 3 to 5 days, and in the freezer for up to 3 months.

INGREDIENTS:

7   LBS. CHICKEN BONES, RINSED

4   CUPS CHOPPED YELLOW ONIONS

2   CUPS CHOPPED CARROTS

2   CUPS CHOPPED CELERY

3   GARLIC CLOVES, CRUSHED

3   SPRIGS OF FRESH THYME

1   TEASPOON BLACK PEPPERCORNS

1   BAY LEAF

CANDIED WALNUTS

YIELD: 1½ CUPS / ACTIVE TIME: 5 MINUTES / TOTAL TIME: 25 MINUTES

1. Preheat the oven to 350°F and line a baking sheet with parchment paper. Place the walnuts on another baking sheet and place them in the oven. Toast the walnuts until they are fragrant, about 6 minutes. Remove the walnuts from the oven and set them aside.

2. Place the remaining ingredients in a medium saucepan and bring to a boil, stirring to dissolve the sugar. Cook the syrup until it is 235°F.

3. Add the toasted walnuts to the syrup and stir until they are coated. Place the walnuts on the parchment-lined baking sheet and let them cool completely before serving.

INGREDIENTS:

1½   CUPS WALNUTS

¼   CUP WATER

¾   CUP SUGAR

½   TEASPOON FINE SEA SALT

Candied Walnuts, see page 663

CROUTONS

YIELD: 6 SERVINGS / ACTIVE TIME: 10 MINUTES / TOTAL TIME: 30 MINUTES

1. Preheat the oven to 350°F. Place the bread in a mixing bowl, drizzle the olive oil over it, and season with salt and pepper. Toss to combine, transfer the bread to a baking sheet, and place it in the oven. Toast the bread until it is golden brown and very crispy, 15 to 20 minutes, stirring occasionally.

2. Remove the croutons from the oven and let them cool slightly before serving.

INGREDIENTS:

4 CUPS DAY-OLD BREAD PIECES

2 TABLESPOONS EXTRA-VIRGIN OLIVE OIL

SALT AND PEPPER, TO TASTE

SHICHIMI TOGARASHI

YIELD: ½ CUP / ACTIVE TIME: 5 MINUTES / TOTAL TIME: 5 MINUTES

1. Place all of the ingredients in a mixing bowl, stir until well combined, and use immediately or store in an airtight container.

INGREDIENTS:

¼ CUP CAYENNE PEPPER

2 TABLESPOONS GROUND DRIED ORANGE PEEL

2 TABLESPOONS SESAME SEEDS

2 TEASPOONS HEMP SEEDS

2 TEASPOONS GROUND SANSHO PEPPERCORNS

2 TEASPOONS MINCED NORI

1 TEASPOON GROUND GINGER

HARD-BOILED EGGS

YIELD: 4 SERVINGS / **ACTIVE TIME:** 5 MINUTES / **TOTAL TIME:** 40 MINUTES

1. Prepare an ice bath. Place the eggs in a saucepan large enough that they can sit on the bottom in a single layer. Cover the eggs with 1 inch of cold water and bring to a boil over high heat.

2. Remove the saucepan from heat, cover it, and let the eggs stand for 10 minutes.

3. Drain the eggs and place them in the ice bath until they are completely chilled. Peel the eggs and serve.

INGREDIENTS:

8   LARGE EGGS

TOASTED RICE POWDER

YIELD: ½ CUP / **ACTIVE TIME:** 5 MINUTES / **TOTAL TIME:** 5 MINUTES

1. Warm a large cast-iron skillet over medium-high heat. Add the rice and toast until it is browned, shaking the pan occasionally.

2. Remove the rice from the pan and use a mortar and pestle to grind it into a fine powder. Use immediately or store in an airtight container.

INGREDIENTS:

½   CUP JASMINE RICE

Croutons, see page 666

PICKLED RED ONION

YIELD: 2 CUPS / ACTIVE TIME: 10 MINUTES / TOTAL TIME: 2 HOURS

1. Place the onion in a mason jar. Place the remaining ingredients in a small saucepan and bring to a boil, stirring to dissolve the sugar and salt.

2. Pour the brine over the onion, making sure it is completely submerged, and let it cool completely before serving or storing in the refrigerator.

INGREDIENTS:

1	LARGE RED ONION, SLICED
2	CUPS RED WINE VINEGAR
1	TEASPOON FENNEL SEEDS
1	TEASPOON MUSTARD SEEDS
½	TEASPOON CELERY SEEDS
⅓	CUP SUGAR
1	TEASPOON KOSHER SALT

CONFIT TUNA

YIELD: 4 SERVINGS / **ACTIVE TIME:** 10 MINUTES / **TOTAL TIME:** 30 MINUTES

1. Place the tuna and olive oil in a small saucepan. The tuna needs to be completely covered by the olive oil; if it is not, add more olive oil as needed.

2. Add the orange zest, garlic, bay leaf, and peppercorns and warm the mixture over low heat. Cook until the internal temperature of the tuna is 135°F.

3. Remove the tuna from the oil and let it cool completely. Serve with toasted slices of baguette or chill in the refrigerator.

INGREDIENTS:

½   LB. YELLOWFIN TUNA STEAK

1   CUP EXTRA-VIRGIN OLIVE OIL, PLUS MORE AS NEEDED

    ZEST OF 1 ORANGE

1   GARLIC CLOVE

1   BAY LEAF

5   BLACK PEPPERCORNS

    SLICES OF BAGUETTE, TOASTED, FOR SERVING

CRISPY WONTON STRIPS

YIELD: 6 SERVINGS / **ACTIVE TIME:** 10 MINUTES / **TOTAL TIME:** 25 MINUTES

1. Add canola oil to a Dutch oven until it is about 1 inch deep and warm it to 350°F.

2. Add the wonton wrappers and fry, turning them frequently, until they are crispy and golden brown, 3 to 5 minutes.

3. Transfer the fried wonton wrappers to a paper towel–lined plate, season them with salt, and enjoy.

INGREDIENTS:

    CANOLA OIL, AS NEEDED

12   WONTON WRAPPERS, CUT INTO STRIPS

    SALT, TO TASTE

JERK MARINADE

YIELD: 1½ CUPS / **ACTIVE TIME:** 5 MINUTES / **TOTAL TIME:** 5 MINUTES

1. Place all of the ingredients in a food processor, blitz until smooth, and use immediately or store in an airtight container.

INGREDIENTS:

1	ONION, FINELY DICED
¼	CUP SCALLIONS, TRIMMED AND FINELY DICED
1	SCOTCH BONNET CHILLE PEPPER, STEMMED, SEEDED, AND CHOPPED
3	TABLESPOONS SOY SAUCE
1	TABLESPOON WHITE VINEGAR
3	TABLESPOONS EXTRA-VIRGIN OLIVE OIL
2	TEASPOONS FRESH THYME
2	TEASPOONS SUGAR
1	TEASPOON FINE SEA SALT
1	TEASPOON BLACK PEPPER
1	TEASPOON ALLSPICE
½	TEASPOON FRESHLY GRATED NUTMEG
½	TEASPOON CINNAMON

CRISPY SHALLOTS

YIELD: 6 SERVINGS / **ACTIVE TIME:** 25 MINUTES / **TOTAL TIME:** 1 HOUR

1. Place the shallots and buttermilk in a bowl and let the mixture rest for 30 minutes.

2. Place the canola oil in a Dutch oven and warm it to 350°F.

3. Combine the flour and cornstarch in a shallow bowl. Dredge the shallots in the mixture until completely coated. Working in batches to avoid crowding the pot, gently slip the shallots into the hot oil and fry until they are crispy and golden brown, 3 to 5 minutes. Transfer the crispy shallots to a paper towel–lined plate to drain.

4. Season with salt and pepper and serve.

INGREDIENTS:

2	SHALLOTS, SLICED THIN
⅓	CUP BUTTERMILK
2	CUPS CANOLA OIL
¼	CUP FLOUR
¼	CUP CORNSTARCH
	SALT AND PEPPER, TO TASTE

Crispy Wonton Strips, see page 672

SPICY CHICKPEAS

YIELD: 4 SERVINGS / **ACTIVE TIME:** 20 MINUTES / **TOTAL TIME:** 24 HOURS

1. Bring 4 cups of water to a boil in a saucepan. Add the chickpeas, reduce the heat so that the water simmers, and cook until the chickpeas are tender, 45 minutes to 1 hour. Drain the chickpeas, place them on a paper towel–lined plate, and pat them dry.

2. Place the canola oil in a Dutch oven and warm it to 350°F over medium heat.

3. Place the remaining ingredients in a bowl, stir until thoroughly combined, and set the mixture aside.

4. Place the chickpeas in the hot oil and fry until they are golden brown, about 3 minutes. Remove the chickpeas from the hot oil and place them in the bowl with the seasoning mixture. Toss to coat and serve.

INGREDIENTS:

1	CUP DRIED CHICKPEAS, SOAKED OVERNIGHT AND DRAINED
2	CUPS CANOLA OIL
1	TEASPOON SMOKED PAPRIKA
½	TEASPOON ONION POWDER
½	TEASPOON BROWN SUGAR
¼	TEASPOON GARLIC POWDER
¼	TEASPOON KOSHER SALT
	PINCH OF CHILI POWDER
	PINCH OF CAYENNE PEPPER

CONVERSION TABLE

WEIGHTS

1 oz. = 28 grams
2 oz. = 57 grams
4 oz. (¼ lb.) = 113 grams
8 oz. (½ lb.) = 227 grams
16 oz. (1 lb.) = 454 grams

VOLUME MEASURES

⅛ teaspoon = 0.6 ml
¼ teaspoon = 1.23 ml
½ teaspoon = 2.5 ml
1 teaspoon = 5 ml
1 tablespoon (3 teaspoons) = ½ fluid oz. = 15 ml
2 tablespoons = 1 fluid oz. = 29.5 ml
¼ cup (4 tablespoons) = 2 fluid oz. = 59 ml
⅓ cup (5⅓ tablespoons) = 2.7 fluid oz. = 80 ml
½ cup (8 tablespoons) = 4 fluid oz. = 120 ml
⅔ cup (10⅔ tablespoons) = 5.4 fluid oz. = 160 ml
¾ cup (12 tablespoons) = 6 fluid oz. = 180 ml
1 cup (16 tablespoons) = 8 fluid oz. = 240 ml

TEMPERATURE EQUIVALENTS

°F	°C	Gas Mark
225	110	¼
250	130	½
275	140	1
300	150	2
325	170	3
350	180	4
375	190	5
400	200	6
425	220	7
450	230	8
475	240	9
500	250	10

LENGTH MEASURES

1/16 inch = 1.6 mm
⅛ inch = 3 mm
¼ inch = 1.35 mm
½ inch = 1.25 cm
¾ inch = 2 cm
1 inch = 2.5 cm

IMAGE CREDITS

Pages 4–5, 6–7, 8, 45, 120–121, 124–125, 144-145, 146, 150–151, 192–193, 199, 204-205, 257, 296, 350, 388–389, 424, 430–431, 508–509, 510, 513, 518–519, 526–527, 530, 536–537, 538, 542–543, 546–547, 550–551, 554–555, 558–559, 562–563, 566–567, 569, 570, 574–575, 578–579, 582–583, 586–587, 590–591, 594–595, 597, 600–601, 604–605, 608–609, 612–613, 616–617, 620–621, 624–625, 628–629, 630, 633, 636–637, 640–641, 644–645, 648–649, 650, 654–655, 658–659, 664–665, 668–669, 674–675, and 677 used under official license from Shutterstock.

Pages 12–13, 17, 24–25, 28–29, 34–35, 41, 42, 51, 52, 59, 91, 94–95, 102–103, 112–113, 130, 140–141, 169, 170, 195, 196, 200, 207, 241, 242, 245, 246, 249, 267, 353, 354, 357, 358, 361, 362, 367, 418, 421, 427, 432, 435, 436, 440, 521, 522, 533, and 670 courtesy of Cider Mill Press.

Pages 11, 156, 514, 529, and 661 courtesy of Unsplash.

All other images used under official license from StockFood.

INDEX

ABOUT CIDER MILL PRESS BOOK PUBLISHERS

Good ideas ripen with time. From seed to harvest, Cider Mill Press brings fine reading, information, and entertainment together between the covers of its creatively crafted books. Our Cider Mill bears fruit twice a year, publishing a new crop of titles each spring and fall.

"Where Good Books Are Ready for Press"

501 Nelson Place
Nashville, Tennessee 37214

cidermillpress.com